The Practitioner Inquiry Series

Marilyn Cochran-Smith and Susan L. Lytle, Series Editors

Jenny's Story: Taking the Long View of the Child—Prospect's Philosophy in Action
PATRICIA F. CARINI & MARGARET HIMLEY, WITH CAROL CHRISTINE, CECILIA ESPINOSA, & JULIA FOURNIER

Acting Out! Combating Homophobia Through Teacher Activism
MOLLIE V. BLACKBURN, CAROLINE T. CLARK, LAUREN M. KENNEY, & JILL M. SMITH, EDS.

Puzzling Moments, Teachable Moments: Practicing Teacher Research in Urban Classrooms
CYNTHIA BALLENGER

Inquiry as Stance: Practitioner Research for the Next Generation
MARILYN COCHRAN-SMITH & SUSAN L. LYTLE

Building Racial and Cultural Competence in the Classroom: Strategies from Urban Educators
KAREN MANHEIM TEEL & JENNIFER OBIDAH, EDS.

Re-Reading Families: The Literate Lives of Urban Children, Four Years Later
CATHERINE COMPTON-LILLY

"What About Rose?" Using Teacher Research to Reverse School Failure
SMOKEY WILSON

Immigrant Students and Literacy: Reading, Writing, and Remembering
GERALD CAMPANO

Going Public with Our Teaching: An Anthology of Practice
THOMAS HATCH, DILRUBA AHMED, ANN LIEBERMAN, DEBORAH FAIGENBAUM, MELISSA EILER WHITE, & DÉSIRÉE H. POINTER MACE, EDS.

Teaching as Inquiry: Asking Hard Questions to Improve Practice and Student Achievement
ALEXANDRA WEINBAUM, DAVID ALLEN, TINA BLYTHE, KATHERINE SIMON, STEVE SEIDEL, & CATHERINE RUBIN

"Is This English?" Race, Language, and Culture in the Classroom
BOB FECHO

Teacher Research for Better Schools
MARIAN M. MOHR, COURTNEY ROGERS, BETSY SANFORD, MARY ANN NOCERINO, MARION S. MACLEAN, & SHEILA CLAWSON

Imagination and Literacy: A Teacher's Search for the Heart of Learning
KAREN GALLAS

Regarding Children's Words: Teacher Research on Language and Literacy
BROOKLINE TEACHER RESEARCHER SEMINAR

Rural Voices: Place-Conscious Education and the Teaching of Writing
ROBERT E. BROOKE, EDITOR

Teaching Through the Storm: A Journal of Hope
KAREN HALE HANKINS

Reading Families: The Literate Lives of Urban Children
CATHERINE COMPTON-LILLY

Narrative Inquiry in Practice: Advancing the Knowledge of Teaching
NONA LYONS & VICKI KUBLER LABOSKEY, EDS.

Writing to Make a Difference: Classroom Projects for Community Change
CHRIS BENSON & SCOTT CHRISTIAN WITH DIXIE GOSWAMI & WALTER H. GOOCH, EDS.

Starting Strong: A Different Look at Children, Schools, and Standards
PATRICIA F. CARINI

Because of the Kids: Facing Racial and Cultural Differences in Schools
JENNIFER E. OBIDAH & KAREN MANHEIM TEEL

(continued)

PRACTITIONER INQUIRY SERIES, *continued*

Jenny's Story

Taking the Long View of the Child

Prospect's Philosophy in Action

Patricia F. Carini *and* **Margaret Himley**

with

Carol Christine, Cecilia Espinosa,
and Julia Fournier

Teachers College
Columbia University
New York and London

Published by Teachers College Press, 1234 Amsterdam Avenue, New York, NY 10027

Library of Congress Cataloging-in-Publication Data

Carini, Patricia F.
    Jenny's story : taking the long view of the child : Prospect's philosophy in action / Patricia F. Carini & Margaret Himley ; with Carol Christine, Cecilia Espinosa, and Julia Fournier.
        p.   cm. — (The practitioner inquiry series)
    Includes bibliographical references and index.
    ISBN 978-0-8077-5051-3 (pbk. : alk. paper)
    ISBN 978-0-8077-5052-0 (hardcover : alk. paper)
        1. Child development—Arizona—Phoenix—Longitudinal studies.   2. School children—Arizona—Phoenix—Longitudinal studies.   3. Racially mixed children—Arizona—Phoenix—Longitudinal studies.   4. Observation (Educational method).   5. Prospect Archives and Center for Education and Research.   I. Himley, Margaret.   II. Title.

LB1115.C278 2010
372.1809791'73—dc22   2009031655

ISBN 978-0-8077-5051-3 (paper)
ISBN 978-0-8077-5052-0 (hardcover)

Printed on acid-free paper
Manufactured in the United States of America

17 16 15 14 13 12 11 10   8 7 6 5 4 3 2 1

Contents

Dedication

With deep respect and appreciation, we dedicate this book to Jenny Williams and her family—her mother Tisa Williams, her father Dennis Williams, and her sisters Julia and Jessica Williams. Their spirit, openness, generosity, and commitment to an education worthy of all children have inspired all of us who have worked on this book.

We also dedicate this volume to the brave and dedicated principal and teachers who made W. T. Machan a beacon of hope in the years Jenny was a student there.

Now, in 2009, teaching at Machan is restricted by state regulations and the consequences of test scores. No Child Left Behind continues to threaten all schools judged to be underperforming. Teachers everywhere are monitored and under peril of reprisal for deviating from prescribed instruction. The state of Arizona has implemented an English-only curriculum, mandated teacher training, and severely restricted bilingual education. For those whose first language is not English, significantly many Spanish speakers, there are four hours a day of drill in English grammar and reading.

This story is now playing out in many schools, in many places.

As we tell Jenny's story and the story of the rich education she received at W. T. Machan, we do so in solidarity with those at Machan and elsewhere in Arizona and across the nation who know that schools can be otherwise, opening doors of opportunity for children, enriching the lives of all children, as Jenny's life was enriched. Jenny's story is a story of struggle against labeling and false assumption. It is the story of a powerful movement for educational and social change. It is a story that, kept alive, has in it the seeds of its own remaking—for a school, too, is a "work"—a work that, as Robin D. G. Kelley (2002) says, can take us "to another place, envision a different way of seeing, perhaps a different way of feeling" (p. 11).

Preface

In this book we tell the story of a child who didn't fit school expectations and was almost mislabeled *slow*—when she wasn't—because the teacher really knew her as an individual and trusted that she would become a reader in her own time and her own way.

We invite you to engage with this child, Jenny Williams, across her elementary school years, through story and observation, through reflection and description. We begin with the *particular* child, in all her engaging fullness, to make the main point of the book—that it is only by attending to each and every child that schooling can begin to achieve its most noble aim of equality of education.

This proposition, which has a long history, challenges the prevailing educational policy and in particular the basic premise of the federal No Child Left Behind (NCLB) act of 2001: that equal educational opportunity can be achieved only at the expense of diversity and by means of one-size-fits-all, state-imposed standards. In contrast, we claim that it is possible to get to know each child as a person, thinker, and learner and from that knowledge to support the child's learning and the child's confidence in herself or himself as a maker of knowledge and meaning.

It has never been easy in education to make the case for a focus on the individual child. Yet it has never been more urgent to do so. Standardized tests, standardized curriculum, and standardized instruction rule the day in schools across the country. It will be years before we know the full damage done by this federal- and state-conducted experiment to the dignity of children, families, and local communities. What we observe in the schools are high stress levels among children and teachers; skills and drill instruction at the expense of curriculum rich in the arts, sciences, and humanities; increases in dropout rates; and surveillance of teachers under threat of school takeovers if test scores do not meet arbitrary standards. Those furthest from classrooms and schools wield the power and dictate practice. The testing and textbook industries are the big winners. Children, families, and teachers, the losers.

Let this be said: Even if NCLB and the associated state mandates and standards were wiped off the books tomorrow, it would not be an easy task to stop the negative forces now in motion and to restore a modicum of power to those closest to the schools. To start again in other and more positive directions will take time, a renewed vision of human possibility, a better connection to history, a knowledge of the resources we can draw from as teachers and administrators and teacher educators, and a deep and daily confidence in the capacity of children and ourselves to be educated and to educate. As Lillian Weber (1994), one of the great educators of the 20th century, reminds us, "We have a depression in our visualization of possibility right now . . . it's both the task and the challenge to keep alive the visions that do exist" (n.p.). *Jenny's Story* is a resource for nurturing the vision of possibility, illuminating the bigger human story of educating that exceeds training and that defies the push for standardization.

In telling the story of Jenny, we root the narrative in a particular place at a particular moment in time. The time is 1993. The place is an urban public elementary school in Phoenix, Arizona, in a neighborhood in the throes of economic changes, a neighborhood composed largely of immigrant families, most from Mexico. By 1993 the practices first introduced in 1987 by a principal who had dared to buck the system were in full flower. She had been joined by teachers eager to learn and inspired by the possibility of changes in schooling to benefit children, and by 1993 the classrooms were mostly multi-age, bilingual, and full of materials for making and doing and learning. In these classrooms, rich in choice and time, there was ample opportunity for teachers to ground their daily practice in the close and caring observation of children and their capacities, giving full attention to children's interests and strengths. It was a place where Jenny could be known and trusted and valued as a learner.

Now, in 2009, for too many children a story like Jenny's would have an unhappy ending—with testing taking away time from attending to particular children and their strengths and passions, with bureaucracy taking away agency from teachers and parents, and with standardization taking away real educational possibilities from many children, especially poor children and children of color.

This is an assault on the schools, an assault on the child's self-making and learning, and an assault on the child's dignity. The weapon is policies and mandates that diminish the child's chance to grow in all his or her fullness and continuity and purpose.

So it is with a real sense of urgency that we offer *Jenny's Story* to highlight the philosophy in action of the Prospect Archives and Center for Education and Research. Prospect offers a *vision* of education based on paying attention to each child's capacities and continuities, on grounding teaching in the potency of particularized knowledge and careful observation, and on drawing knowledge from the collective inquiry of teachers and parents. We tell Jenny's story—not out of nostalgia or despair—but as a powerful reminder of what we can aim for, what we still value, and what we can do in small and big ways.

That is the powerful and politically energizing message of this book. It is a positive message. We *can* do this. We *can* turn away from negating the child. We *can* turn toward the potency of human capacity in children and in ourselves as educators and citizens.

We hope this book creates a context for more and more people to meet, think, and talk about schools and children, about learning and teaching—and to challenge a status quo that privileges testing, bureaucracy, and standardization over teaching, learning, and most tragically the learner herself or himself. We hope to create the conditions for this dialogue.

Acknowledgments

There would not have been a book called *Jenny's Story* without the dedicated work of a number of teachers, administrators, and teacher educators in Phoenix, Arizona. Lynn Davey provided courageous leadership, along with Kelly Draper, at W. T. Machan School, opening up space for teachers and parents to work together for the benefit of all children, to do descriptive reviews of children and their works, and to advocate for an education worthy of all children. In support of their work, the Center for Establishing Dialogue (CED), led by Carol Christine, made possible the seminars and workshops that brought the Prospect philosophy and descriptive practices to Machan and to many other Phoenix schools. We offer here our thanks and admiration for all that Machan and CED stand for and all they accomplish for children, teachers, and families.

We wish to give particular recognition to the teachers and teacher educators who so thoughtfully, generously, and effectively shared their perspectives and insights as participants in the four studies of Jenny and her works that are at the heart of this book. Their names, listed for each study separately, are as follows:

First Spanning Study (Summer Institute II, North Bennington, Vermont, 1996): Louisa Cruz Acosta, Barbara Batton, Maggie (Ellis) Chotas, Abbe Futterman, and Nancy McKeever

Second Spanning Study (Phoenix, Arizona, 1997): Reneé Bachman, Karin Mendez, Karen Moore, Mark Routhier, and Diana Segovia

Third Spanning Study (Phoenix, Arizona, 1999): Reneé Bachman, Cecilia Espinosa, Laurie Fuller, Karen Moore, *all from W. T. Machan School*; and Kitty Kaczmarek, Shahla Nye, Nancy Pape, Cheryl Thomas, and Richard Thomas *from Glendale District*

Mini-Study of Jenny's Works (Prospect Summer Institute II, North Bennington, Vermont, 2006): Joan Bradbury, Louisa Cruz-Acosta, Helen Martin, Gina Ritscher, Ellen Schwartz, and Lynne Strieb

We express to each one individually and to all collectively our deepest gratitude for all they contributed to the richness and depth of the story of Jenny that emerges in this book. It could not have been written without them.

We also wish to extend heartfelt thanks to Lynne Strieb and Betsy Wice, who have read many drafts of this book, each time offering us excellent feedback and suggestions, each time urging us to persevere. We are more than grateful to both for their sound advice and moral support. Beth Alberty's generosity as consultant on the book's design was immensely helpful. We are more than grateful for her thoughtful and prompt responses to our questions, and her unfailingly perceptive eye.

Our debt to series editors Marilyn Cochran-Smith and Susan Lytle is enormous. Though it was a long haul, they never once doubted the value of the book or our capacity to make Jenny's a tellable story. In particular, we thank them for the opportunity to present main threads of the book in a keynote address on Practitioner Inquiry Day at the Ethnography in Education Research Forum at the University of Pennsylvania (February 2009). It was heartening, as we moved toward the finish line, to receive from those attending the session such interested response to the themes and ideas that weave together in the story of this one child—and especially so in an era when attention to the child ranks low among those who write and enforce the one-size-fits-all educational policy that rules the day in all too many schools.

We also owe thanks to the Prospect Board of Trustees for supporting the work on this book over many years and in many ways. We wish to recognize as well the financial support from a small grant to Margaret Himley from the College of Arts and Sciences at Syracuse University.

Margaret wants to acknowledge Robin Riley's patience and generosity, for having a million conversations about this book as it morphed into final form, for making brilliant suggestions, and for saving endless versions on her hard drive. She is a wonderful partner in all of life's adventures.

Pat is grateful, as ever, to Lou Carini for his unfailing support over what has been a very long haul. As he has so many times before, Lou read drafts, listened to parts of the book read aloud, and unfailingly offered intelligent observations and sensitive insights—guided always by his firm grasp of the philosophy of education and of the person, in which all of Prospect's work is rooted.

Finally, Margaret and Pat thank the Williams family, and most especially Jenny Williams, for being the brave and dedicated people they are and for giving of themselves so generously in the making of this book.

The crkol ovv Liyf

i raley Like it Bekas
it has Los ovv kolrs
and Pekas The wrold
is a slsahl Plays
Bot I don tek it
Is varey kolrfol

i Love the wrol
i will kep it saf
For avvrey one

The Circle of Life

I really like it because
it has lots of colors
and because the world
is a special place
but I don't think it
is very colorful.

I love the world
I will keep it safe
for every one.

Poem by Jenny Williams
(first grade)

Introduction

Margaret Himley

The philosophy of education that drives this book was developed over many years at the Prospect School in North Bennington, Vermont. We have written about the philosophy in *Starting Strong: A Different Look at Children, Schools, and Standards,* by Patricia F. Carini (2001), and about the Descriptive Review of the Child in *From Another Angle: Children's Strengths and School Standards,* edited by Margaret Himley with Patricia F. Carini (2000). For those new to Prospect, I will provide a brief review of its history and philosophy before describing Jenny Williams, the heart and message of this book.

WHAT IS PROSPECT?

Prospect School opened in mid-September 1965, with a multi-age class of 23 five- to seven-year-olds from all walks of life and from all across the Bennington community. There were four cofounders, all active in the school and in the shaping of the Prospect philosophy: Joan B. Blake, Patricia F. Carini, Louis Carini, and Marion Stroud, the first teacher. What the school was striving for were learning experiences that, in John Dewey's (1938/1963) terms, would "arouse curiosity, strengthen initiative, and set up desires and purposes sufficiently intense to carry a person over dead places in the future" (p. 38).

From the very beginning, the school's classrooms featured plentiful choices for children; opportunities to make things from a rich array of materials; ample use of the outdoors; and reading, writing, and math taught with individual attention to each child. This was neither a rich nor an elite school, but it was a very inviting scene of learning:

> The small interconnecting rooms and alcoves—filled with scattered tables and chairs, used clothing for drama, papier-mâché dinosaurs, books, children's artwork of all kinds, maps, charts, and aquariums—spread out

in labyrinthine ways across all three stories. Sunlight and the smells of drying paint, paste, and old wood flood through the cluttered rooms. (Himley, 1991, p. 17)

In the midst of all this doing and making, Patricia F. Carini and her colleagues began to observe, record, and describe the children and what was happening in the classroom on a daily and continuing basis:

> The idea was that a school and a staff could create a comprehensive plan for doing this kind of observational inquiry and that such an investigation could be school-based—that a school could itself generate knowledge of children, of curriculum, of learning and teaching. (Carini, 2000, p. 9)

The aim was to fold observation directly into practice, to document children's learning, to develop curriculum out of that inquiry, and so to sustain the school itself as a "moving force" (to cite Dewey, 1938/1963, again) that would lead the teachers and children forward.

From this trust in children as learners, from this commitment to building from each child's strengths, and from this process of collaborative descriptive inquiry emerged, over time and with lots of revisions, what have become known as the *Prospect Descriptive Processes*.

The first Descriptive Process was the *Descriptive Review of the Child*, where a presenting teacher or parent gathers observations and stories about a child, organized under the headings of physical presence and gesture, disposition and temperament, connections with others, strong interests and preferences, and modes of thinking and learning (see Himley with Carini, 2000). The other important Descriptive Process is the *Descriptive Review of Children's Work*. Information from both processes is utilized in this book as we tell the story of Jenny Williams over five years, documenting how a person both stays the same and changes over time and demonstrating how we can come to know others as thinkers and learners, and as persons with particular strengths and interests. Other Descriptive Processes have been used for a variety of purposes, such as the following:

- to gather stories and observations about a child who seems to keep slipping through the cracks,
- to review the grade level standards and promotion policies of a school,
- to understand how a particular classroom activity such as construction works across a spectrum of classrooms and with children of different ages,

- to learn more about a child's particular strengths as a learner and thinker by describing her writings and drawings,
- to reflect on the word *writing* as part of an inquiry into how a writing program is working within a classroom,
- to describe a school library in terms of its physical arrangement, ambience, and social life. (Himley, 2002, p. 4)

All of these processes—rooted in observing a child, a space, an activity—begin with *immersion,* a concept drawn from phenomenology. All have a focus question that the presenting teacher, parent, or administrator has worked out thoughtfully ahead of time with the chair of the review. All are always collaborative, and they have rules and roles necessary for making the inquiry process democratic and inclusive and for guaranteeing the respect and privacy of the persons involved. And most important, all are aimed not at judging or reducing the child but at making the richness and complexity of that person more visible, more fully present. The processes have been and continue to be reworked, but what remains constant is valuing detail and complexity, taking the time to plan and do the review, avoiding judgmental or reductive language, including multiple perspectives, and respecting the child and his or her family.

Works are at the heart of the Prospect philosophy—the works of children and adults, including student writing, drawing and painting, three-dimensional construction, works in other mediums, and teacher records. In 2005, The Archives of Children's Work, together with the program and institutional records of Prospect School and Prospect Center, were gifted to Special Collections at the University of Vermont. Securely housed at Bailey/Howe Library, the archives are readily accessible to scholars, teachers, students, and researchers (for information, contact Chris Burns, Curator, Special Collections, at Chris.Burns@uvm.edu, or go to http://library.uvm.edu/sc/). Of particular interest is the *Reference Edition of the Prospect Archives.* Published in 1985, through funding from the Bush and Noyes Foundations, it is composed of the complete collections of the cataloged works of 36 children, microfiche reproduction of these collections, a subset of color slides, and print documents of teacher narrative records and reports.

Prospect created a teacher education program, collected children's work, documented the school and its curriculum, participated in research projects on reading (Chittenden, Salinger, & Bussis, 2001) and science learning (Chittenden, 1990), developed processes for describing children and their work, and offered seminars, institutes, and conferences for educators across the country. Although the school, always struggling financially, had to close in 1991, Prospect—and the network of educators committed to its vision and philosophy—continue to make an important contribution to the national discussion on education.

In particular, the premise of human capacity, widely distributed, positions Prospect's educational, ethical, and political message at the nexus of conflicted issues in education—most especially, the right to a liberating education for children historically denied that opportunity. The potency of this premise—enacted in the observational, descriptive processes—puts into the hands of teachers and schools a reliable methodology for recognizing the strengths and capacities of each child and of all.

Positioning humanness "as widely distributed capacity, as active making, as value, as resource, as scale, as process, and as responsibility" (Carini, 2001, p. 1), Prospect offers a solid foundation for a liberating public education freely available to all. Prospect's philosophy and Descriptive Processes continue to inform the everyday practice of teachers and teacher educators, as they make space for children's strengths and capacities in even the most constricted classroom contexts in this time of enforced standardization. This is the vision that *Jenny's Story* puts forward and makes doable through the resources of history, philosophy, and Prospect's Descriptive Processes.

WHO IS JENNY WILLIAMS?

Jenny is the middle daughter of Tisa and Dennis Williams, who live in Phoenix, Arizona. She was born in October 1987. She has an older sister, Jessica, and a younger one, Julia. Jenny's heritage from her mother's side is Mexican and Irish, with Welsh and English coming from her father's family. English is her first language. Her grandmother, Nana, speaks Spanish, and Tisa is relearning and Jenny is learning Spanish.

Tisa and Dennis Williams, as well as Jenny herself and her two sisters, agreed to have their real names used in this book because they were eager to have this story told. The sisters' public school, W. T. Machan, was a catalyst for the whole family, as they felt truly invited into the world of education, where parents and teachers worked together for the sole purpose of empowering the children, no matter what background or status, no matter what language or appearance (personal communication to Cecilia Espinosa, August 23, 2007). Names of all other children in the book are pseudonyms.

At W. T. Machan, Jenny was in Cecilia Espinosa's multi-age, bilingual classroom for three years, beginning in kindergarten and continuing through second grade (1993-1996). She moved to Julia Fournier's room, a Grades 2-3 bilingual classroom, for third grade (1996-1997). That summer the family moved to Glendale, Arizona, where Jenny attended fourth grade. Kitty Kaczmarek was her fifth grade teacher at Desert Gardens, where she completed sixth grade and her elementary school education in 2000.

That, early on, Jenny appeared to some adults to be *slow* is key to her story. If the assumption that she was slow had taken root, it could easily have led to judgments that would have worked against her growth and learning. That didn't happen. Cecilia Espinosa's informed perceptions of Jenny, supported by Prospect's Descriptive Processes and the values that underlie them, interrupted this (mis)reading of Jenny. The Prospect processes made visible Jenny's many strengths and abilities and disrupted the all-too-familiar equation in schools of quickness with intelligence.

Jenny's story also marks a particular moment in the history of W. T. Machan. In 1987, when the school was at low ebb, a new principal named Dr. Lynn Davey dramatically turned the tide. She hired teachers eager to join in a mission to create a school open to the community and in partnership with parents. By 1993, when Jenny entered, the school was burgeoning with possibilities for innovation and change. Dr. Davey's leadership and that of her close administrative associate Kelly Draper, together with the dedicated efforts of teachers who shared and enacted daily that vision, had upended the notion that an environment supportive of children's learning and of families can blossom only in white, middle-class schools in suburban neighborhoods. Here was an urban school creating just that.

The administrators and the teachers at W. T. Machan highly valued the involvement of parents, offering to Jenny's parents and others an open door to its educational philosophy. Recognizing parents as the child's primary educators and home as the child's primary context for learning, the school empowered parents to be outspoken advocates for their children. It is no coincidence that in this telling of Jenny's story, her mother's perspective on Jenny as learner, thinker, and person leads the way.

It is also important to Jenny's story that W. T. Machan School was closely connected with a teacher center called the Center for Establishing Dialogue (CED). It was Carol Christine, the director of CED, who invited Patricia F. Carini to come to Phoenix in the autumn of 1989 to talk with teachers and teacher educators about evaluation, about Prospect's Descriptive Processes, and specifically about the role of these processes in documenting children's growth and learning. At three intensive two-and-a-half-day seminars during 1989–1990, teachers across districts were introduced to ways to observe, document, and evaluate classroom settings and children's growth and learning.

These seminars and workshops continued to be offered at CED for more than five years, with teachers from W. T. Machan as regular participants. Summer institutes, allowing for deeper study and reading, cemented the relationship. CED and the Prospect philosophy and Descriptive Processes were important influences on the direction, innovation, and change at W. T. Machan—and on the lives of all the children enrolled there, including Jenny.

OVERVIEW OF THIS BOOK

The four chapters that compose Part I of this book narrate the story of how the (mis)perception of Jenny as *slow* was *jarred*. With contributions from Jenny's mother and her teachers, the story unfolds from the first spanning study in Vermont, through a second one in Phoenix, and then moves across to a different district in Phoenix. By joining in these studies, we learn how Jenny's mother's advocacy, supported by Jenny's former teachers at W. T. Machan, the CED, and Prospect's Descriptive Processes, bridged Jenny from school to school. It is worthy of note that as each transition approached, her mother and Jenny's former teachers made sure to give the new teacher a copy of all previous Prospect spanning studies of the child.

The Jenny that emerges across these studies and through her fifth-grade teacher's observations of Jenny's many contributions to the classroom community has proved compelling to all who have come to know her: Jenny's deep commitments to social justice, her profound ways of learning, her embrace of the world. Getting to know Jenny has been an insistent reminder to us about what education—real education—is all about.

In three essays interleaved within Jenny's story, organized under the collective title "Jarring Perception," Patricia F. Carini brings readers into the philosophy of education—of learning, of making, of meaning, and of participating in the world—that informs the Descriptive Processes. These essays, though brief, position Prospect's political and educational message, wide in historical and philosophical scope, within the actual circumstances of the lives and times of children, teachers, and families. They powerfully and startlingly link Jenny's particular story to the social, political, and historical context in which her story is told, and then retold these many years later.

The four chapters in Part II of the book widen the frame by locating our account of one child in the wider context of history and memory, of conviction and courage, with story as a restorative and generative resource much needed at a time of great duress for schools, families, children, administrators, and teacher educators. We conclude the book in Part III with two chapters that offer theoretical and philosophical perspectives for this book and for the vision of education put forth here.

The book ends with Jenny's voice in an interview Cecilia Espinosa conducted in 2007 with Jenny and her mother, looking back on this work and assessing its value and meaning to them now.

An insert section shows color images of Jenny's work, and there is an appendix: *The Vermont Design for Education.*

CALL TO ACTION

Throughout the book, in the descriptive reviews and spanning studies, in the resonant voices of teachers, in the "Jarring Perception" essays, and through the images, we are reminded of so many other children we know or have taught. We also re-encounter ourselves. In the process we may be moved to action by the most fundamental and most urgent message of the book: For the school to do no harm. For each of us to be the equal of the other. For each child's well-being to be valued as highly as we value our own or that of the child closest to our heart. For the child's essential humanness to be the starting point for education. For the child to be the harbinger of human possibility. For the child's dignity to be the school's first responsibility and guiding principle.

However harsh the present circumstances, there is throughout this book a connection to history and vision, a hope and confidence—engendered by Jenny's own—that the world, the society, the schools, can be made better. Jenny's mission to make the world safe, and the goodness of her resolve, is a powerful awakening to our own resolve for vigilance, resistance, and action.

PART I

Telling Jenny's Story

The Dignity and Well-Being
of the Child

JENNY'S STORY in Part I is narrated through three spanning studies in Chapters 1–3 and a mini-study in Chapter 4. Each chapter introduces aspects of Prospect's Descriptive Processes and highlights contributions from Jenny's mother and her teachers. The picture of Jenny that emerges from age 6 through age 11 particularizes her continuousness with herself even as she is also changing. A main message of Jenny's story is that the child's integrity, announced by this continuousness, is mostly overlooked in schools. The consequences of that failure of attention are foregrounded in Patricia Carini's three brief essays called "Jarring Perception" punctuating Jenny's story.

CHAPTER ONE

Meeting Jenny

Rethinking Schooling

Patricia F. Carini and Cecilia Espinosa

Pat Carini: When I contacted Cecilia Espinosa to ask if she would play a major role in a spanning study to happen at Prospect's 1996 Summer Institute, I knew from her participation in Prospect workshops and summer institutes held in Phoenix that Cecilia had a multifaceted experience with Prospect's Descriptive Processes to draw upon. She was a seasoned participant in the ongoing Prospect seminar series sponsored by the Center for Establishing Dialogue (CED) called "Another Way of Looking at Children," with its emphasis on descriptive observation as the foundation for documenting children's growth and learning. As a teacher in the W. T. Machan School, Cecilia had also participated in a seminar on multi-age classrooms offered in support of the school's decision to regroup children in classes spanning two and even three grades. And she had participated in the summer institutes held in Phoenix, one of which featured spanning studies of children from two Phoenix schools, one of them W. T. Machan. The latter experience meant Cecilia knew that a spanning study employs several of Prospect's Descriptive Processes—typically the Descriptive Review of the Child, the Descriptive Review of Children's Works, a Reflective Conversation, and perhaps, in addition, a Recollection related to the focus of the spanning study. She also knew that a study of this dimension spans several years of a child's school life—and several days of the institute.

PREPARING FOR THE SPANNING STUDY

Pat Carini: I told Cecilia in that first phone call that the theme of the spanning studies for the 1996 institute was children who need more space than schools typically allow—with *space* shorthand for more opportunities to be in action or more time than fits with a school's need to keep children moving right along. Cecilia didn't hesitate for a moment. She said right away that she had a child named Jenny Williams for whom preserving space to grow and learn was essential—space that some adult perceptions of her and recent events at school appeared to threaten.

Cecilia Espinosa: When Pat called and said that the Prospect Summer Institute was going to look at children who need space—emotional or physical space or the space of time—I thought of Jenny, then a second-grader in my multi-age, bilingual classroom. Until a short while before, thinking of Jenny as in particular need of space would not have occurred to me. But something had happened that changed the picture. On a particular morning the Title I reading teacher had substituted for me during the reading and language arts time while I attended a district meeting. Jenny's mother, Tisa Williams, a regular volunteer in my classroom, was also in the room that day. In the afternoon, when I came back to the class, Tisa shared with me that the Title I teacher had seemed concerned about Jenny's reading. She had suggested that Jenny, then in second grade, be tested for reading difficulties. Tisa seemed anxious about what she had heard.

I can't say that at that time in my career I was totally opposed to testing children, or that I even understood the deeper consequences of labeling kids and putting them in special programs. I was very conflicted on these issues. The conversation about the dangers of mis(labeling) kids had just started at W. T. Machan. I was just beginning to understand the complexity of schools. And I knew that the other teachers and administrators at W. T. Machan also cared deeply about the kids and were always ready to work against the system in order to help a child.

Yet, as I listened to Tisa's worries about the comment she had heard that morning, I angrily wondered how someone could identify a child's needs in just one visit. I questioned how we could assume that a test would tell us what kind of reading support Jenny needed. I had known Jenny since she was four years old, when she would come to our class with her Mom because her older sister was in the class. I had a long history with her. For all those years I had seen Jenny grow every day. She is the kind of person who grows in all areas—inch by inch, slowly—and all around at the same time. She is so curious and full of questions. She wants to know the *why*'s of everything. She touches everything, and her touching is related to figuring out how things work. She does this while she talks with someone about her discoveries or while she raises new questions. Learning for Jenny takes longer because she goes so deeply into it, not because she isn't able to learn something out of the lack of a skill.

From my observations and conversations with her, I knew what an intense and deep thinker Jenny really is. During class discussions she would take her time to offer her opinion. She was never fast at saying what she thought about an issue that we were discussing, but when she said something, she could help us see it in a new light, or at a deeper level. She would go to the heart of the issue.

Jenny became a reader by making the book *Henny Penny* her own. She memorized it, and read it over and over, with purpose. She would do choral readings for the kids in the class, often inviting more hesitant kids to join her in her presentation. Eventually, she began to use the book to write her own version of it, *Jenny Penny*. In it, the characters were her classmates. I could see Jenny's work as a reader beyond the struggles we observed when she worked with a different book in a small guided reading group. By the end of first grade and the beginning of second grade, it had been a bit painful to watch her read a book that she wasn't so involved in.

No wonder I thought of Jenny right away when Pat called.

Pat Carini: After telling me about Jenny and how she seemed a perfect fit with the institute theme of making space for children, Cecilia proposed that Jenny's mother, Tisa Williams, and Jenny herself be involved with us in planning the spanning study. As the chair for the spanning study, nothing could have pleased me more. Almost from the first, the teachers at W. T. Machan had been committed to involving parents in Descriptive Reviews of the Child and in seminars offered there and at CED. Tisa Williams was one of those parents. I didn't know Jenny, but I had visited Cecilia's classroom and the adjoining classroom taught by Cecilia's team teacher, Karen Moore. The easy give-and-take between these two teachers and their equal ease with parents could not be missed. I was eager to find out how Jenny would join in the planning—and soon I did.

In my role as chair of the spanning study, I outlined a generic plan to get us started. Teachers come to Prospect's summer institutes from all over the country. It was only logical that once we had all introduced ourselves, Cecilia would picture W. T. Machan School for them and invite them into her own classroom, which, after all, had been Jenny's school "home" for the past three years. There were other decisions to be made. We could start with a reflection on a word related to themes recurrent in Jenny's works. We could start with time for all of us to immerse ourselves in Jenny's works, which would be on display in our seminar room. We could do both of these in combination. Or, we might decide to start with the Descriptive Review of Jenny by her mother and teacher.

Whatever choices we made, as chair I would present the frame worked out by Cecilia, Tisa, and myself in our planning sessions to explain why Jenny had been chosen and to spell out Tisa's and Cecilia's expectations of what the study would yield. As Cecilia and I spoke, I realized that this particular study deserved the name *spanning* for another reason. Because Jenny's mother and Jenny herself would play key roles in the planning and because Cecilia had known Jenny for four years and taught her for three, this was a study reflecting home and school perspectives and spanning Jenny's life from infancy to age 8. Cecilia said she would contact Tisa and Jenny right away to be co-planners. Planning for the study was under way.

Cecilia Espinosa: Tisa and Jenny joined in the planning with enthusiasm. Jenny volunteered to select a collection of her works to send with me to Vermont. At my suggestion, Tisa said she would be the main presenter for the Descriptive Review of the Child. Because Tisa had participated in other reviews, she was familiar with how to organize her knowledge of Jenny (along with that of her husband) according to the headings of the Descriptive Review of the Child:

- Physical presence and gesture
- Disposition and temperament
- Connections with others (both children and adults)
- Strong interests and preferences
- Modes of thinking and learning

I would address the last topic: modes of thinking and learning. The sad part was that Tisa couldn't join us in Vermont. She would, instead, write her presentation of Jenny. Things turned out a bit differently in the long run, but that was the original plan.

I turned my own attention to creating a picture of W. T. Machan and of my classroom, including a glimpse of what school might be like for Jenny on a typical day, though such days are rare in classrooms that make room for children's choices!

W. T. MACHAN SCHOOL (1993–1999)

Cecilia Espinosa: Schools change, and W. T. Machan is no exception. What I am picturing is the school as it was during the years Jenny was a student there. At that time about 900 children, ages 5–11, attended the school. All came from a single neighborhood that had been split into two parts by a freeway that was partially hidden behind old trees, with the noise abated somewhat by walls built for that purpose. Because of the freeway, the neighborhood served by Machan became almost invisible to most Phoenix residents. In the 15 years prior to Jenny's entry to school, the neighborhood had gone through another profound change, turning from a mainly Anglo community of families that were mostly of middle- to low-income status to one composed mostly of recent immigrants who had left their home countries in search of salaries that would allow them to raise a family. Most were from Mexico, and most worked in service industries—hotels, restaurants, child care, construction, lawn maintenance, and house cleaning. The school stood out in this setting for its warm welcome to families, who were greeted upon turning onto 22nd Street by a sign that displayed the school's name and the current weekly announcement in Spanish and English. Inside the school a bilingual secretary was there to greet parents and visitors. In the years Jenny attended W. T. Machan, the door to the principal's office often stood open.

Like many schools in Phoenix, W. T. Machan is a campus school. In the period 1993–1997, there were six buildings, one a new library that held a large collection of children's books written in Spanish—one of the largest in Phoenix. It took a long time to compile that collection. When the new building opened with a librarian in charge who wanted to change the ethos of "no talking and you can only come with your entire class to check out books," Pat Carini facilitated a Descriptive Review of a Space (in this case, the library) that helped that change to come about. For Jenny and for all children at Machan during that time, the library was a place they could go on their own, and where there were story hours for young children not yet enrolled at the school and their moms or dads, as well as dramatic play areas. The library became a place where a child could lose herself or himself in a book in the company of other children.

Unfortunately, the play area facilities and supervision were not adequate even then for the numbers of children at the school. The noise level rose. There were accidents. As vandalism increased, huge metal fences that were locked when the children went home were installed around the playground. However, it is also true that during recess, music was heard inside and outside classrooms. It was not uncommon to see children of all ages on the school sidewalks practicing the steps of a dance to a popular song in either Spanish or English.

Jenny's Classroom

Cecilia Espinosa: During Jenny's time at W. T. Machan, her classroom was laid out as shown in Figure 1.1. As indicated on the classroom map, the room was anchored at one end by the meeting area and my rocking chair. Around the periphery of the room were storage areas for art and math materials and shelves for a big supply of books in both English and Spanish. The sink and the art table were in close proximity—not by accident. Situated on the diagonal were

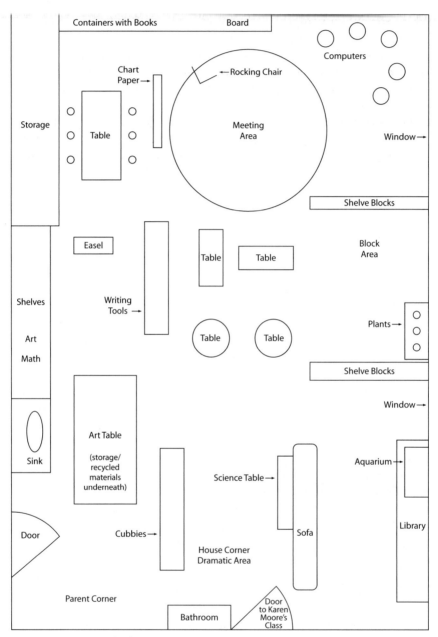

FIGURE 1.1 Jenny's classroom.

16

the parent corner, positioned near the door for easy access, and on the opposite side the mini-computer lab. For most of the children, their only access to a computer was at school. On the wall opposite the shelves for art and math materials was the block area, which was bookended by storage shelves. The science table across from the children's cubbies backed up against the sofa used by children visiting the class library. That section of the room also provided space for plants, the aquarium, and the house corner for dramatic play. Writing tools, the easel, and chart paper were located near the activities they supported. Tables with chairs sufficient to provide a seat for each child were located near the meeting area.

Pat Carini: Cecilia's map provides the bare bones of the classroom—its organizational skeleton. But what is missing is her picturing of how the space was used and how that changed on a daily basis according to the ebb and flow of activity.

Cecilia Espinosa: A space for children to move around has to be flexible. For example, tables would be pushed back to make room for children from one or two other multi-age classrooms who might come and sing right before lunch. The map doesn't show how the space became a setting for a play, a place to practice a dance for a performance, or a gallery where children displayed their work after weeks of intensive study on one topic, such as the Sonoran desert. It doesn't show the children's works always on display on the walls of the room—the poems children wrote placed alongside the poetry of a famous writer, charts with questions that children were wondering about, a section dedicated to parents. It doesn't show the enticing articles and outfits made of interesting textures in the dramatic play area to prompt the imagination. It doesn't show the rich supply of recycled materials and tools used for a variety of projects or the abundance of markers, crayons, color pencils, scissors, glue, watercolors, chalk, oil pastels, construction paper, and other papers. It doesn't show the huge collection of songs and poems that hung from the walls that the children had learned over time. Not only was the collection in both Spanish and English, but the themes were also varied. There were songs such as *Baby Beluga, Old McDonald, Arroz con Leche, De Colores,* as well as songs that speak out for social justice such as those sung by bilingual songwriter Tish Hinojosa. Jenny's class often sang these songs and others with their fourth- and fifth-grade buddy readers. And the map doesn't show that parents were always welcome. Those at first uncertain about a classroom that looked so different from their expectations were encouraged to bring their questions and invited to join in classroom activities.

Let me give one example of what could and did happen in this multi-age (K–2), bilingual classroom when Jenny was a student. The children brought to closure a study of traditional and nontraditional fairy tales by writing and performing a bilingual, nontraditional fairy tale play about Cinderella. Children, parents, teachers, and student teachers worked tirelessly to prepare the performance. Costumes were made, scenery was created, and draft after draft of each scene was written. The children themselves decided that each scene would be told in either Spanish or English without translation. To accomplish this challenging task, they volunteered eagerly to try the different roles even if they had to do it in the language in which they were least proficient. On the day of the performance, they wore homemade and improvised costumes as they helped one another to remember their lines. Our buddy readers and several parents came to the performance.

A Day in Jenny's Schedule

Cecilia Espinosa: Officially school opened at 8:45, though children, Jenny among them, started arriving in the classroom by 8:30. Lunch and lunch recess usually ran from 12:00 to 1:00. The school day ended at 2:45. Between these markers of the day, there were times assigned for reading books, language arts, math, and—on different days—different special subjects (music, P.E., or art), as well as social science and science (alternating); in addition, there was project time at least once or twice a week. There were breaks for snack, lunch, and recess.

Karen Moore (my team teacher) and I wanted the children to be active in the way the classroom worked, in making decisions and choices about their learning, and to be themselves a source of exciting ideas for us to pursue. The children joined in getting the day started by taking attendance, doing the lunch count, contributing news at the morning meeting, and joining in reading aloud a handwritten poem posted on big chart paper.

With the arrival of the collaborating special education teacher, Karen and I divided the group to hear a chapter book read aloud in either Spanish (by me) or English (by Karen). Our purpose was to provide children access to the richness of their own language by reading to them a complex story such as *The BFG* by Roald Dahl (1982) or *Si Ves Pasar un Cóndor/If You Pass a Condor* by Carlos Ocampo (1987). There was also time for the two classroom assistant teachers to work with small groups of children who needed some support as readers. Books like *Henny Penny* in which the language, meaning, and illustrations carry the reader were frequent choices.

Language arts usually followed book reading. A large group meeting made the transition, beginning with a mini-lesson followed by children sharing their current writing projects—poetry, personal narrative, fiction, nonfiction, all kept in the child's writing notebook. Math, science, and social science often included hands-on projects and research. There might be a study of shapes and strength or magnetism or plants. There might be other projects initiated by the children themselves, drawing on the rich supply of materials available in the room.

What I haven't yet mentioned is something that was daily and pivotal: a time following the lunch recess to hear a book read aloud, followed by an opportunity for children to bring forward and discuss any problematic issues that had arisen during the day—or any occasions that were reason to compliment another child's choices and actions. This meeting was truly social studies in action, and Jenny was often a major contributor.

FRAME AND PLAN FOR THE SPANNING STUDY

Pat Carini: Cecilia, Tisa, and I decided to frame the spanning study around the issue of *slowness* that had prompted Cecilia to choose Jenny in the first place. In introducing the study, Cecilia's role was to picture Jenny's school and classroom, to describe how Jenny learned to read, and to tell the story of the intervention of the Title I teacher. We also decided to start the study with an opportunity for all participants to immerse themselves in Jenny's works, probably including reflection on key themes and motifs to support the descriptive process. We decided to have Tisa's presentation of Jenny, with additions from Cecilia, come last because we thought that to begin with their descriptions might unduly influence how we saw Jenny's works. I knew the plan was likely to change in response to participants' insights and ideas once we were in the midst of doing it, but it seemed we had a starting place that was solid and comfortable.

In this description of the spanning study as it actually occurred, Tisa's descriptive review of Jenny is featured for two reasons: to demonstrate the descriptive review process and to call attention to the depth of parents' knowledge of their children (something often overlooked in schools) and to the child's continuity with herself from infancy forward. This continuity has huge implications for how we see children in school and how we educate them.

SCENES FROM THE FIRST
SPANNING STUDY OF JENNY (1996)

Pat Carini: The day the summer institute opened, Cecilia arrived from Phoenix heavily laden with stacks of Jenny's drawings, paintings, and writings—all selected by Jenny—and a bundle of photographs and treasured objects entrusted by Jenny to Cecilia for us to see. Cecilia brought tapes of Jenny talking about and reading her works—and a total surprise and delight to me: a tape of Tisa presenting her description of Jenny. We would be able to hear her live!

Seven of us composed the study circle: Louisa Cruz Acosta, Barbara Batton, Pat Carini, Maggie (Ellis) Chotas, Cecilia Espinosa, Abbe Futterman, and Nancy McKeever. Arranging Jenny's works and her treasure trove of cherished objects in the seminar room that was to be home to us for the better part of the next three days was our introduction to her. It was as we unpacked the photographs and objects that we first came upon a small china box packed with folded papers to which Jenny had attached a note requesting that we not read the papers because they were her prayers and so were private. It was a touching discovery, moving to all of us and to everyone attending the institute who happened to come by to see Jenny's works. We laid out the photographs, Jenny's personal treasures (including the box of prayers with her note attached), her smaller drawings, and some of her written work on a table at the back of the study room. We then mounted the larger drawings and paintings on adjacent walls. As we settled ourselves around the large study table, we were literally (and satisfactorily) surrounded by Jenny.

It is equally true that as we circled ourselves around the table, Jenny was at its center, sometimes present in a work we described or through a tape of her speaking—always through our focused attention on her as a thinker, learner, and person. Circled, and encircling, gathering ourselves face-to-face with each other, prepared the way for a collaborative journey to which each of us would contribute a perspective uniquely her own, with consequent enrichment of our collective perceptions of Jenny and her works.

I convened the group and, according to the plan we had worked out, Cecilia told how she had selected Jenny for the study, offering glimpses of W. T. Machan School and her multi-age, bilingual classroom but giving primary focus to Jenny as a reader and what had happened when the Title I teacher intervened. I framed the study we would do with attention to the Descriptive Processes and to the issue of *slowness* and how that is typically interpreted in schools.

I said we would begin the spanning study with Jenny's works—and we were off. Looking at Jenny's works, handling the treasures she had entrusted to us, it was impossible not to form impressions of what we were seeing and reading. One of us commented on the number of circular forms in the visual works. Another of us added to that the word "full," leading to the further observation of "roundness." Absorbed by the writings, another spoke of how personal the writing seemed to her and how consistently and recognizably Jenny speaks in her own voice. Closer description lent affirmation to these impressions and refined them.

So it was with eager anticipation that one morning we positioned the tape recorder in the center of our large study table to listen to Jenny herself speaking to us about her writings. With rapt attention, we listened to Jenny's voice retelling stories already familiar to us from reading them, including those of Cesar Chavez, Martin Luther King, Rosa Parks, and Harriet Tubman. Later, writing about this experience of listening to Jenny's serious voice, and to her own retelling of these stories, I returned to an excerpt from the tape we listened to. I quote it here in part for the flavor it provides of her retelling and in part for Jenny's description of how the book she wrote with her friend came to be—and how it was created for both of them:

> There was this boy in my class that I liked . . . and at the time . . . we were learning about Martin Luther King and Cecilia was reading lots of books about Martin Luther King. So [my friend and I] decided that we wanted to make a book about Martin Luther King. So it was for both of us and illustrated by us, and it was in English and Spanish . . . and it told about his life and then it told that he, that he liked to play stuff . . . one day his friends, they didn't come to play with him, but they came and told him they can't play with him anymore, and he was really sad and he went home and asked his mom and dad why . . . can't they play with me . . . and then his mom told him about it . . . that when she was a little girl . . . White people didn't want them [Black people] so the White people made them to be slaves. (Carini, 2001, p. 204)

It was from listening to Jenny on tape, together with our descriptions of some of her works, that our inquiry yielded its first rich fruits. Fully immersed now in Jenny's world, we had no doubt that stories of the human struggle for large ideals and causes are a wellspring of inspiration for Jenny personally—and extremely important to her for their larger meaning in the world. One of us observed that these stories are also calls to action. What, we wondered, might that mean for Jenny now and in the future? What we also understood is that it is by the retelling of these stories that Jenny internalizes them. We drew the implication that for Jenny memory and memorizing are key to how she learns, and these are characteristically the ways of learning she herself chooses and trusts. Referring to her habit of pondering and committing to memory—that is, to learning by heart—one of us observed that through doing this reflective learning, Jenny makes the idea or story her own. We recalled what Cecilia at the beginning of our inquiry told us about how Jenny had learned to read: "She memorized the book *Henny Penny,* and read it over and over, with purpose—eventually writing her own version of it, *Jenny Penny*, with her classmates as the characters."

Drawing together what we had thus far learned, we drew the conclusion that what is specifically important for Jenny as a learner is plentiful time to revisit and to do the retelling that allows her to travel deep into an idea or story. We were tantalized by her inclusion of a friend, someone she likes, in making the book about Martin Luther King, and also the emphasis she placed on writing the book in both Spanish and English. Tentatively, we thought this kind of generosity and sharing of ideas and work might relate to her concerns for the rights of others and wondered how the generosity and openness we sensed might play out in the classroom.

With these understandings—some firmly grounded, some still tentative but increasingly trustable—we eagerly awaited the next phase of our inquiry: to revisit Jenny through the portrayal of her in the Descriptive Review of the Child by her mother, with additions by her teacher as needed to fill out the picture. We wanted now to learn more of Jenny herself: what she did at home, what she played with her friends, the quality of her energy, and her ways of expressing herself—that is, her *presence* in the world. Naturally, we were particularly eager to learn how the desires, passions, and ways of learning discovered in our descriptions of her works might figure in the larger story told by those who knew her in the real and daily life of family and school: her mother and her teacher.

We were coming close to the end of our spanning study of Jenny when we gathered around the table, again with the tape recorder at the center, to listen to Tisa Williams, Jenny's mother, describe her daughter. In my role as chair, I provided a bit of context and some reminders. I pointed to W. T. Machan School and to the Center for Establishing Dialogue (CED) for the positive opportunity and experience each had provided for Tisa to familiarize herself with Prospect's Descriptive Review of the Child. That Tisa felt comfortable doing this review was, I said, a tribute to the high quality of work with parents happening at W. T. Machan and fully supported by CED.

I reminded us that a parent's description of a child draws on intimate knowledge of the child accrued from the moment of birth and inclusive of all the many contexts of family life. The fullness and intimacy of what we as listeners would be privileged to hear, therefore, carried with it a particular responsibility for respect and for holding what we would hear in confidence.

My final reminder was that during Tisa's uninterrupted presentation, our role was to keep notes of questions, of connections we perceived with what we had learned from Jenny's works, and of images or themes recurrent in the presentation. At the close of Tisa's presentation there would be a gathering of threads from Tisa's review, which I would begin and to which everyone would contribute.

I prefaced the questions that frame a descriptive review by returning us to the circumstances that prompted the spanning study: Jenny appears to some adults to be slow. She moves slowly; she's slow to speak. Adults are likely to try to hurry her up, and they are likely to expect quick responses and to put her on the spot. Jenny doesn't respond well to that and, in general, she doesn't show up well in new situations.

With that preamble, the framing questions for this review were the following:

- How can this review help other adults see who Jenny is, to value and recognize the way she thinks and learns, and to and appreciate what she has to contribute to the classroom?
- How can the review make visible the kinds of classrooms and learning and social situations that benefit Jenny, as well as the kinds of school practice that work against her capacities and strengths—and those of all children who don't fit the school picture in which intelligence = quick?
- How can describing Jenny break into that stereotype, providing an apt and rich vocabulary that does justice to her and to the many other children who are undervalued in school?

The Descriptive Review of the Child
by Tisa Williams

Physical Presence and Gesture

Jenny is the second of three daughters. When Jenny was born, we had already spent three to four hours inducing labor, but to no avail. We had a cesarean section, and Jenny was born a healthy 8 lb. 7 oz. She was a quiet newborn, brown in color with the most big and beautiful brown eyes. She was already showing signs of her good-natured quality.

As Jenny grew, she was already catching up in height with her older sister. She has a cousin Deborah who was born two weeks earlier, and Jenny was much bigger than her in size also. Jenny's hands are very soft and delicate. She walks slowly, like in thinking movements. We have noticed that she fidgets a lot when she is either sitting on our lap or a chair. Her foot knocks into the side of a table.

Her eyes are brown in color, almost see-through like her uncle's. I like to think of her as representative of our Mestizo background. Her skin color has been a very beautiful brown, and in the summer she gets even browner. Her hair is very straight, and now she likes to keep it down and over her ears.

She has had problems like her dad with growing pains in her feet. She is flat footed and not very interested in running either, although she is very interested in the sport of soccer, she does quite well, and she is a good goalie. Yes, P.E. is not her favorite thing to do at school!

Jenny has always been a big smiler! She loves to show her teeth, and her facial expressions are very joyful. Since she was little, she would put her index finger to her chin when pondering over something, like "Hmmm. . . ." That has tickled Dennis and me. Even when she frowns, she puts her whole face into it!

The most that sticks out about Jenny's physical presence and gestures is her ability to use her whole body at all different times. In my family she is known as the "Best Hugger" because she does it with all herself and body. She is very lovable and physical with her tenderness and caring.

Disposition and Temperament

Since Jenny was a baby, she has been a sweetheart—considerate with others when playing, sharing her toys and her ideas, using her words. I had a day care center in my home from the time Jenny was two until about the time she was going into kindergarten. She really was a good friend to the other children from early on.

From early on, too, Jenny has been known as the observer of the family. She has about 15 cousins, and she would be the one who would check things out first before jumping into anything. She was the one who was looking in. And while she interacted with others, it was apparent that she was in no hurry to finish first or to cause problems with the other children. I remember a girlfriend asking me if I was worried that Jenny was a little slow. How awful that they couldn't see all the wonderful things that Jenny had to offer and all her great qualities that she was teaching us already. That was my first experience at the cruel statements said intentionally or unintentionally about Jenny without really getting to know her first. The second came from family. Because all her cousins were so close in age, and one of them was the same age, Jenny was compared a lot to others. For example, she doesn't run fast, or why doesn't she hurry over there to get the candy from the piñata before it is all gone? Well, maybe because she doesn't see sense in pushing each other over, grabbing at things even to the point of hurting yourself and others just for some candy?

I think Jenny is a lot smarter than us adults.

As she grew older, her curiosity grew. Her nickname was Curious George. I love watching her watch things. She is the one to remind me to slow down. Her desire to know the *why*'s and *how*'s of everything has increased. At the grocery stores she is the one asking the clerk how this or that works, and she will eventually position her whole body around the cash register and stand there until the store clerk answers her questions. She still goes behind the register, but now she is a pro at it!

Jenny loves talking to people—all sorts of people. She is very polite and friendly and also very respectful. I think at times others may have thought she was out of line by her persistence and curiosities and thought she should just be still and not speak until she was spoken to. But Jenny still would not waver, even when mom or dad would say, "Not now, Jenn" or "Don't bother that person."

Her respect for things also carries over to respecting nature, her love of the desert, for people of all colors, for herself. Differences in people have come up quite a lot in conversations with her over the years. She has a compassion for others, for things that matter.

Jenny loves the water. Her other nickname was Water Baby. We were often frightened before she learned how to swim, because we thought that she would be the one to fall into the swimming pool or into the river. The water attracted her from very early on. She is a very good swimmer now. She is also one to spend the most time in the shower or bath too. I'll never forget seeing her on our vacation when she was seven. We were in Puerto Peñasco, and there was Jenny—out of all the family and friends in the ocean—playing and splashing, floating on her back, still and fluid, with her eyes to the sky, her body floating like she was on a cloud alone, with the whole world around her! It was magic. She really inspires me to stop and look at all that is around me!

Jenny has grown to be very confident in herself, but also very natural in that confidence. With her work at home, it doesn't matter if she isn't the first one done with the clay or with her artwork. She just enjoys doing it, enjoying it, and seeing the end result. She also is very generous with including others. She will invite neighbors over to play (sometimes to mom's dismay). One particular neighbor girl is Hannah. Her mom put her in my day care program. She was about four and Jenny was three. Hannah was very much an introvert and extremely shy. After about two years as neighbors and eventually close friends, Hannah began to come out of her shell and really became a delightful little girl, participating in a lot of activities. Her mom said that Hannah became outgoing because of me, but I think not. I am sure it was because of the friendship she had with Jenny. Jenny has a joy and enthusiasm that attract others. She opens her heart to what matters to her, and her friendships are very high on the list.

Jenny has a great sense of humor. She was the first in our family to impersonate Elvis Presley saying, "Thank you very much," with her lip curled up to one side like he does. She loves playing dress up and doing shows for us. She is very courageous in that she will put her whole self out there, even at the risk of being embarrassed. But most of the time she is never embarrassed.

Since Jenny was little, we noticed that we had to call her name quite a bit to get her attention. We are not sure yet if she has a hearing problem (she is currently being tested and retested) or if it is because she doesn't always pay attention. At home we are used to having to call Jenny's name quite often either because she is engrossed in what she is doing or she is just not in a hurry to answer us. I have learned that being patient with her and giving her that extra time is the best because she works hard once she gets to it. I notice too that she does wander off thinking about other things. This has been somewhat of a sore subject for her at home and with her extended family. I notice she really has to work hard at being there when her uncle or aunt calls her for an activity or something. She struggles with that, I know. It is very sad that she can be judged *slow* or *not all there*.

Jenny has a very spiritual side to her also. She is very interested in the stories of the Bible and asks us to read from it more often than any other book. Afterwards she talks about the stories and tries to relate them to the present. She attends Catechism class on Sundays, and her teachers have told us what a leader she is in the class and how she gets the other kids to participate by watching her. She said that Jenny comes up with such huge ideas, thoughts, and comments. She is also very articulate in her praying. I think this is an important part of Jenny that some might not know. When we say grace at the dinner table, Jenny is the one to really dig down deep and say the most beautiful words. And she has no reservations about who is sitting with us. This reminds me of how serious Jenny is about things that matter to her, about issues and people that concern her, and her belief that what she is praying for will be taken care of. She prays for her family, her sisters, her Nina, friends, teachers, for the homeless, for people to not be mean to each other, for her dad to get a new job so he doesn't have to work so much, for her to have a good week at school, for us to be able to move to a bigger house soon. Then she thanks God for her family, her friends, for the food at the table, and for keeping us all safe.

Jenny is a very special daughter to me. She is caring, intuitive, easy-going, lovable, a joy to be around! She is eager to learn new things, open and giving of her relationships with others, sensitive to issues, concerns, things that matter.

Sometimes I wish I could stop more often, smell the roses, look at rainbows in my mind, and enjoy life a little at a time with no hurry like Jenny does!!

Connections with Others

Jenny is the middle child of three sisters. Her older sister is Jessica. Her younger sister's name is Julia. Jessica is Jenny's first mentor. Jess has dawdled, hovered, watched, nurtured, protected, and just plain taken care of her little sister. Jenny has been very lucky in that way. She still looks up to Jess. Except now Jenny is as tall as Jessica! Jessie is not sure if she likes it all that much, since she is the oldest and the one who taught Jenny everything she knows! (Or so Jess says!) But they have a terrific relationship.

Jenny hasn't quite figured out what to think about her younger sister. They have their difficulties. Julia is very aggressive. Jenny thinks she gets too much attention and that everyone thinks she is so cute! (You know, the youngest one syndrome!) But Jenny tries, and Julia tries. Every now and then we get a tender moment from the two, or both of them will get their skates and go skating together. They like to play dress up together and have a threesome relationship with their cousin, Deborah. Jessica, however, has been her inspiration.

The sisters have been in a multi-age class together. Jessica was in second grade when Jennifer entered kindergarten. Jess showed Jenny how to do everything, making sure she had a pencil when it was time, or showing her where to sit, or helping her get her lunch in the cafeteria. She showed her all the ins and outs of the school! After a while Jess started feeling a little annoyed and didn't really want her sister following her around. Jenny accepted it pretty well, and soon began her first friendships with other classmates. (Her neighbor Hannah and Jenny are still best friends, but Hannah goes to another school.) Jenny met Pamela, Andrea, and Cynthia. They were in the first grade. This began a wonderful time for Jenny. Not only did Jenny have a great imagination already, full of excitement and wonder, but with the help of these girls, it grew even more. They became inseparable. Jenny and Pamela were especially close. Pamela offered a lot to Jenny and Jenny to Pamela. They read books together, wrote poems, and explored different places in their imagination. When they were outside playing, I might find them either experimenting with mud and eventually seeing how it felt to have their whole body in it, or quietly having a tea party in China, dress-up clothes and all. When Pamela moved on to third grade, the two had a difficult time. Jenny missed Pamela terribly in the classroom, but she also knew that she would still be able to see her at other times. She felt confident and sure that they were going to remain friends no matter what. And Jenny was excited too about entering second grade. It was another voyage, another journey, but this time she was going to be the big kid in the class!

In school Jenny has connected well with her teacher, Cecilia. She became an important role model for Jenny. Jenny would see how hard her teacher worked and wanted to do the same, like her sister Jessie. When we would do homework together, I would want Jenny to work on a problem a certain way, and she would say, "No, Mom, Cecilia doesn't do it that way! She wants us to do it this way!" Jenny also fell in love with all the things that Cecilia taught in the classroom and all the projects that they worked on. She would comment on how interesting the things Cecilia says are. After the second year that Jenny was in her classroom, she was even talking like her! I think that says a lot about how big our role as educators is. I mean, look at how students can copy us. We are not just in the classroom as a separate entity, just a body only there to give information, and not to give ourselves. We expect our kids to give their all, inside and out, but do we give our self?

Jenny also connected very closely with student teachers and teachers' aides in her classroom. More than once I've heard her comment about wanting to be like her, or admiring that teacher for sharing her artwork and showing her how to do some of her pieces. This is where Jenny's ideas and freedom of expression grew—in the classroom. I am sure of it. But this was also the beginning of worrying about whether Jenny was reading like she was supposed to. "When is she supposed to anyway?" was a question my husband and I talked about often. Jessie learned and excelled early on. Julia, of course, had just begun preschool and was not required to read yet. But for Jenn, it was to be when she was ready. I am thankful to her teacher for giving me research on the subject of kids and reading, and for taking the time to talk with me about when a child is supposed to be reading and how to teach them. I remember my husband Dennis and I sitting in Jenny's conference at the beginning of her second-grade year, and Dennis asking Cecilia about why Jenny wasn't reading well yet and wondering if having her in the bilingual class was such a good idea. But he just needed to learn, to study more about reading and about how kids learn things at different times and about what the child has to offer *now* that maybe some other kid who reads well doesn't offer. What are Jenny's strengths and how do we use that to support her? So began our journey, my husband's and mine!

Anyway, back to Jenny.

Jenny really connected a lot with the people she studied at school over the years: Frida Kahlo, Helen Keller, Georgia O'Keeffe, Cesar Chavez, Martin Luther King. She learned many things that sparked her interests in causes and justice. From then on, she would stick up for the underdog, and befriend those not so popular.

My sister Carmel is a very important person in Jenny's life. She is her godmother and she calls her Nina. Carmel lives in New Mexico. Jenny has visited her frequently over the years, and they have developed a very special bond with each other. Carmel gives Jenny so much love and attention. They travel together and write letters to each other, and Carmel shares with her own life experiences. Carmel has become very spiritual, and Jenny understands that. Jenny is very lucky to have her! (We all are!)

Jenny is very connected, I've noticed, with many women in her life: her Nana, Grandmother, sisters, friends, mom, teachers. She is very open and invites them into her heart. She likes spending the night with her Nana and her Grandma. She has real appreciation for who they are in relation to our family. Jenny loves to be in the kitchen with them helping cook. Then she likes waiting on us too, taking orders like a waitress, and serving company is one of her favorite things to do. I think she connects really well with adults and wants to hang out. She likes to share her poems, stories, pictures, anything she has worked on with everyone. She is a talker, but not just chatty stuff. She talks about the news, or she'll ask you to do math problems with her and then talk about how she worked them out. When she learns about famous people, like Martin Luther King, she likes to talk with family and friends about it, seeing how they feel or what their opinion is, and she carries it a step further by adding her own thoughts and ideas and how it relates to us.

This past year Jenny has developed some new friendships in her classroom. She has expanded her relationships with females and now has included some boys in her life. She made a new friend of a boy named Alberto. Alberto has had some difficulty as far as being accepted by others and excelling in school activities. Jenny has looked beyond all that exterior and found some wonderful things in Alberto, and he has in her. Jenny befriends a lot of kids. She is much more giving and accepting of people, and she amazes me with her convictions. I remember a student teacher in Jenny's class telling of her concern that Jenny was hanging out with Alberto and how maybe he was rubbing off on her because she was getting in trouble a lot more lately. I remember asking Jenny why she liked Alberto: "How did you get to be so close?" She said, "Because he likes me, mom. We like to talk, we like to draw pictures together, and I just like him." I was thinking later how damaging it is to have someone say that he's a bad kid and your daughter shouldn't hang around him. The student teacher expressed her concern to Jenny, and Jenny admittedly told the student teacher, "I'm not getting in trouble because of Alberto. It's because I was helping this other kid catch his dog and it took a little bit longer that I thought." Jenny was very hurt by this. She didn't understand why the teacher would have thought that way.

I think Jenny is the smarter one by looking beyond appearances and by liking someone for what was inside them. She is a good friend to Alberto even still.

Strong Interests and Preferences

Jenny loves to play dress-up and put on shows for us. She also gets the microphone and likes to sing with her sisters. She likes to play board games that are strategic, and she likes playing card games. She has several notebooks and pads lying around the house, and she likes to interview us and write the questions and answers down. Oftentimes she will take her pad in the car or outside and jot words down or draw pictures of whatever is on her mind.

Jenny hasn't really been interested in sports, although, as mentioned earlier, she has taken an interest in soccer and plays with a lot of determination and zeal. She enjoys rollerskating and often goes up and down the sidewalk by herself, especially after school—almost like a release or getaway or something. We go rollerblading as a family in the park, though both Jenny and I choose to rollerskate rather than those blades, and Jenny does great! She keeps going and going! Some say that she is uncoordinated, something that I am quite familiar with, as my brothers often told me that when I was young. It adds to the generalizations about her *slowness*. But I think not. Just the other day she and her cousins were at the pool, and Jenny was the only one to go off the diving board, not only once, but twice. She amazes me with her courage and fortitude. She is so determined to get past the appearances of life and get on with being herself. She is so courageous. I know that sometimes it bothers her when people make comments about her size, or they compare her to some other child when it comes to sports or activities. When we go shopping, I know that she struggles with clothes not fitting her, and that she wears a bigger size than her older sister Jessie, but she handles it with so much bravery. She counts on people loving her and accepting her for HER. Just Jenny. That's her.

I have to say, though, that Jenny is my television watcher! She was the first one to figure all the control buttons on the remote when we bought a new TV. She likes playing music. She is very smart about working stereos, or things of that nature, things that take figuring out.

She is the first one up in the morning—bright, shiny, and cheerful. She likes to greet her dad and me with a big "Good Morning!" and then plop herself on the couch with the remote! We have to be on her about that. But it's interesting to me that she likes to get up so early.

Jenny also likes to sell things. She and her friend had an idea to make cards and sell them. Since they liked to draw, and just knew that their pictures were works of art, they thought, why don't we make more and sell them! Their sale went very well, and the cards were a hit! Many times Jenny has set up a table outside our home and had mini-garage sales. She makes her signs, sets up her items with a price taped onto them. Last week she finally got to try out what she has always wanted! That was to have a lemonade stand. She did it on a Friday evening and a Saturday afternoon. There she was . . . her sign . . . her cups . . . her lemonade . . . her money can . . . and she would shout, "Lemonade! Lemonade! Come get your lemonade!" What a beautiful sight!

It is somewhat difficult to conclude this review of Jenny. I guess I have so much in my mind about my daughter. She is such a joy to all of us. When she was starting kindergarten, I remember her little face, full of excitement and so eager! She had the standard outfit on: brand new, first-day-of-school beautiful pink-with-flowers dress, brand new shiny black shoes, and her hair up in a ponytail with the most beautiful pink bow and her bangs curled under. She was beaming! She was ready and excited!

Did we know that she would have comments and assumptions made about her ability to read and write? That because she wasn't speed reading like another student, she wasn't smart? That she would be judged for the time and space that she needed in and out of the classroom? That a test would determine what she knows instead of all that she brings to the classroom and her own life experiences and knowledge?

And what would have happened, I wonder, if her teacher wouldn't have taken the time to teach her father and me about looking at Jenny's strengths and giving us literature that explained kids developing at their own pace, their own time? Finding what interested her and using that as a tool to help her with her reading and her writing. Teaching parents along the way . . . we need it.

Because if we had been any other place, I might not have learned all I know now about Jenny . . . (and still am learning) . . .

And Jenny might not have been the lead actor in the Cinderella play . . .

Or danced at the Cinco de Mayo celebration . . .

Or written and published her first book, *Jenny Penny* . . .

Or had her poem picked for the District Poetry Contest:

Flowers

Flowers are colorful
The stem is my body
The leaves are my arms
The petals are my fingers
And a flower is my life.

—Written by Jennifer Lee Williams
Dedicated to mom and dad

Pat: Following Tisa's description, I turned to Cecilia for any additions about Jenny's modes of thinking and learning. She told a story of another significant occasion when Jenny reached out to a child, as she had to Alberto.

Cecilia: For several years, we have had a tradition in our class that on Friday the student of the week gets to invite two classmates to have lunch in the classroom rather than in the cafeteria. This is a very special date for them and for me. When it was Jenny's turn to ask her two guests to come to our class for lunch, she did something that really surprised me. Rather than invite her closest friends, she invited John, a boy new to the classroom who consistently got into a lot of trouble. He tended to hurt people with his words and also physically. Most of the children were fearful of him. I have to confess that I was a bit exhausted by the consequences of his actions in the class.

Jenny not only invited John, but also the one girl he teased tirelessly. Jenny treated all of us as if we could all get along and could like and respect each other. We were equals at the table, all past actions forgotten. Jenny moved us forward.

Pulling It All Together (for Now)

Pat Carini: It was exciting, and at moments overwhelming, for us to hear Tisa's calm voice as she talked about Jenny: Jenny, the quiet newborn; Jenny, the swimmer, the Water Baby; Jenny, the Best Hugger; curious Jenny wanting to know the *why*'s and *how*'s of everything; generous Jenny, always ready to share; serious Jenny, unembarrassed to pray with heartfelt devotion. Jenny so absorbed in thought she doesn't hear what is said to her. Jenny reaching out to other children, making a friend of a boy disliked by others while standing her ground in the face of adult criticism of that friendship. Jenny seeking out a boy who teased and also the girl he made his main target. Jenny, by making herself the bridge, opening the circle to include both, and also her teacher.

Listening, we recognized the Jenny who in daily life reaches out to those excluded by others and the Jenny who relates Bible stories to *now*, as the Jenny we knew from her works—the Jenny who joins wholeheartedly with history's heroes and martyrs, who in their lives exhibited courage and so made contributions to all.

For some of us, Tisa's choice of the word *unembarrassed* was an arresting description, connecting for us at several levels. Unembarrassed to pray, digging deep for words to express her love for her family and her thanks to God. Unembarrassed to ask questions that matter to her. Unembarrassed, too, to persist in figuring out the *why*'s and *how*'s of things even when others grow impatient. Unembarrassed to show her feelings openly and wholeheartedly or to make friends with someone others look down on. We wondered whether perhaps this lack of inhibition means, among other things, that what Jenny believes to be right and true she unswervingly puts into action. We thought her friendships with boys excluded by others offered an outstanding example Jenny's values in action. We wondered whether perhaps Jenny's bravery in this respect springs from her stern belief that every person has a right to respect and justice.

The picture of Jenny as a thinker and learner that emerged for us from Cecilia's account of how she learned to read and from our descriptions of her work and from listening to Jenny on tape had alerted us to her capacity for story, for retelling, for committing what matters to her to memory. From Tisa's description, we understood that the polar capacity to Jenny's reflective power is her power as an observer. Her curiosity and determined persistence in getting to the bottom of how things work abet both of those powers. Jenny is eager to learn new things and, for her, conversation and talking with people is a trusted way to do so. We learned that Jenny also has a vivid imagination and talent for performance. We concluded that Jenny is out there in every sense while at the same time delving deeply into big ideas and large social issues, not in the abstract but as ground for action. Jenny takes the ills of the world seriously and to heart. Listening to her mother's description, reflecting on her works, it seemed to us that ultimately it is people who inspire her life and her learning—her family, her friends, her teacher, and all those who in living their lives have made the world better.

With all this to contribute, with these many strengths, not only as a learner but also as a person capable of deep commitment, what is it, then, that some adults at school find lacking? Summing it up, we found it to be a short—and telling—list: *Jenny didn't learn to read according to the school timetable. Jenny doesn't always listen or pay attention to adults when they want her to do something. Jenny isn't physically agile, appearing to be somewhat uncoordinated. Jenny isn't competitive or quick to jump into things.* In brief, Jenny's pace is at odds with school standards of efficiency for yielding measurable results on schedule.

In other words, Jenny doesn't fit the mold. Finding her not fitting into their expectations, school adults who don't know her leap to judgments. For us who had participated in this study, Jenny's mother's advocacy and Cecilia's, together with the multi-age grouping of children at W. T. Machan, provided Jenny's greatest protection against these judgments. The multi-age grouping, in particular, relaxes pressure on time while simultaneously promoting strong bonds among a group of children—both of which benefit not only Jenny but also the many other Jennys who don't fit snugly and promptly into the school mold.

We talked about how valuable it would be for expanding the picture of children who don't fit for there to be future reviews—in Phoenix, with teachers who know Jenny and with those who don't but will surely have encountered others not unlike her. Referring to the questions I posed at the beginning of the spanning study, the group concluded that it is attending to a child's strengths and capacities that breaks through the stereotypes and jargon that slate children for failure. The words Jenny had taught us about herself through her works and through the particularity of her mother's and her teacher's descriptions were testimony to that: *wholehearted, unembarrassed, deep, reflective, committed to putting her ideals into action, observant, questioning, loving.*

The spanning study proved to be an intense adventure, one that brought us close to Jenny and also inspired us, individually and collectively. Meeting Jenny through her works, her desires, her expressiveness, and her passions prompted our own memories of childhood. It was also a reminder of our own strong desires, our burning interests, and how these sustained each of us intellectually, imaginatively, and spiritually in our lives.

The Politics of Attention

Patricia F. Carini

The following essay, the first of three positioning Prospect's philosophy and methodology in a wider context of ideas, connects a mere glimpse of a very young child to world-scale historical happenings. The juxtaposition sends a startling educational and political message.

A little girl, perhaps two years old, at a stretch two and a half, is unhesitatingly scissor-stepping, one leg crossing over the other, down the seats of a row of airport lounge chairs, keeping close to the backs of the chairs, using them as a support but not holding on. What I take to be members of her family are at the end of the row of chairs she is nimbly negotiating, laughing and talking with a couple of other people sitting in the row across. The waiting area is almost deserted at this early hour of the morning. They pay no apparent attention to the little girl. My attention is caught by her agility and concentration. Her slightly inclined head suggests she is focused on her legs and feet. Occasional armrests in the down position are no apparent obstacle. Perhaps her family are so accustomed to her nimbleness they no longer take any particular notice. Perhaps they are confident she won't fall, that once she reaches the end of the row she will reverse course. Watching her criss-crossing legs as she makes her way down the empty row of chairs, I wonder how she "learned" to do this leg-crossing walk. Or is this perhaps a new discovery occasioned by the row of chairs? I wonder what claims her attention outdoors, at a park, or on a playground. Even as I am wondering, one of the adults comes and scoops her up as a flight is called. She is gone.

What has happened here isn't unusual. Travelers are known for finding something of interest, something once noticed that, dispelling tedium, claims their attention. A detail of a landscape glimpsed out a window. Other travelers.

Overheard conversation. I might not have noticed a child. I might not have been alone, but with others and engaged in conversation. I might have been buried in my book, which I would have been except the child caught my eye. There was no interaction between the child and me—not a glance exchanged or a word spoken—yet she has made a claim on me, set me wondering, sparking my interest. I have never seen her before and will undoubtedly never see her again, yet she is woven into my memory. I feel fortunate to have started my day with her. I regret her departure. There is a sweetness about what I have witnessed.

But wait. To pay attention doesn't always gift the eye, inspiring interest, refreshing the spirit. There are circumstances when to look, to notice is painful—so painful that revulsion and despair blind the eye befallen by unimaginable horrors. To explore this idea, to jar our thinking, I turn to one of those unimaginable horrors. In *On the Natural History of Destruction*, W. G. Sebald (2003) masterfully depicts this blindness in his telling of what happened to the German people in response to catastrophic bombing during World War II. The bombing enveloped whole cities in flames, leaving behind unbelievable devastation, sometimes roasting alive inhabitants of the buildings destroyed.

In the wake of such catastrophe, Sebald writes, the "quasi-natural reflex engendered by feelings of shame and a wish to defy the victors, was to keep quiet and look away" (2003, p. 30). To look away. To not attend to what is. To fix attention elsewhere. It was as if, he says, "[there was] a tacit agreement, equally binding on everyone, that the true state of material and moral ruin in which the country found itself was not to be described" (p. 10). In support of that analysis, Sebald calls attention to eyewitness accounts written at the time, noting the tendency to relapse into generalizations and clichés that, as he says, serve to "cover up and neutralize experiences beyond our ability to comprehend" (p. 25). Not looking, not attending, leached language of its descriptive potency, leaving banned images, horrors swallowed up in generalization, unmediated, festering, lying in wait, doubtless pushing up unbidden (and unspoken) at unexpected moments, haunting dreams.

Cliché and generalization obscure the particular, depriving the local, the immediate of its power. This is not without consequence, for it is the particular's sensuous resonance with body and soul and the feelings that resonance stirs that jar complacency. Aided and abetted by trite words, albeit in the face of the utterly unreal, the patterns of day-to-day routinized habits of living filled the perceptual void. As Sebald reports, "With remarkable speed, social life, that other natural phenomenon, revived. People's ability to forget what they do not want to know, to overlook what is before their eyes, was seldom put to the test better than in Germany at that time" (2003, p. 41).

In testimony to this, Hans Erich Nossack, one of the few German writers who at the time recorded the immediate aftermath of the bombing of Hamburg, describes his sense of unreality at what he witnessed—in the midst of utter devastation, children raking a garden, a woman washing the windows of a lone undamaged building left standing in the midst of rubble, and perhaps most strikingly, this scene in one of the suburbs spared by the bombing: "People were sitting out on their balconies drinking coffee. It was like watching a film; it was downright impossible" (cited in Sebald, 2003, p. 41). To which Sebald, in response to Nossack's incomprehension of what he has witnessed, suggests:

> [His] sense of alienation arose from seeing himself confronted, as it must have seemed from the point of view of one affected, by a lack of sensitivity bordering on inhumanity. You do not expect an insect colony to be trans-fixed by grief at the destruction of a neighboring anthill, but you do assume a certain empathy in human nature, and to that extent there is something alarmingly absurd and shocking about drinking coffee in the normal way on Hamburg balconies at the end of July, 1943. (p. 41)

Normalcy . . . life goes on . . . words, hollow of content, paper over horrors . . . feeling, frozen. . . . Do not trouble the surface. Do not look. Do not say. Do not tell. Keep the secret.

The example is extreme, rendered so by the magnitude of the circumstances, made tellable only by Sebald's sensitive handling of its content. Yet it is not difficult to see in it a wider application. What Nossack reports calls sharply to attention the fact that *not* attending to what is—falling back on custom, on cliché, taking recourse in a reality that on closer inspection might not with-stand scrutiny—is as common as mud.

Do not look, at least not too closely, at the fate of children in a society driven by wealth for the few. Do not look, at least not too closely, at the fate of the poor and the uninsured. Do not look, at least not too closely, at the consumer-ism and waste that grease the economic wheels. Do not look, at least not too closely, at the falling standards and failures of regulation that glut the market with cheap, defective goods. Do not look, at least not too closely, at the fact that special interests control the government. Do not look, at least not too closely, at who it is that benefits from misbegotten wars. Do not look, at least not too closely, at failures to regulate banking practices, causing untold misery through loss of homes and jobs. Do not look, at least not too closely, at the fact that this society heads the list for numbers of citizens imprisoned. Do not listen, at least not too carefully, to the clamor for safety and certainty at any price, not excluding the human rights of the citizenry.

Do not look, at least not too closely, at schools for warehousing the children—mostly poor and of color—who don't make the grade. Do not look, at least not too closely, at the decimation of school curriculum, reduced to skill drills in decoding and computation. Do not look, at least not too closely, at the practice in schools of diagnosing, medicating, and outsourcing children because they are disruptive (ADHD) or don't read on schedule or in some other way threaten the school's accountability.

Do not look. What's out there is too big, too overwhelming. Just live through it. Survive. Keep your head down. Find distraction where it's findable—buying sprees, gluttony, drugs, television, spectator sports. But, of course, that isn't the whole story. It isn't either the whole story that the entire German population kept their heads down. Some didn't. A few plotted the overthrow of the regime. A few did keep diaries of the facts on the ground as they saw them, or recorded details relayed from others. The others, the population at large, clung with averted eyes to old habits, taking uneasy refuge, as Sebald phrases it, in "the unquestioning work ethic learned in a totalitarian society" (2003, p. 12). They kept busy. They restored "order." They did so with efficiency. All this industry kept their attention fixed squarely on their "work."

Is it so different here and now? Isn't work, the economy, the big thing? For some, it means wealth and status while for those earning minimum wage or less, forced to hold two or more jobs just to make ends meet, work is all that keeps the wolf from the door. Now, with the economy in recession, many have lost jobs and, unable to find work of any kind, subsist on unemployment benefits. Humans kept that busy attending to work, or finding it, don't have a lot of time to spare for wonder and imagining, for dreams of what might be. Memory foreclosed, imagining shut down, the power to envision the future in terms other than an interminable now is short-circuited. Attention is elsewhere.

CHAPTER TWO

Meeting Jenny Again
Reimagining Ourselves as Teachers

Patricia F. Carini

"There is neither a first word nor a last word. The contexts of dialogue are without limit." This quotation from M. M. Bakhtin (1986, p. 170) has place of honor on the masthead of *Centerspace,* the newsletter of the Center for Establishing Dialogue (CED). How does a teacher center in Phoenix, Arizona, connect with Bakhtin's remarkable assertion? What does it mean that there is neither a first word nor a last word, that the "contexts of dialogue are without limit"? What I hear in Bakhtin's words I have experienced in action at CED. Though CED is no longer, it was a location where words and ideas and practice were plumbed, and then plumbed again, where stories were told that invited other stories, where conversations might pause but did not end, where one speaker invited the next.

I didn't anticipate when I accepted the invitation to offer the seminar "Another Way of Looking at Children" that the dialogues begun in those seminars would spill over to other seminars on multi-age classrooms, mathematics, book study groups, and even to reunion days, which brought together generations of teacher participants in the seminars—not to mention conference days, the annual occasion for the year's participants to chair and present Descriptive Reviews for colleagues from their schools, who in turn were drawn into the conversations about issues, children, teaching practice, and books. What I couldn't know until I was at CED was that Prospect's commitment to multiple perspectives and contexts as a way of looking and knowing was a near perfect fit with CED's commitment to dialogue. As my respected colleague Bruce Turnquist would say, "glove to hand" (2008, p. 6).

Knowing CED as I did, I had no doubt that when the teachers and teacher educators who were part of the 1996 spanning study of Jenny in Vermont urged a parallel study in Phoenix, such a study would happen. I don't think Cecilia doubted it either. I don't think we even discussed it. What I knew—and maybe Cecilia did too—was that the Vermont study would be picked up and woven into the ongoing dialogue about children that could be counted on to happen at CED. This time the focus would be Jenny and the teachers participating from W. T. Machan. Yet this dialogue, already begun in Vermont, would almost certainly reverberate in future conversations, while echoing back to others.

CED is testimony in action to the truth of Bakhtin's words when he says "the contexts of dialogue are without limit." Teachers drawn to CED didn't come there just once or primarily with "what to do on Monday" on their minds. They didn't even come primarily to select which of the beautiful children's books to purchase or to browse among the professional books in CED's library. They came to question their practice, to learn from each other, to rework their art, all in the interest of making schools and their own practice better. These weren't teachers who had settled comfortably into familiar patterns, who resented any disruption of well-worn paths. These were searchers and change-makers.

Dreya Johannsen, a poet, a student at Arizona State University, and a secretary at CED, comparing the teachers who came to CED with her own art—poetry—and that of a musician friend, wrote compellingly in *Centerspace* of how much it asks of the artist to revise, to change—and to continue to revise and change—and how in that process the art itself is made truer. In her words:

> Since I started working at CED, I've become aware of revision happening across the Valley, in the classrooms where you teach, in your teaching. So many of you are coming to our office and looking for materials to aid you in the revision of your practice. So many of you are meeting with each other and discussing your work, the teaching that is your poetry, your music, and stripping it down to the foundation so that you all can see what needs to change in order to have a truer classroom, a truer practice. How humbling this is, how admirable you are for doing it. (n.d., p. 1)

CED created the room for change to happen from the ground up, drawing inspiration from teachers' urgency and belief that it is possible for schools to be remade and for their own practice to be truer. CED itself held a vision and created a history true to its commitment to the potency of dialogue and the power of the voices of those closest to children and to classrooms—parents, teachers, school administrators—to speak out for an education worthy of the child, that took as its starting point the child's own agency.

SCENES FROM THE SECOND
SPANNING STUDY OF JENNY (1997)

Since the 1996 Vermont spanning study, there had been changes for Jenny and her family. In the autumn following that study, Jenny herself, now a third-grader, moved on as anticipated to Julia Fournier's Grades 2–3 multi-age, bilingual classroom. Even as that move was happening, there was news of a further and bigger transition for Jenny and her whole family. The Williams family was moving to Glendale, Arizona, a city close to Phoenix, a move that would take them to a new district and so also to a new school. Happening in May, just weeks before the close of school, the move would mark the close of Jenny's and her sisters' education at W. T. Machan. That event shaped the plans and the focus for the 1997 spanning study.

Carol Christine, CED director and chair for the 1997 study, chose in consultation with Julia Fournier a close iteration of the question that set the course of the 1996 study. With a major transition looming, however, the question was accented with greater urgency:

> The question framing this study and Julia's review is how to have adults see who Jenny is, to value and appreciate the way she thinks and learns and to appreciate what she has to contribute as a person and to the classroom.

Julia added to this frame a specific request from Jenny's parents, Tisa and Dennis, for help in communicating with teachers in a new school setting the kinds of classrooms and learning and social situations that benefit Jenny, as well as those that work against her strengths and limit her possibilities for growth. Julia pointed out that to do this effectively, Tisa and Dennis were in need of a vocabulary that suited Jenny and could help the teachers in the new school understand what Jenny had to offer.

There were other links with the 1996 spanning study, including Cecilia and Tisa, each of whom would contribute to this study. Five teachers from W. T. Machan School—Reneé Bachman, Karen Moore, Karin Mendez, Mark Routhier, and Diana Segovia—completed the study circle. Like Julia Fournier and Cecilia Espinosa, the other teachers from W. T. Machan brought to the spanning study their prior experience with Prospect's ideas and processes, including Descriptive Reviews of the Child conducted at Machan, seminars, book study groups, summer institutes, and reunion days. Carol Christine, many times a chair for Prospect-related summer seminars, would play that role again for this study.

On May 30, the first day of the spanning study, and on the morning of May 31, a Descriptive Review of Jenny's Work, a reflection on the word *embrace*, and Tisa Williams's description of her daughter set the stage for the concluding session: Julia Fournier's Descriptive Review of Jenny. As we enter, Julia has restated the framing questions, and is beginning her description of Jenny.

The Descriptive Review of the Child
by Julia Fournier

Physical Presence and Gesture

I think of Jenny walking with her body forward, leaning into the wind, when she does something. When she dances, when she walks, when she does anything, she's just going into it. Jenny sometimes wears her mother's clothes to school and always has an outfit on that makes me think of famous people who have had a unique way of dressing, like Francine in the *Arthur* books, or Annie Bananie, or even Annie Hall, and like our art teacher, Susan Timmer. She has a real distinct way of dressing up. No one puts an outfit together quite like Jenny. We started a little joke this year, where I would look at her, trying to figure out which article of clothing she was wearing belonged to Tisa. She impressed all of us at the swimming party by wearing her mother's bathing suit. She gave me the whole history of that bathing suit: "This was her old bathing suit, but now she has another one that's black."

Jenny does not move quickly, talk loudly, or draw attention to herself; however, I always know where she is. She has a strong presence. Her talk is slow and measured and strong. We wait for Jenny to finish, and we know it will be worth it. Jenny has earned the respect of getting the class' attention, since she has always listened to every word of every other person. Jenny uses her hands a lot to tell a story, and she does these kinds of movements when she doesn't know something and is trying to remember the word. She goes like this a lot: she rolls her eyes and uses her head as well.

I know the word *big* has been used to describe Jenny, but she was not big in comparison to the other girls in my class. I think she was right in the middle.

Disposition and Temperament

Jenny is pretty even most of the time. In the middle of an argument, she can just start to smile. She'll realize the argument is getting ridiculous, and she'll just start smiling. But when she's really passionate about something, she will not back down and will not compromise. It's difficult as a teacher, because she seems to need an answer or an ending in order to be able to move on. Sometimes it's just not possible. At the beginning of the year, one of the first questions was whether boys or girls have it harder. This huge discussion started, and it was just sort of innocent, but it turned into something else. At that time I had a boy who said really rude and inappropriate things, and so he was just saying all these blanket statements about how important men were and, basically, how unimportant women were, and she just went ballistic. She started with, "My dad works in construction, and there are women who work at construction jobs," and all this stuff, and it was really hard to calm it down, because she really wanted an answer. Then a girl said something that was just really innocent and funny, and we all started laughing, and that was the end to it. There has to be some kind of closure for Jenny, and at that point it was the humor that this girl had.

Jenny got really upset twice during the year, and both times involved the same girl in the classroom. The first time Jenny had been caught being undiplomatic, which is un-Jenny-like. She said something really mean, and there were witnesses, and she tried to say she hadn't done it. She was so upset, because she was really embarrassed and ashamed of herself for having been that way. The fight had been about how this girl was manipulating people in the room and saying things that people were doing in the class that they really weren't doing, and saying that Jenny and other girls in the class were talking about another child in the classroom that was never happening. It was time to go to computers, but there was no way this was going to be over, and so every single girl in the room got involved in the discussion. The boys went to computers, and the girls stayed and talked about it.

Jenny struggled with this girl all year, and one day I said, "I think you have a sister that's pretty much like this. How do you deal with this at home?" And then all of a sudden a light went on. After that, Jenny would choose to work with her, and it was really, really good, because it was a real struggle at the beginning of the year. After we found a different way to look at her, Jenny started to choose to work with her.

Jenny likes to go to the nurse, and I think it's the growing pains that Tisa was talking about, because she'll go and come back maybe after 30 minutes and not say anything about it. She'll say, "My finger hurts," or it will be things like "My arm hurts." I usually let her go. She can ham it up, but she doesn't really like to be the center of attention. I noticed that when she brings snacks, she puts her head down—she's really shy about it. She's not comfortable being the center of attention in that kind of way or context.

Connections with Others

Of course, the relationships I am most aware of are those with her family, which ground, anchor, and define Jenny. Her relationship with Pamela is also something that is strong in her life.

The relationship I was able to observe the most was between Janice and Jenny. I really enjoyed watching these two girls work and was glad that they were able to get to know each other through the classroom. They were similar in their manners and mannerisms, and supported each other throughout the year. Through Jenny, Janice learned about social justice and worldviews. Through Janice, Jenny learned moderation and compromise. They were not friends who blindly followed one another. They held a gentle check on each other, mostly Janice on Jenny. When Jenny asked Janice to validate a fact during a dispute, many times Janice would think carefully and modify or tone down Jenny's version.

The girls worked on many writing projects together. I wondered aloud to them at the beginning if the work was being shared by both. Jenny assured me that it was. As time went on, Janice expressed more frustration about not getting to do the actual writing more. They worked this out. At one point in the year, the two girls made a decision to consciously work with others and not only with each other, and they sort of announced it to everyone: "Well, we've decided to not work together all the time." I think that was their New Year's resolution. Of course, I had mixed feelings. They said, "It's not fair to the younger kids because we can help them, and it's not good for friends to work together all the time." They often helped each other speak, and finished sentences for each other.

Anita was another strong friend, along with these two. These three were the "outside girls" at the sleepover at my house. I had an inside group and an outside group. It was Anita, Janice, and Jenny who slept outside, and I think they were really scared, but together they were strong, and they stayed outside all night in a tent. Then the next day they were trying to be smug about it, but it's really not their way. One of the other girls was saying, "You were afraid," because the boys told them there was a headless woman in the backyard. When the boys slept outside at their sleepover, they made up all these stories about how scary it was. Jenny was the first one to figure it out. She said to me, "Tomas didn't even sleep over at your house, did he?" I said, "No," and she said, "And he was the one who said all the stuff about the headless woman!" The three girls were just really enjoying the fact that they'd done it together.

Jenny was such a kick to have around, but she never really felt like she was one of mine. Having had Cecilia for three years and having her mom working at the school lessened any teacher/student dependence. It was never like Jenny belonged to me. Our relationship was more like swapping stories or kidding around with each other.

I struggled to find a way to deal with how Jenny works and uses time, and that was hard because she was just with me for one year. Kids are individuals, but as a teacher I'm also trying to set a standard for transition, so the kids can find their own way. Jenny never, ever, ever would comply with it. I just wanted to say, "Jenny, just play the game for two weeks." But she never would. She would always start and finish when she wanted to.

Sometimes she would say, "Did you read my homework yet?" and then snicker, because she would have a special joke for me in her homework. We communicated a lot through journals. We would often talk about what we were talking about in journals outside of journal time. So it wasn't enough for something just to be in the journal; she would have to ask what I meant by an entry, or she would want more of a story. Jenny seemed interested in the adult world, in finding out how it works. She tried out her theories with different adults and kept having to adjust her perceptions. Like when she was asking me about being a Catholic: "Are you?" I guess Tisa had said, "I think Ms. Fournier was raised a Catholic," and so Jenny started asking me, "Were you baptized? Did you make your first Communion? Did you go to Confession? Do you still go to church?" I replied, "Yes, yes, yes, no." And when she was looking at my wedding pictures at my house, she said, "Oh, these must be all your friends." I said, "No, those are my brothers." She was making assumptions about other adults in her life and asking questions and then going, "Oh." I think she does that a lot.

At the end of the year, she was complaining a lot about not having enough time to finish things, and I was really having a hard time with her because she was really trying to do everything—trying to say good-bye to everybody, doing everything, still trying to get her work done, and then complaining about, "Oh, I'm not going to get my autobiography done, because I don't have enough time to do it and we need more time." And I said, "Well, what about that Friday you took off to go to Disneyland? That could have been time to work on your autobiography, and maybe you need to come in during lunch." But, you see, she had other stuff to do during lunch, so she couldn't do that. She had a really big idea about all the stories that she wanted to have in her autobiography.

Jenny also took a day to go to Student Council. It's so funny, because she wanted to be the student rep so bad this year, because . . . well, her sister is President of the Student Council, for one. I'm sure that's one of the reasons . . . but she didn't feel comfortable doing it. She liked the idea of doing it, but didn't really want to do it. And then another child was chosen—Anita. A couple of times Anita was absent so Jenny was the backup, and then they just started going together all the time. I don't know how they maneuvered it, but they became the Student Council reps together, and before I knew it, they were going on the Council's field trip together. I was a little perturbed about it, because that was another date she was gone, that Friday and Tuesday of the last two weeks of school, all the while complaining about not having enough time to get her work done.

Strong Interests and Preferences

Flowers, plants, nature, and the desert. African Americans and other people of color. American heroes and status-quo changers. Building blocks, junk construction, three-dimensional geometric work. Adult life, especially marriage and how that happens. Families. Numbers, and large numbers. Artists. The world. Friendship. She likes old things like antiques and vintage clothes and anything that has a history attached to it. Travel. Spanish language. I think it was a really big deal for her when she wrote a Spanish book and read it in front of the whole class. I can picture her reading it. I can just see all these kids, and she's reading and she had a child sitting behind her to help her if she forgot a word or didn't know a word.

Modes of Thinking and Learning

Jenny makes meaning of the world by knowing who she is. She becomes what she learns, and then that becomes more of how she makes sense of the world. Jenny is a reader and writer, but mostly a talker and listener. I'm not sure she could stand the reading and writing without the talking and listening being a part of it. The social nature of learning and life is crucial to Jenny's way of learning and knowing and seeing. There are times when Jenny is almost in a trance, writing alone, head down and concentrating hard. This usually occurs at the end of a work session when time is running out. Jenny does her work fully. She never has time to finish what she's working on, but she somehow manages to complete most of her work. Her work is also done very thoroughly, very well. The worst thing I could say to her would be, "Just leave it." There is no such thing as a rough draft or outline for Jenny.

Jenny likes all kinds of books. She really enjoyed the author studies my team teacher, Mr. Bentz, did on William Steig and Chris Van Allsburg. She likes the deep books, the crazy books, the scary books, all of them. Her real passion seems to be nonfiction. As long as she is finding out, Jenny is happy. She searches for the deeper meaning in everything. She's never content to take things at face value.

The other day the kids were doing their country studies, and she kept asking all these number questions like, "How many people live in the capital of India?" She likes big numbers. Then the people who were presenting on Italy said, "and Italy is shaped like a boot." She raised her hand and said, "Why is Italy shaped like a boot?" Like it was a symbol or something, like the boot was a symbol, because we had talked about the symbolism in flags, like the colors of flags. My student teacher, Erin, and I looked at her; it was just such a great question, like, "So are we going to get into the formation of the Earth now?" She was really thinking Italy was formed that way because it had a special symbolic meaning. I pulled down a map and said, "See, Jenny, it's shaped like a boot because there's all this water around it." Then she just started laughing because she realized, it was kind of like she got caught in a time warp or something.

Jenny's writing is rich and full. Her writing style is like a reporter. Jenny has learned the conventions of written language, like punctuation. She is using periods, capitals, and quotation marks in her writing. Jenny has good invented spelling and knows many strategies for spelling words correctly. She rarely uses these strategies when she's in the midst of writing, because I think stopping to consider that really interferes with her creative process. I sometimes worry that someone new to Jenny might misinterpret her invented spelling as a lack of knowledge, because that happens a lot.

She likes numbers. Dates also fascinate her. She likes to read large numbers out loud and ask questions related to "how many?" She's getting to know large numbers and really understands them. She likes just reading them, four million, five hundred forty-three thousand, whatever. Andrea was doing a report on Colombia, and kids asked, "How many people live in Colombia?" Andrea didn't know, and she just made up a number, and Jenny smiled because she knew that couldn't be the right number. It just sort of let me know that she does have this understanding of big numbers and muchness and that she knows how many people should live in a country. Jenny makes models for the mathematical problems she is solving. Three-dimensional construction/destruction was very big for her this year. She told me that she likes it.

Jenny challenges herself and works to find multiple solutions to problems, such as making a net for a particular 3-D shape. She finds more than one way to solve the geometry challenge or finding. If I say, "I want you to make a prism that has an area of four," she finds more than one way to do it. Jenny understood her role as an older student in the class, and when given the choice of whom to work with in mathematics, she usually chose a younger child who was struggling with these concepts, or many times an energetic child who had problems concentrating on the focus activity.

Jenny asks questions, questions, questions. People like her questions because she asks them to really learn, not just to hear herself talk.

We spent two days a month at a nursing home, and Jenny and Janice were given a special project to work with a noncommunicative resident. Both girls took this assignment very seriously and did a great job with her. They massaged her and spoke with her, with little or no response. They informed me if they ever thought there was a change. I think they both believed their work with her would make her better.

Jenny really wants to be a bilingual speaker. She has tried so hard this year. She put herself in situations that would help her learn more Spanish. I think Jenny really needs a bilingual environment; it is really a part of who she is.

Jenny has been leaving Machan all year. Just as Jenny transitions in her own way from one thing to another in schoolwork, I see her doing that with leaving the school. She had an autograph book and told people she would be taking "a little bit with her" in the book. I think she will still be transitioning when she is in her new school. When I drove my assistant teacher, Claudia, home on Thursday evening, Jenny wanted to come with me. She kept saying over and over, "You know, I've known Claudia for four years." There is so much in what she was trying to say, like the time she'd spent that had passed and had been her formal education, and how it has been defined, pretty much, by one teacher along with her two sisters.

Jenny makes me think of the moral in the fable *The Tortoise and the Hare*, "Slow and steady wins the race," and of another worn saying, "Good things come to those who wait." Her transition is overlapped. She'll let go of one thing when she's been able to grasp onto the new and has been able to make it part of the way she sees herself and her learning.

Pulling Together the Threads

Themes standing out from Julia's description paved the way to additions and to the dialogue within the study circle that followed: a child who sets her own time table, sometimes at odds with school time; an admirer of history's heroes, of changers of the status quo; a questioner; measured in speech, a diplomat; respected by other kids; able to undo her own misjudgments or a mean action; more Julia's companion than her student; a storyteller, with a love for anything with a history equaled by a love of numbers; uniquely herself, from dress to how she learns—"making meaning of the world by being who she is."

When Julia finished her presentation, Jenny's mother added to the observation of Jenny's love of numbers her fascination with the *Guinness Book of World Records*. Tisa's addition brought to Julia's mind a recent and related incident:

The other day we were walking down the street from Matt Bentz's house, and she said, "Do you think anybody thinks these are all your children?" And I said, "Well, remember the *Guinness Book of World Records* and the most children by one mother is 69, so I guess these could all be my children, except they're all kind of pretty close in age." It's funny, because she is always thinking about that kind of stuff.

Clarifying Questions and Dialogue

Adhering to the usual pattern of a Descriptive Review, Carol as chair called next for questions of clarification and other observations in response to Julia's portrayal of Jenny. These went straight to the heart of Jenny's challenge to school time, with a request to hear more about how Jenny's relationship with time influenced what happened in the classroom. Julia responded:

> It's time to go over to Mr. Bentz's class and she's not ready to go. She's like hanging out in her cubby, talking to her friends, while over in my room, we've started a chapter book in Spanish, and Matt Bentz is waiting for her to come over to start his class. Or, it's time to start writing, and she's doing all this talking before writing, which would be fine if, when writing time is over, she'd stop, but she hasn't gotten all her time to write so she keeps on writing. It's always waiting, which was okay once I knew her and everybody else knew her, and we knew we weren't going to wait for her to start, because I don't think she wanted that or expected it, and we really couldn't do it.

There was a further time-related question about Jenny missing out by being late, not getting what was going on in class—for example, not being able to follow the book that Matt Bentz was reading. Julia said she didn't think that was the case since Jenny was likely to go get the book and read it for herself.

As the conversation continued, a distinction was drawn between Jenny's noncompliance and that of "a group of kids who habitually come in from recess 15 minutes late because they can't put the ball down and couldn't care less about the chapter book." Julia interjected that adults, too, have preferred times and ways for doing certain things. Offering an example, she said the hours from 5:00 in the morning until 7:30 are her own best time to write. Why wouldn't it be the same for kids? Julia said the book *Dumbing Us Down* by John Taylor Gatto (1992) makes this point and helps with thinking about children in relation to how school structures time, and how artificial that is. For example, when subjects are compartmentalized into in tightly scheduled slots, what we are teaching the kids is to never care about anything—because how can you care about something when you have to stop doing it when the bell rings.

Others joined in with examples, some of Jenny getting in trouble because she challenged strictly enforced demands to be on line or to stop or start an activity—not by arguing, but by simply not conforming. How would that non-compliance be greeted in a new school, and how might that influence Jenny's transition?

There was a suggestion in response that Jenny's habit of setting her own schedule and going her own way might not transfer to a new situation: "Here, at Machan, she is so at home, so comfortable." Others were less sure that Jenny would respond to pressures to conform, which in turn prompted speculation on how Jenny might handle or accommodate future demands—for example, the rigid scheduling typical of high schools. The conversation ended (for the time being) on the thought that it seemed not out of the question that Jenny might be herself a system-changer, a challenger of the high school status quo.

Supporting Jenny's Transition

Carol, noting that we need kids like Jenny in high school, reminded the study circle that transitions are exactly the focus of the dialogue Jenny prompted: transitions of time. The time it takes to be comfortable, to become familiar with new structures, to let go of what is being left behind while trying to find a place and a way to be in a new place. Gauging the moment to be right, Carol invited suggestions and recommendations in response to Julia's framing questions for the review:

> How to support Jenny as she makes the move from Machan to her new school and how to help her parents find words to speak with teachers on Jenny's behalf.

Carol also pointed out that while all suggestions were welcome, and were to be listened to with respect, neither Julia nor Jenny's parents were expected or asked to take specific action in response to them.

In the conversation that followed about supports for Jenny and her parents, most suggestions hinged on following Jenny's lead and counting on her own strengths as a maker of community. The idea of talking with Jenny about how she works in a group and what is important to her seemed the starting place—possibly adding to that conversation a discussion of the value of giving priority during the first days in school to developing a social relationship with her new teacher. A suggestion followed that Jenny might initiate that introduction with an open letter to the fourth-grade teachers or even by interviewing them: This is who I am, these are the things I've learned about, and these are things that are important to me and that I hope I can study. Another participant in the spanning study thought that requesting interviews could be interpreted as inappropriate or threatening, and wondered if there might not be other ways to make a connection.

With that interjection, Julia returned the dialogue to Jenny's *own* capacities as the key to making the move to a new school:

> I think Jenny's going to find a way. She's going to find ways to turn things around. She's going to help build a nice community in the classroom. It just may take a little bit longer because it will be a bigger mission than what she had to do before. But I don't think she would be happy living in a situation without trying to make things better. That's what she sees as her goal, to find ways to make people like each other, to help people feel better about themselves.

Carol in turn summed up how Jenny's parents, Tisa and Dennis, can be present for Jenny in the school, bringing a positive message of who she is:

> It seems like it's important for you to have a presence in the school, so you will also know about what's happening first hand. You clearly helped create the picture Jenny had of Machan and helped connect school to home. That's going to be important in the new school as well. It also seems really important not to talk about Jenny at the new school as being *slow* in any way. That needs to be erased from the picture. What may be helpful is to practice talking about what Jenny brings that are clearly strengths, to work on phrases and words for talking about her that present her ways of doing things as positive contributions to the classroom. This study can be a resource for that, for putting into words her interests, the kind of learner she is, her many valuable contributions to making a classroom community, just as Julia described them.

Another cluster of suggestions pooled the names of teachers in the new district, mostly members of CED and for that reason known to Carol and others in the group. These were colleagues who could be contacted by Tisa and Dennis for guidance and might be able to steer them in the direction of classrooms from which Jenny would benefit. With these teachers as bridges to the new district, the move away from Machan and into the new school began to feel more secure, more doable—not only for Jenny but also for her sisters and her parents.

ENCOUNTERING JENNY/ENCOUNTERING OURSELVES

The descriptions of the spanning studies that form the heart of this book document their cumulative yield for Jenny and her family. Each study generated cogent suggestions for supporting Jenny's strengths. Each contributed to a vocabulary apt and specific to Jenny. Each broke the school mold of categorization of individual children according to a generalized standard. Each forwarded Jenny's opportunities as a learner, thinker, and person. In that sense, each spanning study can be viewed as complete unto itself. Separately and together the spanning studies had an alerting and also a widening effect, focusing the attention of us, the describers, not only on Jenny but also on "all the other Jenny's" out there who don't make a neat fit with the school agenda.

What has not yet been portrayed is the impact of the spanning studies on those who enacted them. In other words, what happened for us, the adults—the teachers, parents, teacher educators, and administrators—who participated in the descriptions of Jenny and her works? In a final session set aside for this purpose at the close of each of the spanning studies, those participating reflected on the experience of doing these collaborative studies and on ways that what we learned about Jenny resonates in our own lives—both professionally and personally. Sharing these reflections, usually written, we reentered the studies, this time with Jenny as mirror to our own selves.

Time Inhabited and Time Measured

Time was a theme encountered recurrently in each of the spanning studies, so it is not surprising that it resurfaced with parallel frequency across our own reflections. Neither is it surprising that for many of us, the jarring tensions between Jenny's pace and rhythm as a learner, thinker, and person and school time, with its high priority on quickness and efficiency, evoked a powerful response. As one of us wrote:

> Jenny *forces* us to look at time. When *we* take time, we are forced to look at whether quickness *is* something we should value. We are forced to look at how time (limited time) plays a [role] in evaluation—testing, circumscribed projects, etc. Jenny draws us to other values: generosity, compassion, rights of others.

And, tellingly, this participant went on to raise a bedrock ethical and philosophical question: "What should we value in schools?"

For another of us, being forced by Jenny to look at time spurred a reimagining of his practice and classroom:

As a teacher, I was thinking during the [study] how often I am worried about time in the room and how I react to children who do not (seem to) listen to my directions. I react quickly, usually not looking at/from the student's point of view. . . . Listening to Jenny's relationship to time helps me to reimagine how things can be in my room—more time for one thing—not half hour or even hour for blocks, but hours and even days to allow the full embrace of ideas, activities, and ways of doing things.

And then, more personally, the same writer observed: "I also see my own need for time and space and that jumping around from activity to activity does not even work for me." In confirmation of the desire for a less hectic pace, another teacher wrote poignantly of being reminded by Jenny of how time in our kind of society tends to trap us all: "Jenny taught me that as adults we allow ourselves to become prisoners to time and lose our love for what we do and our ability to just stop and take in the world around us."

Others echoed the educational necessity for larger blocks of time, for opportunity for a child to delve deeply and with full concentration—as one of us phrased it, "to put their whole selves into their work." Another pointed out the disjunction of conflicting values woven into the school fabric: "We want children to care about their education and to be involved on an intellectual level with their work, yet we want them to start and stop at particular times and be content to leave things unfinished." The value question at the root of this disjunction is inescapable: "How can we expect [children] to be dedicated to something if you have them stop in 15 minutes?"

Yet another voice connected time in its deepest human dimension with memory and with Jenny's own passion for history, her deep desire to discover her own location in life through the lives of others:

For Jenny history is so important . . . her own history as well as world history. She was able to work through issues and bring them back to her own life. I think about other students like Jenny and the importance of history, of knowing who you are, what has helped form your thoughts and opinions.

This sampling of the thoughts stirred for those who joined in the spanning studies is sharp reminder of the engrained practice and the routine acceptance of slicing and dicing time in schools. There is the rarely questioned pressure to "cover material" paralleled by the necessity to move children along at a standard fast forward pace. There is the recognition that these pressures have consequences—not only for Jenny, but for all children, and for teachers, too.

There is depletion of inhabited time: that is, time in which to abide, to revisit, to remember, to imagine, to pursue dreams and desires. Time depleted, time fragmented, undercuts the intellectual dedication of both children and teachers. Inevitably, speed devalues deeper thought, working against the child's desire to make his or her own connection with ideas, with history—to be a part of the world. The high value given to quick response, to the ability to shift gears, to getting it all in holds both children and teachers hostages to clock time.

Going beyond this critique, there are the positive values Jenny illuminated for us and, through her story, for others—values indispensable to learning, to social contribution, to a fulfilling life, but necessarily submerged if speed and efficiency drive school standards. Among these are caring, dedication, passion for what we do, generosity, sharing, and stopping to look closely and to take in the world. As those who participated in the spanning studies recognized, all these acts of devotion themselves take time: time to reflect, time to muse and wonder, time for enacting and for return. As Jenny's teacher, Cecilia Espinosa, phrased it, this was the time needed for any child, a child like Jenny, "to rework her ideas and passions . . . [to] embrace the world . . . [to] make her studies become part of her and then [to give back] to the world what she has learned."

Unlocking Our Own Stories

Reading the words of others who, like me, learned from Jenny, I was reminded of how our human lives and stories are interwoven, of how Jenny's story cannot do other than unlock our own. For example, there is the experience of a participant in the study who had been declared *slow* as a child that tells Jenny's own story from the perspective of its consequences over the long term:

> When I was little I was called *slow* by everyone in my family. That is what I remember. I don't know if anyone took the time to look at that way of being from a different perspective, as we have done here today. I do know that I began to believe what people said, so that my slowness became a way of being.

This comment serves as an important reminder: how we are called—quick, slow, bright, a day dreamer, lazy—all too easily becomes a self-fulfilling prophesy. As Toni Morrison says, words are indeed acts—acts with consequences (1997, pp. 13–14). Jenny's parents' refusal to type her, and the support of the spanning studies for a positive way of seeing her, guards Jenny from becoming what others call her by making room and time for her to become wholly who *she* is.

Another participant told how Jenny reflects her own childhood experience of time and challenges her as an adult to re-engage that experience:

> Thinking about Jenny reminds me a lot of me of when I was a little girl and that time didn't really matter to me back then—that I thought *alone*, that I asked questions . . . that I really cared about what happened to the people around me . . . that relationships were important. . . . I thought that *I* could make things better. These were all very important feelings and ideas I had swimming around and wondered why no one else seemed to have felt that way. I was just a little girl.
>
> *Now* that I am *supposedly* an adult I feel the way I have changed and how I have surrendered to time, but that is *not* how I want it to be. . . . It was ironic to hear/participate in this child study [at] a point in my life where I would like to revisit who I was and not be concerned with time. I don't want to fall into the trap that I see others run into. The trap of "I *have* to do this." The trap of "They're expecting me to do this."

Then, as if to remind herself of how time can be other, of how in poetry, in song, in dance, in the narrating of life and innermost feeling we *dwell* in time, the writer returned to Jenny:

> I think of Jenny's poem about poetry in which she refers to it as "being like a song but that you can put your own beat to it." That's what is so beautiful and strong about how I think Jenny probably feels about life and how much she knows what her beat can offer to the world around her.

It is a lovely image: a song we are all singing, taking different parts, each putting our own beat to the part that is ours to sing—or a story we are all telling, with each story a variation on the others. Because we are human, because we have longings and passions and beliefs, a song we can't help singing, a story we can't help narrating. As another writer told us:

> The work we did with . . . Jenny, resonates strongly because of its essential humanness. Her freshness and wholesomeness remind me of what is possible when I have an open heart and a confidence in humanity. When Jenny says, "I will keep the world safe for everyone," I believe her. Putting such trust in a young child re-awakens me to my own work— that I, like Jenny, have the power to create safety.

Expanding on these big human lessons of safety and trust, another wrote, "I am most struck by how I was able . . . to see Jenny as an equal: a human being whose well being is as vitally important as my own. . . . I felt the urgency of her safety." And she went on to say what was true a decade ago, and what achieves an even greater urgency in these darkened times: "It is frighteningly easy for well meaning persons to judge hastily and by doing so [to do] harm. Jenny renews my commitment to the kind of vigilance it takes to avoid harming."

Reading these affirmations of humanness and of education as a human endeavor recalls the words of Lillian Weber (1997): "The school exists and so one continues the effort to make it better. The first principle of making it better must be to do no harm . . ." (p. 179). And paired with Weber's words, there are these from a sermon by G. Morgan Campbell delivered at the turn of the 20th century and cited by Marian Wright Edelman in *The Measure of Our Success* (1992): "If the child is safe, everyone is safe" (p. 79).

Jenny as Compass to Value

One way to talk about what happened in the spanning studies is that standing alongside Jenny, describing her and what she wrote and drew, had an awakening effect. Seeing from Jenny's perspective called into question our own values, and beyond that the values foundational to educating, schooling, and teaching. By her example, searching questions, questions that strike to the value roots of educating and being an educator, are brought to full conscious awareness. Is what I am doing in keeping with what I say I value? Is what the school is doing justified in human terms? What is the primary obligation of the school, of the teacher, of the parent, to the child? Isn't it not to do harm? What does it mean for educating if the school reduces time to a schedule and curriculum to coverage? What is the school's obligation for nurturing the child's intellectual dedication? What are the conditions for intellectual commitment to be nurtured? What kind of time is required for that to happen? And taking that another step by returning to a question posed earlier, what should we value in schools?

These are questions jolted loose by dissonance, by the discomfort of conflicting values. Their own value is their power to penetrate the veneer of school culture and of practice routinized to fit within its boundaries. Arising from the close company kept with a particular child and within the immediacies of the daily life in a school, these are not abstract or generalized questions posed by an external expert or authority eager to promote a new model or ideology for schooling or teaching. Rather, these are urgent questions, questions that by their personal and moral weight force a relooking, a reevaluation of fundamental issues, because what is at stake is consequential both personally and for humanness more generally.

With Jenny as anchor, these are questions that can profoundly change the questioners, personally and collectively. If I am reminded that the child's safety is fundamental, then I have to ask, what is safety anyway? If I am reminded that intellectual commitment is a worthy educational aim, I have to ask, what fosters and what gets in the way of that commitment? If I am reminded that being on time and in step with the school schedule trumps the time needed for deep learning, I have to ask, how can room for big learning and big educating happen?

In other words, these questions are not merely academic. These questions are philosophy in action. They are questions "that chart a course, that exert a high value pressure . . . [that] *provide a reliable moral compass*" (see Chapter 10). They are questions carrying too much weight to be merely set aside. It is the aim and accomplishment of Prospect's philosophy and Descriptive Processes to construct conversations that raise these fundamental questions, that stir memory, that sharpen attention to the value roots and meaning of what it is to be human, of what it is to envision a humane education. Because the processes are collaborative, because they exact attention and respect for the child or work described and, equally, for each describer's perspective, these conversations create a territory roomy enough and sufficiently safe for big questions to be asked and explored.

The Power of the Particular

Patricia F. Carini

The second of three essays bearing the collective title "Jarring Perception," reconnects with the child glimpsed in the airport and the catastrophic events taking place in Germany during and in the aftermath of World War II. In this essay, paying attention—and where attention is paid—juxtaposes the particularity of the child with generalized perceptions of childhood and of the world at large. The political and educational message it sends pivots on ethics and ethical standards.

Attention is elsewhere. In *Freedom Dreams* (2002), Robin D. G. Kelley speaks eloquently to the deadening impact of a society diverted by economic interest and busyness. In his words,

> In a culture dominated by the marketplace ... the conditions of daily life, of everyday oppressions, of survival, not to mention the temporary pleasures accessible to most of us, render much of our imagination inert. We are constantly putting out fires, responding to emergencies, finding temporary refuge, all of which make it difficult to see other than the present. (p. 11)

Kelley is speaking of the society at large, but it is no different in the schools. Putting out fires, responding to emergencies, managing the routines of the day, keeping pace with demands for accountability, leaves little time to think in terms larger than replacing one model of instruction with another touted as better able to deliver the goods: improved scores on tests, adequate yearly progress, closing the achievement gap. Effectively, these demands and the routinized habits of "doing school" occupy attention. Filtered through the accountability screen, individual children are attended to mostly to the extent they deviate from school expectations, perhaps threatening the school's ability to deliver the goods. This isn't new in schools. It was, though, dramatically exacerbated by No Child Left Behind (NCLB), which put schools on notice that the stakes were high. Measure up or be privatized. Measure up or be taken over by the state. Matched with the well-established practice of being on the lookout for children who deviate or stand out or don't fit, with the aim of diagnosing and labeling them, what attention was given to a child was scrutiny for evidence of deficiencies or delays or other problems.

The idea of noticing a child like the one glimpsed in the airport, for her own sake—noticing what draws her attention, what excites her interest, what inspires her imagination—falls outside the well-established practice of lumping children together and sorting them out again by achievement and grade level, a practice deeply engrained in schools long before NCLB. Such habits of attending—and not attending—aren't easily jarred. For scales to fall from eyes, for possibilities to be put in motion, for new directions to be found, there has to be vision of something other than what is. Incremental change, some tinkering around with the establishment model, inevitably fails, drained by its own inertia. Old habits prevail. Hope dwindles. Adjustment is made.

The saving grace lies where it ever has—in the collective resistance and actions of teachers, parents, and students. It lies in resistance and actions sufficient to keep alive the possibility of something other, sometimes by connecting with a history at odds with engrained habits, sometimes inspired by dreams of revolution, sometimes by connecting with a vision of humanness—of the child—exceeding the narrow confines of school jargon and tiny ideas. It depends on a joining together of those able to imagine in the present something other in the future. It depends on practicing seeing afresh.

It depends most especially on the primary necessity of depth of experience and on particularizing that experience. For it is in the particularity of what is attended to that courage to move on to the next step and the next is found. It is particularity that sets aside reliance on ready-made solutions, that nurtures poetry and a poetics of educating. Kelley says it this way:

> In the poetics of struggle and lived experience, in the utterances of ordinary folk, in the cultural products of social movements, in the reflections of activists, we discover the many cognitive maps of the world not yet born. (2002, p. 10)

Attending to the particular is where this three-part essay started, offering an ever so brief glimpse of a little girl. A snapshot, a child caught for a moment in action, is unequally matched with the weight of the horrors of postwar Germany and what went unattended in response to those horrors. What is one child against the backdrop of 200,000 dead, many burned alive, in Hamburg? Less dramatically, but no less at odds in scale, what is the weight of one two-year-old against the backdrop of the tired, moribund habits of mass schooling? What of value can calling attention to one child cross-stepping down a row of chairs accomplish, positioned as it is, in the midst of ravaged cities, in the midst of the betrayal of promises of a worthy education for all children?

Sebald (2003), drawing on descriptions by travelers to postwar Germany, casts light on the value of the particular. One example suffices. Its source is a series of reports written by Victor Gollancz for the British press detailing the deficient diets and consequent rises in tuberculosis and other illnesses afflicting the populations of Hamburg, Dusseldorf, and the Ruhr. Sebald singles out as "the most startling . . . a brief piece titled 'This Misery of Boots,' about the wretched footwear of the Germans . . ." and, continuing, explains that the report is "startling, not so much for the text itself as for the photographs that illustrated it" (p. 38). Sebald reprints two of these in his own text: a foot wrapped in rags; a sole seemingly fashioned of roughly hewn wood, held on with thongs, a thin cloth covering shielding a naked foot. In the latter photograph there is also visible a well-shod foot, perhaps that of the author. What is important about these photographs? Why insert them in the text of Sebald's own well-documented account? As Sebald tells us, for this reason: "Photographs like these, mak[e] the process of degradation visible in very concrete form" (p. 38).

This is the power of the particular: to join us humanly in the concreteness of what is. It is the power experienced when viewing the Vietnam Memorial. Name by name. Life by life. Or in the aftermath of September 11, reading one by one the brief biographies published in the *New York Times* of those who perished that day. Or in the image of a child atop the roof of a house half submerged in flooded, post-Katrina New Orleans, signaling for help. Or in the photograph taken in the depths of the Great Depression of the gnarled hands of a man, hands with no work to do, undoing knotted string.

The boots don't tell the story. The boots make the story tellable. Here the unequal match of a tiny girl negotiating a row of chairs and massive catastrophe are joined. The photographs of the boots by particularizing unspeakable degradation chip the surface of normalcy, name false the façade of life as usual.

The glimpse of the child, brief as it is, or perhaps for that reason, particularizes human capacity, shining a light on the peculiarly human gift for learning the world, for imagining it, for seeing and making it anew. In Sebald's words, that glimpse, that snapshot lends concrete form to childhood experience and its gift to the world. In her body's response, chairs acquire new possibility. The chairs, in turn, occasion opportunity for exploring and perfecting the possibilities of her own body. Significantly, the child did this of her own accord, without instruction, without goading, revealing in her concentration on the task, her pleasure in doing it.

Viewing this chair play chips the surface of such well-worn clichés as "toddler" routinely applied to children under the age of three, while it simultaneously calls attention to the child's own resources, her own deep-seated desire to engage with the world, her ability to discover opportunity even in so unlikely and unpredictable a *resource* as a row of chairs. Equally, who can watch the child's concentration without wondering what the wider implications of her intentness of purpose may be? Who can help but wonder where her sure-footedness, focus, and confidence of body may take her in life? Who can watch a child so un-self-consciously out there, so intent, without a welling up of regard for her welfare and hope for her future well-being and dignity as a person? Who can watch this child in action without other children, or one's own childhood, being called to mind? One particular invites another.

In brief, the child glimpsed in action, dancer-like, defies childhood as a generalized event. Her purposefulness raises sharp questions of the assumption that it is necessary to "motivate" the child to learn and of the restrictions imposed in schools on children's bodies and expressiveness in the name of order and acquisition of skills according to a strictly legislated time schedule. What happens if the child's attention is forcibly diverted from where her own interests lie? What happens if no one is noticing, if attention is elsewhere, if she doesn't measure up as an early reader or reverses numbers or wriggles around when made to sit still?

Attending to the particular moves us to remember, to join with, to reach out, to imagine. Of major importance, attention to the particular awakens us, jars us, shakes old habits, forces us to look, requires us to see and to say the unsayable.

Edward Said (2000), commenting on phenomenological philosophy, and specifically the contribution of Maurice Merleau-Ponty to that philosophy, says that it is "a way of intensifying participation in human experience" (p. 5). Its subject is the particular: the particular child, a particular work, a particular teacher, a particular school. It is immersion in the particular, whether it is a child, a work, a place—or what passes for boots in postwar Germany—that enables the "intensif[ied] participation in human experience." Further, it is immersion in the particular that jars the twin habits of generalized and judgmental response, opening the way for novel perceptions and understandings to enter.

That is what Prospect's Descriptive Processes are about: how something is looked at matters. Each act of looking is inevitably an act of valuing. What is perceived may entice (the child in the airport) or repel (the degradations inflicted by the firebombing of German cities). What is perceived may stir recognition, regard, and caring or, equally, disregard and neglect—and the whole span of feelings and valuings that fall between and perhaps exceed these. A look can harm and hurt and stop. It can call forth and benefit and liberate. To change how someone or something is seen changes how it is valued and redirects actions toward it. What is held in low regard or is not seeable is easily tossed aside. What is cared about and perceived as having high value, value equal to or greater than one's own, is treated with regard, respect, and, yes, love.

Prospect's descriptive methodology, by making the child or a work or a practice or a place the subject of attention, with the aim of intensifying participation, of seeing what is there in its complexity, fullness, variety, and possibility, is an education in the art of valuing. The dimensions of this kind of liberating change are not heroic or final or absolute. Yet, borrowing a phrase from Margaret (Peg) Howes, to "unfreeze what was frozen" (cited in Carini, 2001, p. 146), to set something in motion, has its own sufficiency.

The presence and participation of others, all focused on the effort to see and to value, is key to this unfreezing. Something about a child or a painting or a place that catches the eye of one viewer is helped by what catches another's. Both are enlivened, often challenged, by the perspectives of others. There is refreshment in these many and novel perspectives, each complementing or jarring against the others. Setting aside judgments and preconceptions, describing the child or an artwork from multiple perspectives and with attention to how the child or the work changes in time and across contexts, makes space for the individuality and uniqueness of expression of each to stand forth. In the doing of it, describing that begins with tentative impressions gathers energy as each description builds on the next. As if taking on a life of its own, the describing itself becomes a collective work, a creative act. The experience of doing this collective work can be likened to awakening—to, suddenly, seeing someone or some object more fully, more dimensionally, more itself alive and in motion.

In this respect, Prospect's methodology announces an ethical position and sets an ethical standard. It is a discipline and an ethic that by disengaging describers from the habit of generalized response enables them to see beyond conventionalized perceptions and knowledge, and most especially beyond the labels and categories that by cloaking the child or work or teacher or school render them at best unidimensional and at the extreme, invisible. A nonreader.

A disadvantaged child. A failed school. A substandard teacher. These are definitions that de-face and immobilize. The definers are confirmed in their prejudices. Conventional perceptions and generalized knowledge go unchallenged. Nothing much happens for either the defined or the definers. The status quo is preserved, though at a cost. Future possibilities are foreshortened or shut down.

To challenge conventional knowledge, to disrupt the status quo, to make visible the wide distribution of human capacity and the contribution each life and work makes to the world is also a political act. Unfreezing and mobilizing the child, the teacher, the maker of works is a liberating act—and an act of welcome. It is a radical idea, a politically potent act, to take the child, each child and every child, as starting place and endpoint for education. Prospect's methodology translates that democratic idea and ideal into doable, positive practice. As Robin D. G. Kelley (2002) advises us, "The most radical art is not protest art but works that take us to another place, envision a different way of seeing, perhaps a different way of feeling" (p. 11).

CHAPTER THREE

Taking the Long View of the Child
Trusting the Person as Maker of Meaning

Patricia F. Carini

At the 1997 spanning study of Jenny, with her family's move from W. T. Machan imminent, much discussion focused on the transition. There was a new school to be found for all three daughters, with attention to classrooms that would be supportive of each of their strengths. The recommendations from 1997 placed emphasis on Tisa's and Dennis's continued advocacy for their daughters, with particular attention to a fourth-grade classroom sufficiently spacious to make room and time for Jenny's strengths to be recognized. How this worked out in practice figured in the 1999 spanning study, not as the main focus, but as context for the description of Jenny presented by her fifth-grade teacher, Kitty Kaczmarek.

THE TRANSITION YEAR (1997–1998)
by Tisa Williams

The move from W. T. Machan was not without glitches for the family as a whole and for Jenny in particular. In the summer following the 1997 review, we started our search for a place for the girls by visiting a neighborhood school, riding our bikes there because it was that close. I talked with the principal and told her we were coming from Machan and how I was looking for a school something like that. She told me that her school wasn't the place for us. Then, of course, I went back to Machan, and Julia told me about another school. So I went there, met with the principal, and told him what we were looking for. He was very open to what we wanted so I registered the girls that summer. He set the three girls up in their classrooms.

Jessie's placement in sixth grade was fine, but the fourth grade where Jenny was placed felt gloomy. I walked into the room and thought, maybe it's just today. The room was dark. There was nothing of interest on the walls. The bookshelf was just a table with a shelf on it. It had about ten books, all the same. To me, it didn't really look like a literature study section. It looked like plain textbooks and that was it. There weren't any animals. To me, it all felt strange. There was a big cutout of a tree on the wall. I couldn't tell what it was for.

I volunteered in the class starting on day one. The first paper we got that first week Jenny was there was a description of the teacher's expectations of the kids and the reward system if they were good, which was that they were going to get big apples put up on the tree on the wall. So that was a little clue. But I thought, give it a chance. I'm just used to Machan. Be more open-minded, Tisa. Then, about two or three weeks into the term, the teacher had an emergency and had to leave school. There were substitutes. We were thinking the teacher would be back. We went through three substitutes in four weeks. The teacher wasn't coming back. It was not a good scene. The third substitute saw me walking to the car, and she came up and said, "Oh, I just wanted to tell you that here's the name of a school that I think would be better suited for your daughter, it's more. . . ." She didn't say "structured," but I knew. And I knew we would have to go. I told Cecilia, "I'm on my second school here. Help me." Cecilia gave me two names. I drove all around and couldn't find one of the schools I was looking for. When I did, I couldn't get a variance for the girls to be moved there. I'm crying in the car thinking, I've got to find a place for Jenny.

It was the end of October when, with help from Cecilia and Julia, we finally found the right place. The teachers were just more than open and willing for us to be there. I knew right away that we had found a place that welcomed children. It was the atmosphere. It was the teachers allowing children to be individuals, allowing them to have their space—knowing that they are all unique, knowing that it's a learning center for everyone, including the teacher.

SCENES FROM THE THIRD
SPANNING STUDY OF JENNY (1999):
LOOKING BACK AND BEYOND

Tisa Williams's description of finding a fourth-grade classroom for Jenny added a new element to the 1999 spanning study. In other respects the 1999 spanning study mirrored the two previous studies. There were two Descriptive Reviews of Jenny—one by Kitty Kaczmarek, her fifth-grade teacher, and another by her mother, Tisa Williams. There was a description of Jenny's work, and a reflection on the word *courage*. Those participating in the review were Reneé

Bachman, Cecilia Espinosa, Laurie Fuller, Karen Moore, all from W. T. Machan School, and Shahla Nye, Nancy Pape, Cheryl Thomas, and Richard Thomas from Glendale District.

Carol Christine, in her role as chair for the third spanning study, pulled forward salient points connecting Tisa's strong advocacy for Jenny and her other daughters during a difficult transition with what was discussed and learned from the 1997 spanning study. She emphasized that Tisa knew what to look for in a fourth-grade classroom—and what not to tolerate. In this respect, all she had learned at Machan and from the 1997 spanning study proved to be an invaluable resource.

Kitty's observations of Jenny that follow are testimony to the yield of Tisa's persistence and advocacy. Each set of observations confirms Jenny's strong presence in the context of activities ongoing in the class and in company with peers. Each set of observations also offers a variation in perspective. Each contributes a facet to the picture of Jenny across time, continuous with herself and also changing.

Jenny in Action
by Kitty Kaczmarek

Advocate for Fairness

As I sat down in the rocking chair facing my fifth- and sixth-grade students, I knew this classroom discussion would be like no other. It was the day after the Columbine shootings. The newscasts were full of terrifying scenes, and these could not be ignored. I asked my fifth- and sixth-grade students to come down to the carpet to discuss their thoughts and feelings. My own heart was racing. It would not be business as usual today. All of the students sat cross-legged except two, Jenny and Reggie, who were standing at the back of the group. I opened the conversation by asking if the kids had watched the news last night or this morning. Several kids shared their perspectives on capital punishment as well as gun control. One child expressed concern that people on the radio were happy that the shooters had killed themselves. Other students wondered aloud about where the teenagers had gotten their guns.

The next voice was Jenny's. She was discussing the listeners' comments from talk radio that morning. Many people were calling in to say that kids should wear uniforms and that uniforms would eliminate part of the problem of school violence. Jenny was visibly agitated. Forehead pinched, eyebrows raised, she said, "Just because kids dress a certain way doesn't make them bad. Adults should trust kids more. All kids are not like those kids at Columbine."

Jenny is known in our classroom as someone who speaks out for the rights of others. She will step in to defend the underdog and rally for social justice. For example, earlier in the school year, the kids had participated in the Kids Voting Program. There were fiery classroom debates on propositions for and against cockfighting. Some students had relatives who owned fighting roosters, and shared their perspectives with the entire class. We had discussed all the gubernatorial candidates and their stances on the issues. Jenny led the conversation regarding one candidate who was advocating school uniforms. Jenny made very clear that this candidate's stance on school uniforms meant he wouldn't be receiving her vote.

The third observation I'll share of Jenny's alertness to rights, and the ethics involved in infringements on those rights, had to do with testing. No time is more stressful in an elementary classroom than the month of April. Students must endure test after test. It seems that I can see my students' heads sinking into their shoulders, as if the weight of their testing performance bears down on them like blocks of concrete. But, this day's testing conversation began a little differently. Jenny noticed on her test answer sheet that under ETHNICITY, someone had bubbled in her ethnicity as HISPANIC. Her mother is Hispanic and her father is Caucasian. She felt that she should bubble in both CAUCASIAN and HISPANIC. At this comment, there was a fluttering of paper as the other students flipped to the ethnicity section of their test answer sheet. Douglas commented that someone had bubbled in AFRICAN-AMERICAN on his test, and since his mom is Hispanic, and his dad is African American, he should bubble in both. Angela also mentioned that she wanted to change her test booklet to show her Asian as well as her Hispanic heritage. As a result, three students bubbled in a second ethnicity on their test that day.

What did I do? I would love to have a snapshot of my face, because I was truly amazed as I listened to this discussion. I mentioned to the kids that sometimes computers have been programmed to read only one choice per category. Their comments made much more sense than my feeble justification. Jenny's response to my justification was that I should talk to our principal about this because it did not seem right. Jenny, once again, had spotted an untruth, initiated a discussion, offered a solution, and persevered against what didn't seem just or fair.

What I have reported are all events that happened in the classroom, but Jenny also meets problems head-on on the playground too. She always lets me know when she thinks someone has been wronged. Jenny will confront other students on the playground and tell them they have wronged another person. If she can't resolve the problem on the playground herself, she will seek adult help. The kids see her as their advocate.

Speaking Out/Persevering

Jenny speaks up for herself too, and once committed to a project, she is persevering. From my observations of Jenny taking hold of a project and speaking out for it, I have chosen three incidents to recount. The first is recent. It's May at last, a wondrous time of year, because testing is done and our classroom routines can return to normal. On this day, Jenny and Angela approached me with a bundle of dog-eared papers and told me that last year in fourth grade they wrote a play on the Underground Railroad. They didn't have a chance to perform the play, because they had barely finished writing it at the end of the year. They wanted our class to perform this play, design the scenery, etc. The two girls wanted the job of student directors, and I was soon to find out how seriously they took that role. They set up a process to select the actors for each role. They decided which scenes needed rehearsal. They informed their peers when they were too noisy during rehearsal. They critiqued the acting performances of all the characters. They made lists of which props were needed and then asked their classmates who could bring the items from home.

Another time, earlier in the school year, Jenny approached me in class one day asking me to please not schedule any more field trips on Tuesdays and Thursdays, because those are the days she has violin lessons. I sometimes have to remind other students about their band or orchestra lessons, which are part of the school day, but not Jenny. Once Jenny has committed to something, she carries it through. I thanked Jenny, told her I hadn't realized our trips all fell on those days, and assured her I would keep her request in mind when I planned the next field trip.

On another occasion, Jenny asked me, "How do I get into the Film Group?" Our principal had started the Film Group, which met twice a week to plan and film public announcements and school news reports. These are shown on the TV monitors in the classrooms at the start of the school day, right after the Pledge of Allegiance. Eight students in our classroom had decided to work with the principal, and I think Jenny was worried the principal would say no since our classroom was so well represented already. I said, "Well, let's ask the principal and see." And of course she said yes to Jenny's request. Jenny started to film school news and announcements along with the other students. In this circumstance her capacity to speak up for herself seemed to me to be matched with a strong desire to perform and speak publicly and to a larger audience.

Two further observations of Jenny connect her pace to her determination to tap every resource she needs to pursue her interests. As to pace, and as the following observation supports, Jenny does not like to feel rushed or hurried. The students had been working on their human body research projects, for which

I usually allot 40 minutes. As we were cleaning up and organizing our research folders, Jenny raised her voice to be heard over the noise: "Can we have more research time tomorrow? When you put research up on the schedule on the board, will you make sure we have more time than we did today?" So 40 minutes did not seem like much time for Jenny, and she was not afraid to tell me so.

As for determination, once Jenny gets her fingers into a project, she doesn't let go until she has completed it. She uses me as a resource, but she is equally assertive and confident when it comes to asking for help from other students on projects. When our research on the human body was well under way, we decided to make a Jeopardy game using the information from their research to serve as questions and answers. Douglas had completed his research and volunteered to help anybody needing assistance with their Jeopardy questions. I noticed that Jenny went right over to Douglas, and sat down with him to discuss the writing of her questions and answers.

I happened to be sitting at a table near Jenny and Douglas, working with another student, so I could see and hear much of their discussion. Jenny's topic was menstruation, and this was a brand new topic to Douglas. So there sat Douglas, his eyes squinted, intently listening to Jenny. I overheard Jenny explaining the menstrual cycle to Douglas, and his response: "And this happens every 28 or 30 days?" Some kids might have shied away from discussing this topic with a member of the opposite sex. Jenny didn't think a thing of it. She needed help putting her information in the Jeopardy format, and Douglas was the person to help her.

Another factor may also have been involved. Douglas had earned Jenny's respect at the start of our study of the human body. I had said to the class, "Some of you are whispering the names of body parts. Are we going to be doing this all month?" Douglas was the one who chimed in and said, "Yeah, in the research group today, someone was wanting to say the P-word, you know, penis. They were laughing about it." Other students, following his lead, said, "Yeah, we're going to study this at the middle school anyway, so we better get used to talking about these things." Jenny had seen how Douglas handled himself in these classroom discussions. I think she trusted him to be mature enough to handle the new information she had discovered and to guide her in writing the Jeopardy questions.

Questioning/Persisting

Jenny is both inquisitive and persistent. She doesn't leave questions hanging in her mind. She seeks out resources to help her find the answers, whether it's a book resource or a human resource. At the end of research time one day,

I told the class, "Okay, everyone, let's get our research areas picked up. We're going to stop for the day." I saw Jenny, book in hand, wading through the students organizing folders and putting books away. She started talking to me as if I knew exactly what she was thinking about, as if I could read her mind. She pointed to the book and said, "And women have to have this test done every year?" She was pointing down to the page that was talking about gynecological exams and Pap smears. I say, "Oh, okay, yes, that's right, every year." It did cross my mind at this point that I could tell her, "You will probably want to go home and ask your mom further about this if you have any other questions."

Then I thought to myself that I was not being up front with this information. So I took another stab by saying, "It's really important, too, because you know how we were talking about cancer and the different places you can get cancer. You can get cancer anywhere in your body, even in your uterus." Jenny said, "Well, and the doctor, does he just shove this in?" And I said, "No, gently, gently that goes in. This is something that happens when you're in your late teens, and then you go in to the doctor every year." She said, "OK, OK."

Later I talked to her mom, because this was a sensitive subject indeed. Her mom had already taken her to the library to check out several books on the menstrual cycle, including the book that was in her hand when she approached me. No doubt there would be further discussion of these issues in the home, but I was impressed with Jenny's need to know that information at that moment, her deep concentration, and her strong desire to get the answers she wanted.

There was every reason to be proud of Jenny's finished research on blood and the menstrual cycle. She wrote: "You have it everywhere, and it's blood! A period is sort of like something invisible, because you are the only one that knows about it. If you don't want to tell anybody about it, you don't have to." Jenny had been thinking that the whole world would know when your period started. She had been worried about this, and she dispelled that myth during her research. When she wrote about macrophages, she said: "You are probably thinking, oh my gosh, what the heck is a macrophage? But, it is in your body, and you should be glad it is. It is like a weapon they use in the war, except this weapon is on your side. It is a kind of white blood cell. Right now it is killing some germs in your body." Jenny is an impressive writer with a strong, confident voice, able to bring information she has gathered alive. It has occurred to me that her style and voice are just right for nonfiction texts for children. All her research projects show her questioning mind and her drive to find the answers to her questions.

How Others See Her

I have already said that other kids see her as an advocate, as a fair-minded person. The last two observations I will share confirm the recognition of Jenny as a strong presence in the classroom. The first in particular offers a perspective on Jenny I haven't previously emphasized. It was January, and the fifth- and sixth-graders were deep into their Ancient Egypt research projects. They had selected topics of interest focusing on that theme. On this day, small groups of four or five students were sitting on large pillows reading nonfiction books. Some students were designing a cover for their research, while others were conferring with me. There was a quiet hum of activity.

Just that morning we had received a new student, named Nadia. For a classroom that had been a close learning community for several months with few students leaving or entering, it was an unusual event. Who broke the ice? It was Jenny who leaned across the table and said to Nadia, "Come over and be with our group." Sensing that Nadia might be feeling on the outside of the circle, and wanting her to feel at home, Jenny invited her in. So, that was how Nadia entered our classroom, by joining the Egyptian jewelry and clothing group. Jenny didn't wait for me to assign Nadia to a group. She took the initiative and extended her hand. Jenny wants everyone to be included. No one should feel left out.

My other observation turns the tables, with Jenny the one to be invited in. It, too, relates to the Ancient Egypt research. This time the students designed various ways to present their new knowledge and learning on this theme. Some of the groups chose to write a play about Ancient Egypt. Others designed a chart or poster to explain what they had learned. Others decided to write a script and film a movie. One research group was studying Queen Nefertiti and King Tut. Though Jenny already had her own research group busily engaged in designing clothes and jewelry based on pictures in their Ancient Egypt books, this group invited Jenny to be in their movie. The invitation to Jenny went something like this: "We'd like for you to act in our movie. We'd like for you to be like a reporter." Jenny took their invitation very seriously, even though accepting it meant she had a very large speaking role to memorize. In addition, she gave this group her two cents about several script changes. In response to Jenny's suggestions, the group actually rewrote the ending of their script. I think the invitation shows the level of respect the class has for Jenny. I think Jenny felt really proud that another group had invited her to be in their movie.

Pulling Together the Threads from Jenny's Fifth Grade

From Kitty's observations, it is clear that Jenny had, as Julia Fournier predicted, "[found] her way." Julia's confidence in Jenny's capacity and deep desire to make things better, to be a builder of community wherever she might find herself, is affirmed at every turn in Kitty's description of her presence in the classroom. In that description, Jenny emerges as a respected contributor to the classroom able "to help others feel included and to like each other"—a capacity vividly demonstrated through Kitty's observation of Jenny extending a welcoming hand to a child new to the classroom.

There are other themes and key words highlighted in Kitty's description of Jenny's presence in the classroom that similarly confirmed the picture of Jenny emergent from the two previous spanning studies: Jenny the questioner, intent on learning about the world; Jenny persistent in her efforts, not easily deflected from a question or from completing what she has set out to do; Jenny setting her own deliberate pace; Jenny a changer of the status quo; Jenny a vigilant advocate for others and for fairness; Jenny able to speak up for herself and for others; Jenny alert to making room for all to be included; Jenny a lively and thoughtful writer.

Though subtle, there are also changes in the picture of Jenny, now a fifth grader, nearing the completion of her elementary education. Notable among them is extension of her fascination with story and storytelling to drama and dramatic performance as evidenced in the Underground Railroad play carried over, Jenny-fashion, from one year to the next; her determined and successful effort to join the principal's Film Group; and the invitation readily accepted to take a major role in the Ancient Egypt movie. Equally notable is that Jenny not only entered into these dramatic activities with her customary wholeheartedness and carry-through, she took charge: changing a script, casting the roles, organizing the cast to obtain props, overseeing the quality of the production as a whole. Jenny's capacity for seeing and implementing a large-scale project, and her capacity for involving others in her vision—hinted at in the earlier presentations—emerge here full flower. By 1999 there was no question Jenny was on her way.

POSTSCRIPT ON SIXTH GRADE
by Tisa Williams

Jenny's elementary school years ended well. As she was about to enter sixth grade, Dennis and I were a little nervous, because she wanted the same teacher as her older sister Jessie had had. This teacher was very good, but had a fast pace in her classroom and held high expectations of the children. That was good, but we did not know how far she would go if a child wasn't keeping up with the rest. Would Jenny's self-esteem be on the line every day, or might she feel unworthy or misunderstood?

Jenny flourished in this classroom! We had given her new teacher a copy of all the Descriptive Reviews that her teachers and I had written, and I think that really made a difference.

Jenny became a true leader in her class, she was a friend to everyone, and she could always be counted on to help or to be a part of whatever was going on in the classroom. She really had an impact in the sixth-grade classroom for the entire year.

Body in Motion

Patricia F. Carini

It is Prospect's way to juxtapose close attention to the details of the daily life of children and classrooms with close reading of philosophical texts, novels, and poetry. In this final essay of the three parts of "Jarring Perception," the philosopher Maurice Merleau-Ponty's likening of the body as work of art is pivotal, as is his assertion that "we are condemned to meaning (1962, p. xix)." This essay reconnects once again with the small child glimpsed in the airport and, through her, with our own self-making.

Paying attention to the child in motion, with herself, with the world, jars against generalized notions foundational to such laudatory aims as "putting the child at the center" or "taking the child as starting point for education." The child in the airport doing her chair dance sidesteps the static language of "whole child." Applying the designation "unique" or other well-worn phrases of "agency" in her own learning, flattens rather than heightens attention to what is going on in this chair play. That said, it is as important to note that though the words, threadbare from use, are clichéd, they are not for that reason false.

It is true that the child is more than the sum of her parts, and as parents of more than one child can affirm, it is equally true that no two children—not even identical twins—replicate each other. Each baby born inaugurates the world anew, bringing to the world a refreshing perspective. While there are resemblances and complementarities, the weaving together of modes of expression, of ways of greeting and engaging the world, embodies a complexity that far exceeds the additive.

These points tend to be missed in the schools. Attention is elsewhere. Nearly always it is uniformity that is sought. Differences of any kind threaten the smooth running of things. Unruliness, quirkiness, stepping outside the established boundaries are seldom accorded a high regard in schools. In schools, the child as a number, a statistical average or percentile rank, obliterates the child's expressiveness and complexity. In particular, the body—the very locus of expressiveness—is denied. Adventuring into unknown territory, kicking over the traces, and breaking free are inseparable from the energetic body and its unpredictable gestural potency. In this configuring of the body as locus of expressiveness, as vital force in making and remaking both self and world, the body according to Merleau-Ponty (1962) is likenable to a work of art, his argument hinging on the individuality of each artwork and the impossibility of separating the body's expression from what is expressed—say "the dancer from the dance" (Yeats, 1996, p. 215). In Merleau-Ponty's words:

> A novel, poem, picture, or musical work are individuals, that is beings in which the expression is indistinguishable from the thing expressed. It is in this sense that our body is comparable to a work of art. It is a focal point of living meanings, not the function of a certain number of mutually variable terms. (p. 151)

The comparison of the body to a work of art, a source of meanings extending beyond itself, for which it is the focal point, signals a radical departure from usual ways of seeing the child (or ourselves). What has marred the conceptualization of the child as "whole" is the tendency to compose that wholeness from discrete parts: social, mental, emotional, and so on—all in the interests of preventing failure to recognize that there is more to the child than mental competency, that nutrition and the child's general well-being are also at stake. As a conceptualization, this view is useful and also lacking. It misses the potency of the human drive for meaning, the passion for living fully on the cusp of life, the burning intensity of desire. Most significant, it misses the body, replete in its gestural expressiveness, its passions. Missing the body, it misses play as the generative channel for the child's passions—those lived meanings to which, as Merleau-Ponty says, *we are condemned* (1962, p. xix; emphasis in original).

"Condemned to meaning" is a startling assertion. To be condemned brooks no option. The desire for things to make sense (even when they may not seem to), married to the strong desire that whatever it is that attracts and drives desire *matters* (even when that may be called into doubt), is overwhelming in its urgency—and in its implications. For things not to make sense, for things not to matter, undoes intention, aim, purpose—unravels the web of being. Hope of the future vanishes. Educationally, to start from the child's passion redirects attention away from "learning" as external to the child, something that

requires instruction at every turn, something that must be imposed on the child. Reoriented to the child's desire, attention is directed to particularizing the child's passions, to where it is in the world the child seeks the meaning to which, being human, she is "condemned," and the significance (or value) of what she encounters in her search. Attention is shifted to the mediums, the stories, the archetypal human themes roomy enough to channel her desires, spacious enough for her to find her own place in the world, sturdy enough to bear her weight, bridging from the here and now to a future not yet foretellable, but beckoning, holding promise of more to come.

To pay attention to the child as a work of art stretches the imagination, dramatically challenging the truisms of "uniqueness" and "wholeness." The child in kinship with works of art is not a closed or sealed system. A poem, a musical composition, a dance, a painting calls out to other poems, other compositions, other paintings—and, equally, to the makers of these works. A constellation of works inspires the making of more, like to some, arguing with others.

So, too, with a child. Even as I am watching the child in the airport, I am remembering stories of my own nimble-footed sister, walking at nine months, a skilled climber at the age of a year or so, anticipating in these feats future athletic proficiency. Children drawing side by side trade ideas and stylistic elements. Open to others, the child is open to the world. Notwithstanding all the suns drawn by children, each adds a nuance, an element of novelty. Novelty defies identity while contributing to the ever-increasing, never-repeating congregation of suns, creating kinships with other sun makers. Trees are figured in dances with arms curved to make the crown or held close to the head, palms flattened together, in depiction of stately pines. The child, the artist, is gifted with capacity to become whatever it is in the world that commands attention—to gesture it, to draw it, to tell it, to write it; in brief, to remake it.

To what purpose all this profligate making and remaking, this knowing of the world by being it—happening now all over the world, as it has for so long as the human race has existed? What is this passion for making about? What light does it shed on learning, on educating? It is about self and self-making. It is about making and remaking experience and engraining it in the body, in memory. It is about the satisfaction of reaching deep and extending far. It is about accomplishment and usefulness and contribution. Work and works are not divisible. The worker's satisfaction measured by whatever standards she holds to be acceptable, whatever for him has a rightness or beauty about it, is worth the striving it exacts for the confidence it instills and its generative potency. The maker is at one and the same time grounded and propelled into a future replete with possibilities. The poet Jimmy Santiago Baca (1992) writes movingly of his own experience of this satisfaction, this grounding and launching, achieved by learning to read and write in prison by listening to the words of poets read aloud by other prisoners. In his words:

> When I at last wrote my first words on the page, I felt an island rising beneath my feet like the back of a whale. As more and more words emerged, I could finally rest. I had a place to stand for the first time in my life. The island grew with each page, into a continent inhabited by people I knew and mapped with the life I lived. (p. 7)

Focusing on the child as maker, attention is drawn to the child's particularized expressiveness in play with the world, with others, with her purposes and her ways of being. Attention is drawn to where the *child's* attention is and what it is that compels her interest—as her own legs were compelling for the child in the airport—perhaps for just a moment in time. Perhaps foretelling a future yet to be discovered. In the glimpse of the child in the airport, her medium is her body, specifically its rhythmic capacity expressed in the repetitive criss-cross of her legs. The gesture to the future is foretold in early agility and her enjoyment of this expression of it readable in her total concentration. The body as medium for expressiveness is a place to start. The educational question is how to expand opportunity for that expressiveness, attentive to other mediums that may intensify pleasure in the rhythms of the body and the world: dance, gymnastics, music, rhymes and poetry, the cycles of the season, perhaps patterns more generally.

Guiding each such glimpse of a child is the necessity for response to what the child is drawn to (and repelled by), values (and dismisses), attends to (and turns away from)—and especially what the child burns for with insatiable desire, cherishes and yearns for with a terrible longing. Attentive to the child as maker, as herself a work of art, what overwhelms the teacher, the parent, is not the *paucity* of the child's capacities, but their muchness, variety, and complexity. It is a story most fully told in the child's own making of things, the reciprocating works of art that spill out from her expressiveness, her engagement with mediums and the world. For in the making of things, the maker authors her own self as well. This is a story, always partial, never fully knowable, not even to the maker—and assuredly not to the onlooker, however lovingly attentive. Yet—and this is of utmost importance—though ever partial, the story of the child's making of things, and of her own self-making, is sufficient, and more than sufficient, as guide and inspiration for her education.

CHAPTER FOUR

Describing Jenny's Writings and Drawings
Authoring Works/Authoring Self (2006)

Patricia F. Carini

When Prospect School opened its doors in 1965, among its furnishings were paints, sand, blocks, paper, crayons and markers, cardboard and wood scraps, clay, sewing materials, and more, all accessible to the children. For the first 45 minutes to an hour in the morning, there was a hum of activity as the 23 children, ages 5–7, took charge of these materials. To say the children took to these materials is an understatement. Works poured out on a daily basis. The proliferation of what the children made was like a waterfall—unstoppable. Looking at children's works was inescapable for the simple reason there were so many of them. What took longer was to learn how to look more closely.

At first, it was how the children went about making things that claimed my attention. Some moved around, touching different materials, sort of getting the feel of a medium before settling on what appealed. Others dove for a prized material that, given the choice, they were quick to claim. Some stayed with one material the whole time, while others fitted in two or three. As makers, children were sometimes so quick to decide on *what* to make that it seemed the decision had been taken beforehand. At other times, their activity was exploratory—a kind of testing of the possibilities of the medium. For some, especially those deeply engaged with story, or what is sometimes called imaginary play, materials—even as props—seemed superfluous.

These differences in preference and ways of working intensified my interest, and the more so as I began to notice that across time, a child's works display a continuity of themes and motifs and style, nuanced by experimentation and by increasing facility with preferred mediums. Bound up in the making, and observable in the works made, were the child's gestures and expressiveness, his or her ways of engaging the world.

Paying attention to these continuities and ways of engaging, I came to understand that works and the making of them are arrows to what I think of as a child's—or any person's—internal furnishings: to memory, to narration and story, to imagination, to an aesthetic identifiably that child's (and no other's). That is, the integrity of a child's works matches to her or his own integrity. A child's works map a path to what the child values, strives for, holds to as expression of self. In brief, works mark a path to the child's self-making.

At Prospect, the things children made were sometimes photographed. Many went home. A lot got left at school. Keeping those left behind, and later more purposefully collecting what children made, we encountered the question of what to do with all the works we had gathered. For a while, the approach was to organize them by theme and motif. We learned a lot from taking this slant. Among other things, we were struck by how many houses, trees, and suns got made, and that even so, these elements seemed not to be exhaustible. One child's suns weren't duplicated by another's. The trio of house, tree, and sun figured in countless drawings, yet each rendering was fresh. What did the novelty and freshness with which each child imbues these motifs mean?

DESCRIBING CHILDREN'S WORKS: A PROCESS

These kinds of observations and questions turned our attention to finding a way to look more closely at children's individual collections. Yet we were also hesitant. Mostly, children's art has been categorized developmentally or in accordance with personality theory and other typologies. We knew we didn't want to engage in this kind of psychologizing of the work as a tool for categorizing the child and, as we saw it, dismissing in the process both the maker and the work. We wanted something else: to see a work more fully and, in particular, to understand better how it reflects a child's pursuit of meaning. Description without passing judgment or assigning the work to predetermined categories seemed better fitted to our purpose of learning to see works without trying to explain them away. Here we had some experience, for it was already the practice in the school to describe children in this way.

It was Beth Alberty, a frequent visitor to Prospect who brought with her a strong background in art history, who pushed us over the edge, with the suggestion that we devise a process for describing works in parallel with the one for describing children. With her help, we began. Coupled with this venture was the decision to reorganize the collections of children's works according to child. This wasn't an idle whim. The questions driving it were ones we were already grappling with: What did it mean that a child's work was so identifiably her or his own even as it changed? What did it mean that for any given child certain themes and motifs where recurrent across the body of work? How did the continuousness of the child's gesture and ways of orienting herself in the world connect with the continuousness of the works she made?

After experimentation, a remarkably straightforward process for doing description of children's work emerged. There is a planning session in which the teacher or parent of the child whose collection is to be explored and a chair who will conduct the review meet to get an overview of the works and choose a work for description—most often because the work plumbs a vein in the works richly represented in the collection. Once the chair and presenter have chosen the focal piece of work, a word for reflection is chosen—a word tied directly to the focal work or to works recurrent in the collection. If there is enough time available, the planners may include the opportunity for response to additional works from across the collection, either before or following the description of the focal work.

This chapter provides a concrete example of the process in action as we turn to look closely at Jenny's works. Descriptions of her works, along with reflections on words these works called to mind, played a part in each of the spanning studies, beginning with the taped version of her retelling of the Martin Luther King story, and followed in the 1997 study with a reflection on *embrace* and description of a tri-fold collage. Jenny's fascination with drama and information gathering are featured in the observations of her fifth-grade teacher.

These descriptions of Jenny's works were by no means mere add-ons, although her mother's and her teachers' descriptions of her in the classroom and at home have so far in the book held center stage. Featuring Jenny's works as a fourth perspective on her unfolding story now focuses attention on her own expressiveness, her choices of medium, and the motifs and themes recurrent across a body of her works. It isn't that approaching a child's story through works tells a whole new story. It doesn't. It does, though, tell that story *differently,* often adding dimension and complexity to the one narrated by those observing the child—however loving their attention.

SCENES FROM THE DESCRIPTIVE REVIEW OF JENNY'S WORKS (2006)

The opportunity to focus solely on Jenny's works came up fortuitously. There was an afternoon during the 2006 Prospect Summer Institute in Bennington, Vermont, when it proved possible to assemble a group to do a three- or four-hour mini-study, with me playing the role of chair. Six institute participants volunteered to join the study circle: Joan Bradbury, Louisa Cruz-Acosta, Helen Martin, Gina Ritscher, Ellen Schwartz, and Lynne Strieb. Along with me, Louisa Cruz-Acosta had been a participant in the 1996 Spanning Study, which was also held in Vermont. All others participating in the mini-study would be look-ing closely at Jenny's works for the first time, bringing to the works, and to Jenny herself, fresh eyes and perspectives.

As I have explained for other aspects of the review process, several key deci-sions are made in advance. Although Margaret Himley would not be able to participate in the review, her familiarity with Jenny's works was key to these decisions. Together we settled for this mini-study on high-quality color copies of 20 works spanning Jenny's elementary school years. Looking through them, we noticed, not for the first time, that many blended visual and written mate-rial. We decided on a composition Jenny made in first grade that paired a poem and a drawing as the focal piece for description, with primary attention to the poem (see Figure 4.1). The title of the poem written in Jenny's hand was "The crkol ovv Liyf."

The piece also recommended itself for its embodiment of elements recurrent in the other pieces we had at hand: circles, hearts, color, world among them. Plumbing the meanings of any of these words would have yielded rich mean-ings. After some weighing of options, we chose *world*. To keep attention on the focal piece, another decision was to wait to display the body of works until after the description of "The crkol ovv Liyf." With these decisions made, we moved on to create a plan we hoped would use the four hours to the maxi-mum—a plan I introduced at the start of the study, just prior to the reflection on *world*.

Starting Up

The introductions that usually open a Descriptive Review of Work were omit-ted because all in the group were acquainted. I explained the reason for taking this opportunity to focus exclusively on Jenny's works. I also explained the advance decisions Margaret and I had made, and outlined the plan for the study, giving some emphasis to the allowance of a generous amount of time held in reserve following the description of "The crkol ovv Liyf" to view other works, with individual study of those works to follow. In outline, the plan looked like this:

- Reflection on *world*
- Description of the focal work, "The crkol ovv Liyf"
- Overview of additional works representing a span from early to later ele-mentary school years (a total of 19 works)
- Individual study of works selected from among the 19
- A final go-around to gather threads from the mini-study as a whole

I reminded all of us taking part of the dual requirements of respect for Jenny, her family, her teachers, and her works and of preserving the child's privacy by keeping the afternoon's proceedings in confidence.

Reflection on *World*

Reflecting on a word is quiet, solitary work, each person delving into her memory for phrases, words, and images evoked by the word, writing these down as they come to mind. The point of a reflection is not to winnow or define a word. The point is to uncover some of the richness of layered meaning the word embodies. In the reflection on *world,* my own first response happened to be William Blake's "The world in a grain of sand." Later, in the sharing of our responses, another speaker phrased that thought otherwise, with the observation that anything looked at closely—a flower, a leaf, a seed—opens up a world.

The one of us who started the sharing began, though, not with the infinitesimal but with the immensity of the world—and all that it encompasses—and then, in counterpoise, came her own observation that each of us, though living within the immense world, makes worlds of our own. Children make "small worlds" using whatever comes to hand—twigs and leaves and acorns, Legos and blocks. Teachers create a classroom world. A family makes a home.

The bigness of the world came first, too, for another in the circle, but for this speaker it was from the angle of how the world has beckoned humans to explore it—an exploration that chronicles a long human history of discovery of new territories and the mapping of these. As she reminded us, it is a bloody history. Entire populations have been decimated by explorers. Eco-systems have been destroyed.

With variations, there were references by several speakers to the world as contained, bounded by its own circumference, itself a tiny part in an ever-expanding universe. Exploration taken from another slant called attention to the deep, driving human desire to know, to understand the world—and ourselves within it. Myth and science. Diaries, stories, chronicles, and histories. Dreamers and inventors and prophets and poets and teachers.

That a book can create a world, a world the reader enters and becomes a part of, added yet another dimension, leading on to how people as makers of traditions, of rituals, of all manner of ideas and belief systems, and of things, have told the world over and over again—culturally and historically—changing it and themselves. All of these slants and more were shared, including stories from our own lives.

The crkol ovv Liyf	The Circle of Life
i raley Like it Bekas	I really like it because
it has Los ovv kolrs	it has lots of colors
and Pekas The wrold	and because the world
is a slsahl Plays	is a special place
Bot I don tek it	but I don't think it
Is varey kolrfol	is very colorful.
i Love the wrol	I love the world
i will kep it saf	I will keep it safe
For avvrey one	for every one.

FIGURE 4.1 "The crkol ovv Liyf," by Jenny Williams (first grade)

Looking across the responses, the polarities of the immensity of the world with the infinitesimal, of the physical, geographic world with worlds imagined, of world as bedrock and world as remarkable, of the world's expansiveness and its boundedness are strikingly recurrent, with examples and words chosen by each speaker contributing nuances of meaning.

We let the reflection on *world* settle, to find its place, not as a lens through which to read Jenny or interpret her works, but rather as context shared among us. How *world* figures in Jenny's thinking and works, and what from our reflection might make some connection with *her* telling of *world*, we would discover by way of the work itself.

Describing "The crkol ovv Liyf"

Immersion and First Impressions. In keeping with the usual practice when describing children's writing, we listened to "The crkol ovv Liyf" (Figure 4.1) read three times aloud, by three different readers, each voice intensifying our experience of the poem, providing the opportunity to immerse ourselves in it, to experience it together as a whole. Listening to the poem, it was impossible not to form impressions of it. Sharing these allowed us to edge a step closer to the poem itself. One of us called attention to the roughly circular drawing that separates the two stanzas of the poem while others spoke to the bigness of the title ("it's huge") and to Jenny's references to color. We were all puzzled by what we saw as ambiguities in the poem, especially in connection with the word "it."

Description of the First Stanza. The ambiguities were the lead-in to a closer line-by-line reading and description of the poem. This descriptive reading is a sometimes slow, even painstaking process. There are times when a particular reading of a line is confirmed by other describers—but not always. Divergent perceptions of the same line, each supported by the describer's explanation of the basis for her reading, aren't reconciled. Each is allowed to stand. There is no cross-talk and no need to justify. The descriptions heard, one following the other, simply layer. Periodically, there is a pause to pull together threads of the description.

The following samples offer a taste of our first forays into the description of Jenny's poem, starting with the title:

Although the title has only four words it's huge, conveying all the cycle of life . . . the weighted words are "circle" and "life." A circle has no beginning or end. By putting "life" alongside "circle," there is a sug- gestion that life can be like that—that it has no beginning or end.

The next describer observed that there is no explicit mention of the circle of life in the poem, going on to say: "Neither do the words 'circle' or 'life' appear, leaving the relationship of the title to the poem somewhat ambiguous, though describing the poem itself may clarify the relationship."

The next rounds of description focused on the first six-line stanza of the poem, which was initially read and responded to as couplets, beginning with the first: *I really like it / because it has lots of colors.* The first describer said:

Because the line begins with "I" there is a personal tone confirmed for me by the writer's equally personal response of "liking it." It might refer back to the title or it might refer to the drawing.

The next describer called attention to the use of "really" and "lots": "Those words lend emphasis to 'like' and richness and perhaps variety to 'color'." The third describer agreed with and also qualified this comment: "Yes, there is emphasis but even so, all the words used are ordinary and unelaborated."

From these first forays, the tempo picked up. The next rounds of description tended to have a larger scope, providing a more confident rendering of how the poem works—and what makes it work.

I'm responding to the whole first stanza. The first couplet begins with "I," the second with "and"—which seems to make a transition. And then the third line begins with another conjunction, "but"—suggesting an

exception. The "but" appears to position the third couplet in contradiction to the first: lots of colors and *not* very colorful.

Other contributions to the next two rounds of description called attention
to the dominance of verbs and the absence of adjectives. The exception—
"special"—could apply to many things, but in context we understood Jenny to
mean "special" in the relational sense: the specialness of the world to her. One
of us suggested that though "world" might refer to her drawing of it, this line
may also mark a transition point in the poem, moving on from the picture to
the actual world and Jenny's feelings about that actual world. Picking up on
this reading of the poem, another describer pointed out that the first stanza is
readable as prose: "It has a conversational quality and a softness of tone, ascrib-
able perhaps to the lack of punctuation and ordinariness of the language."
We took another look at the first stanza as a whole, paying particular attention to the verbs "like" and "think." To several describers, these seemed to make
another transition:

> Not only is the reader possibly being moved from one location (a draw-
> ing) to another (the actual world), "think" shifts the ground from feel-
> ing to analysis. It's as if the writer takes a step back to have a second
> look—an evaluative look: the world is a special place but it isn't very
> colorful—and color is something the author asserts she really likes—
> *lots* of color.

Collectively, we were puzzled. There appeared to be a contradiction. Was
that contradiction calling attention to the colorfulness of the drawing and
relative lack of color in the actual world? Lacking the descriptive evidence to
resolve this question, we deliberately left it hanging. We also reminded ourselves that ambiguities are anything but uncommon in art works, visual and
written, and that this is true of works by adult artists and authors a well as
children.

Description of the Second Stanza. The description of the second stanza
returned us to verbs, taking us deeper into the compositional structure of the
poem. That starting point also served to pull together several threads from the
description of the first stanza.

> ***First describer:*** I want to talk about verbs. She starts with "I really
> like," followed by "I think." "Like," as we said, is a statement of feel-
> ing. "Think" is mental. Then there's the break between stanzas. Then,

"I love the world," which is another but even stronger verb. "I love the world," like the title, has four words. It is a very direct statement. There's something about the tone. "Love" and "world" are both huge. The tone changes in this stanza. There is something about this poem that brings to mind a sonnet. I know it isn't a sonnet, but it shares with that form a description followed by a conclusion—in this case a promise: "I will keep it safe." I love, I will keep. What happens is an action, but at the same time it is a holding. It's not an acting on the world. It's a holding of the world to preserve it: to make the world not a dangerous place, not just for her but for everyone. It is the tender tone of this stanza and its message that makes that first part that can be read as prose, not prose—but poetry. It is like the Circle of Life: the ending is circling back up and changing the tone of the first stanza.

Momentum gathered from this braiding together of several strands from the description. One of us had been counting words and mulling over the words used and the particular locations in which they appear:

There are only 26 words in this huge poem, and they are all words we use every day. The writer uses "I" four times, making the poem personal—her feelings, her thoughts, her intentions. "Color" and "world" each appear twice as the subject of her feelings and of the poem. "Safe" appears only once. "Everyone" appears only once and at the end. That enlarges the promise and moves the poem from "I" to "all."

Picking up on what moves the poem, and where the author stands in relation to it, there was this observation:

Until the line "I don't think it is very colorful," the feeling has been outward: I really like it; the world is a special place. It is, as we have said, a stepping back, to look from a different angle, to evaluate. It is a private statement, as if said to herself. It is as if every line or couplet turns the poem a little bit. It's a back and forth between her and the world so that even though it is for everyone, it feels exceedingly personal. If this is a piece of school work, I have to wonder what gives her the internal freedom to move to this deep, tender thoughtfulness, to make herself so vulnerable.

The gentle power of the poem moved us, just as the author's love moves the poem:

The writer is a little, little girl, perhaps only six years old, but the poem is a statement of power. Or at least, she assumes she has power. It is great love that is its source and is also what motivates her to keep the world, this special place, safe. I couldn't help thinking of Superman: making the world safe for everyone. But she isn't Superman, she's a little girl.

The time for describing the poem was drawing to a close. Yet, as so often happens when describing works, the poem, now internalized by us, continued to speak and to connect. That the poem and title work together was thought provoking. Though the connection isn't direct, the poem circles back in a manner akin to the title. Both are huge in feeling and in concept: an unending cycle of life, the bigness of the world.

Paused at this point of consideration and wonder, we were not quite ready to let the poem go. What was said next helped us to do that:

> I've been thinking that this poem calls up some other poet but I couldn't get to it. It's Langston Hughes. It is the way she uses language, but it's also a particular poem by Hughes. . . . I wish I could remember the poem, but anyway, Jenny's poem reminds me generally of Langston Hughes's very soft, direct way of using language and how that expresses tremendous feeling but is never overstated.

This same speaker went on to mention two other things that had caught her attention:

> I was looking at the original. In it, in her own hand, she wrote "everyone" as two words: "every one". Read that way, it isn't a generalized "all" for whom she is keeping the world safe, but each and every person in the world. Also referring to the original, it could be that what we have read as "n" in the word "don't" is a "w"—which, if so, would make the line read, "But I dow (do?) think it is very colorful". It's hard to say without the transcriber of the poem to help us.

Jenny's Presence in the Work. And what of Jenny? What glimpses of her did we catch by describing this single poem? As one of us said, "Here is a child, a very little girl, thinking very big thoughts, for whom feeling seems an important mode for relating to the world." In confirmation, another of us said, "The Jenny we meet in the poem knows what she likes and what really matters to her; in this poem, the world." We also learned that this liking and valuing isn't a passive or merely academic interest: it moves Jenny to the promise of action—action for the benefit of others. We caught glimpses, too, of innerness, powers of reflection, contemplation, and capacity to penetrate to the heart of the matter. The Jenny we meet in "The crkol ovv Liyf," we said, has the capacity to be self-reflective, to stand back and take another look—a look that is both analytic and evaluative.

With this picture of Jenny, we brought our study of "The crkol ovv Liyf" to a close. To shed a bit of light on the title of the poem, which for so many of us had a familiar ring, I showed a copy of the cover of a book bearing the same title supplied by Jenny's first teacher, Cecilia Espinosa. It was a book Jenny really liked, and for that reason, Cecilia thought it might have influenced Jenny's choice of the title for her poem. The full title of the book is *Ceremony—In the Circle of Life,* by White Deer of Autumn, with illustrations by Daniel Sans Souci (1991).

The poem by Langston Hughes wasn't available the day we described Jenny's poem. Ellen Schwartz, who had noted its similarity to Jenny's poem, later found it. Inserting it here seems a fitting way to conclude the study of "The crkol ovv Liyf."

Poem [2]

I loved my friend.
He went away from me.
There's nothing more to say.
The poem ends
Soft as it began—
I loved my friend.

—Langston Hughes (1995, p. 52)

Connecting "The crkol ovv Liyf" to Other Works by Jenny

Turning our attention to the larger array of Jenny's works, we drew on what we had learned from our collective description of "The crkol ovv Liyf." Certain connections reflected in the body of works jumped out at us, among them the presence of words even in the visual works and Jenny's persistent predilection for curvilinear forms. Circles greeted us at every glance. To pursue these connections and to search out novel elements or elaborations of persisting themes, we each selected two or three works for closer inspection, with the understanding that we would each keep notes of our observations.

When we re-gathered after this period of individual study for what would be the final session of the mini-study, we brought with us, besides our observations, works from among the larger collection to illustrate what we had learned:

Triangle instructions (Figure 4.2)
Old Abe (Figure 4.3)
Portrait of girl with red sun (Plate 1)
Collage portrait of girl in yellow (Plate 2)
Note to dad (Plate 3, parts a and b: cover and interior)
Letter to Mr. Bentz (Plate 4)
Note to Cecilia (Plate 5)
Georgia O'Keeffe (Plate 6)
Mother's Day acrostic (Plate 7, parts a and b: cover and interior)

(*Figures 4.2 and 4.3 appear on the following pages. The plates are included in a separate color photo insert section.*)

One of these—portrait of girl with red sun (Plate 1)—effectively illustrates the persistence of curvilinear forms that caught our attention when we first inspected the larger array of work. Drawn when Jenny was eight years old, it depicts a circular sun, a circular face with circular pupils, a red circle on the girl's shirt, and another tiny circular face with tiny red circles to depict the eyes—circles within circles. Another smaller drawing, also curvilinear (Plate 5), made a further connection. Bearing this heartfelt message to the recipient, "This is all . . . of my love and I made this for you," it mirrors in its fullness and embrace the love for the world so fervently avowed by Jenny in "The crkol ovv Liyf." The word "love" in this piece (and others) also confirmed for us the larger, perhaps dominant, theme of bigness we observed in "The crkol ovv Liyf." In this instance the theme was reflected in a wholeheartedness of feeling freely and unreservedly bestowed on those close to her, especially her family and teachers, but inclusive of the world at large.

Noticing the omnipresence of "love," we made note of other relational elements in the works. Some of the written pieces, like Jenny's message to her father (Plate 3), are letters with a specified recipient. Others, like the explanation of how to make a triangle (Figure 4.2), imply an audience, a reader, though none is specified. This observation turned us in two directions: the conversational, engaging style of Jenny's writing exemplified in "The crkol ovv Liyf" and Jenny as questioner. As we looked at examples illustrative of both, their convergence strongly suggested to us that *conversing, speaking, asking questions* is for Jenny a powerful, perhaps her most powerful, mode of learning.

In this respect, the explanation of how to make a triangle says it all: conversational in style, implying an audience, and then at the end posing a question that leaves the conversation open, inviting the reader to join in. The work is undated, though given the content it was most likely written when Jenny was in second or third grade. Hearing the piece read aloud, we thought that it

FIGURE 4.2 Triangle instructions

seemed probable that it was written in response to a school assignment asking the student to explain in words how you make a triangle. Jenny starts by doing that but then, as one of us said, the writing takes a different turn:

> It's as if she's thinking about the person reading this, almost as if she were asking, "so, if I were to give you these directions, what would keep you from doing another kind of shape than a triangle?" It is as if there is a kind of stepping back or stepping out of the assignment at this point to reconsider, to evaluate that brought to mind a similar reflective moment in "The crkol ovv Liyf" when Jenny appears to take a second look at her drawing of the world (or perhaps at the world itself) and observes that perhaps after all it isn't really very colorful.

It seemed to us that taking these second looks tends to move what she writes to a deeper and unexpected level. In "The crkol ovv Liyf" that moment opens the way to the second stanza with its expression of love of the world and the promise to keep it safe for every one. In writing about how to make a triangle, Jenny goes beyond the assignment to ask what does it *mean* to try to put making a triangle into words? What is to prevent the directions from being misunderstood, if someone tried to follow what she has written? Then, having set herself this complicated task, she asks the reader, "What would you do?" To which we could only reply, "Good question!"

Looking at this work and others in which questions are prominent (Plates 3 and 4) prompted the further observation that to ask a lot of questions puts the questioner out there. Thinking about that, noticing the directness of her questions, one of us said it made her think how spunky Jenny is, and in support of that, to read and comment on the note to Mr. Bentz (Plate 4):

> What was Ira
> Seas good bye about?
> I was gone in the
> morning. was it a
> funy book? I rilly like'
> Ira Slep's over. Did you
> like it? From:
> Jenny Williams

That's a lot of questions. She missed the morning when the book was read, but that doesn't stop Jenny from wanting to know what it's about and what Mr. Bentz thinks of it. And this is to me striking: She does it not as student to teacher but conversationally—just as we said of her poem. [It] takes confidence . . . to ask a lot of questions, to permit yourself to do that. For me, it is related to Jenny giving herself permission to write so openly and freely of her deepest feelings in the poem, to make herself vulnerable.

Time for describing the focal piece of Jenny's works was coming to a close. Customarily, in my role as chair for the Descriptive Review, I would have drawn together the main threads from our description of "The crkol ovv Liyf" and the other pieces. This time, it was the next speaker in the circle, Ellen Schwartz, who integrated the themes from our description of the poem and the other works, with particular attention to Jenny as its author:

Writing seems so useful to Jenny, something she likes to do. Thinking about this, I paid attention to her poem in response to Old Abe [Figure 4.3]—which is, of course, by Langston Hughes (1995, p. 103)!

Lincoln Monument: Washington

Let's go see Old Abe
Sitting in the marble and the moonlight,
Sitting lonely in the marble and the moonlight,
Quiet for ten thousand centuries, old Abe.
Quiet for a million, million years.

Quiet—

And yet a voice forever
Against the
Timeless walls
Of time—
Old Abe.

—Langston Hughes

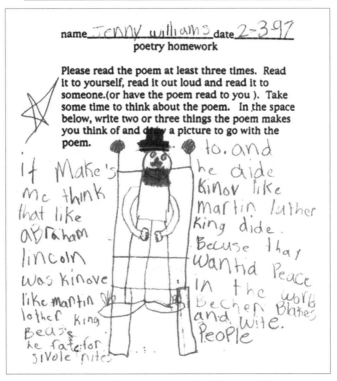

name Jenny williams date 2-3-97
poetry homework

Please read the poem at least three times. Read it to yourself, read it out loud and read it to someone.(or have the poem read to you). Take some time to think about the poem. In the space below, write two or three things the poem makes you think of and draw a picture to go with the poem.

It Make's me think that like aBraham lincoln was kinove like mantin lother King Beau's he fate for sivole nites

to. and he dide kinov like martin luther king dide. Becuse that wantid peace in the world Bechen Blakes and wite. people

FIGURE 4.3 "Lincoln Monument: Washington," by Langston Hughes, and Jenny's response

Joining the two poems there is a similar rhythm and there is a similar sense of the very, very large. There is in both a pause in the middle. It makes me think how Jenny is observant as a learner and how she looks to other artists—like [the drawing] that has "Goga o Kefe" written in the corner [Plate 6].

Initially, the hugeness I was thinking of in Jenny's work were the big ideas in her poem and reflected in the title. Those sorts of big ideas. And then when I looked at her response to the poem about Old Abe, written when she is older, I started to think that this is a way she thinks about the world. She sees the world in a way that frees her to respond however she wanted to this poem. Hughes's poem doesn't talk about Lincoln and his political actions. It's descriptive of the monument and alludes to a voice forever, but it's really not specific about what Lincoln did. *It was Jenny's own self that connected Old Abe with Martin Luther King.*

That's a big leap, and it's also about another kind of big idea: justice. That she would choose to make that connection is a big kind of thinking. I keep putting that bigness of idea and thinking alongside all the tenderness of her poem, the colors, the love she shows to her family and to her teacher. The ideas are big, but they are close to the heart at the same time. And we are only looking at a small amount of work.

These comments, pulling together multiple strands from our descriptions of Jenny's works, concluded the mini-study.

Afterthoughts

Listening to these observations, I was reminded how often during the original spanning study in 1996 the phrase "brave Jenny" was on our lips—and how that was affirmed by this study of her works. A child free to think big, to think deeply, to question, to observe, to probe beneath the surface, to take every occasion as an invitation to think, to question, to act. A child for whom value and feeling and thinking are intimately joined.

I heard other connections between this 2006 study with the picture of Jenny formed in the earlier studies. For example, the abundant questions in the works we studied in 2006 echoed something Julia Fournier said in the 1997 spanning study: "Questions, questions, questions." And added: "People like her questions because she asks them to really learn, not to hear herself talk." I thought how Jenny's drawings and writings flesh out and enrich that observation. I thought how Julia's comment that people like her questions fits with, and is extended by, the description of her writing as a way of relating, a way of striking up a conversation, and a way of learning and thinking. I was reminded how the piece on explaining to someone how to make a triangle corroborates Julia's observation that "Jenny sets herself challenges"—ending with (what else?) a conversational question to the reader: "How would you do it?"

I was struck that the picture of Jenny emergent from her works as someone who "puts herself out there" is almost an exact quote of a conclusion reached at the end of the 1996 spanning study: "Jenny is out there in every sense." When I said those words as I drew together of the threads from the 1996 spanning study, I positioned "being out there" and her bravery alongside her capacity to delve "deeply into big ideas and large social issues, not in the abstract, but as ground for action."

Now, from this 2006 study of her works, I found I was altering that conclusion. It isn't only that Jenny is *drawn* to big ideas. *More precisely, bigness of idea is for her a way of thinking.* In connection with Old Abe in the Langston Hughes poem, that bigness is described as a leap: "It was Jenny's own self that connected Old Abe with Martin Luther King. That's a big leap, and it's also about another kind of big idea: justice. That she would choose to make that connection is a big kind of thinking."

Describing Jenny's works a decade after the first spanning study yielded a picture remarkably congruent with those drawn earlier, adding to that picture important insights about Jenny as writer, questioner, and thinker. The congruency, though, was startlingly present, and that was true even though this time the persons composing the study circle had only her works as source and, except for me and one other, had never had the benefit of hearing a Descriptive Review of Jenny herself. What was previously learned about Jenny through the spanning studies had stood the test of time—so had the Descriptive Processes that yielded that knowledge.

What was strikingly different in 2006 is that there is no mention of *slowness*. There were questions raised as we went along about illegible handwriting and misspellings and how this might affect perceptions of her in school. There were none about her commitment and capacity as a reader and writer, as a learner and thinker. Describing Jenny's works confirmed the vocabulary of depth, delving, questioning, commitment, and resolve, and further articulated a capacity for thinking carried into action by its bigness of resolve and its tenderness of feeling.

I left the 2006 study of Jenny's works pondering the dimensions of the bigness of an education commensurate with the bigness of Jenny's capacities—as a thinker, as a learner, as a person intent on contribution. What would such an education look like?

PART II

Imagination Unloosed

History, Memory, Conviction, and Courage

THE FOUR ESSAYS in Part II pivot on the generative potency of story, as Milan Kundera (1988) phrases it, "to connect the past with the future" (p. 19). Each essay situates Jenny's school life in the 1990s in the wider context of history and memory. The first essay, by Patricia Carini, describes the history of an era as it is exemplified in a powerful statewide policy document particularized and enacted at the Prospect School. The essay following, by Cecilia Espinosa, explores memory as vital resource for the teacher's own self-making—and for the poetry of teaching. The third essay, by Julia Fournier, explores story itself through the provocative claim that the stories we tell of our lives and what we make of them have defining power—that we become the story told, that our conviction is linked to those stories. And in the final essay in this section, Carol Christine joins the teacher's self-agency with the mutuality of working with others as entwined stories, in which one leads on to the next, each contributing dimension to the larger story of what it is to be a teacher and to have the courage to act on behalf of all children.

CHAPTER FIVE

History, Vision, Struggle

The Vermont Design for Education

Patricia F. Carini

Jenny's story as told here is now more than a decade in the past. So, too, are the exhilarating days at W. T. Machan School at the peak of its remaking—recalled so vividly in these pages by Jenny's teachers, Cecilia Espinosa and Julia Fournier. That Jenny landed in the school at that moment in time, that her education began when energy and enthusiasm for change were running high, is not incidental to her own story. What if the school had at that moment been ruled by tests and mandates enforced by surveillance? What if it had been strictly stratified by ability groupings? What if . . .? It is the same for us all. Our locations, temporal and geographic, at key points in our lives are not without consequence. Should you and I have happened to land at the same time and place, our experience and narration of those circumstances and their impact on choices we made, the directions we took, would differ. But for each of us that particularized location and point in time, though not determining, contextual-izes our lives, profoundly influencing our perceptions of self and the world.

For Jenny, it meant that her first school experience was in team-taught, multi-age, bilingual classrooms providing a continuous opportunity for her growth and learning and for her teachers to come to know and take seriously her capacities as a learner, thinker, and person—and her contributions to the class as a whole. Let it be noted that to embrace multi-age groupings and bilingual education was not without risk and personal cost, for these are daring steps for a school to take—steps that challenge school convention and that upend the usual expectations of what school should be and should look like.

On a broader scale, Machan's history connects through the vision it enacted and the educational experiences it provided with the liberating aims of schools and movements, past and present, similarly inspired: to remake schools in the image of the learner, to unmake outworn conventions for schooling, to enlarge possibilities and choices for children and their families. One of those points of connection was with Prospect. By 1989–1990, the year the first Phoenix seminars were offered at the Center for Establishing Dialogue (CED), Prospect was a center with sturdy ties to schools in many locations, offering *another way of looking* at children and at schools and a descriptive methodology for enabling that to happen. Prospect also brought to Phoenix its own history as a school (1965–1991) and that of the location and era in which it was founded (for the fuller story of Prospect and its philosophy and methodology, see Himley, 1991; Himley with Carini, 2000; Carini 2001; Himley, 2002).

AN ERA OF CHANGE:
THE VERMONT DESIGN FOR EDUCATION

Originating as it did in the mid-sixties, Prospect anticipated by a few years the impact of a wider movement in education then gaining momentum in Prospect's home state of Vermont and across the country. As it turned out, 1965 was an auspicious moment to launch a school, ushering in as it did an era in which there was burgeoning hope for revitalizing the society and the nation's schools. There was a growing confidence among educators and social activists from all sectors that a society more open, more pluralistic, more diversely textured was possible, with the public schools a major contributor to the accomplishment of that aim. New visions of schools flourished—less rigid, better able to engage children in their own learning, roomy enough to comfortably include the full spectrum of the nation's children. Hope flourished—hope that the schools could make a liberating education a reality for all children.

In Prospect's home state, the Vermont Design for Education, one of the most important policy documents reflective of this vision, was published in 1968 and reissued in 1971 (see Appendix). Dedicated to "the individual's strong, inherent desire to learn" (p. 4), the Design's commitment to the positive value of difference and to the wide distribution of human capacity is a cohering thread across the 17 educational premises set forth in its brief 25 pages. As I reread the Design a few years ago, after a lapse of 20 years or more, every page was a reminder of that commitment. Equally, every page posed a challenge to the "now" world in which standardization, uniformity, and deficiency are the educational watchwords. Here is one of many passages that caught my eye—and made its own connection with Jenny and W. T. Machan School:

> Students are as diverse intellectually as they are physically, having different backgrounds and experiences, feelings, ways of thinking, personalities, and ways of working and learning. In order to be effective, schools

must allow and encourage students to work at their own rate, to develop their own unique style of learning. . . . Learning experiences must be geared to individual needs rather than group norms. (p. 10)

And then there is this key sentence—and another reminder—addressing the school to its mission: "The school's function is to expand the differences between individuals and create a respect for those differences" (p. 6).

Think of it. Think of the boldness of that assertion—not mere tolerance of difference but affirmation of the positive value of difference. Think of it especially in the context of now. The function of the school asserted in the Design— and in practice at Machan when Jenny entered—was not, as now, to establish group norms and to enforce compliance with those norms. The aim was not to prune each and every child to fit a standardized, one-size-fits-all model of schooling. Instead the focus was on the *uniqueness* each child brings and on the school's responsibility to respond to and nurture that uniqueness. What was to be valued was not sameness, but what *distinguishes* each child, and the richness these differences contribute to the whole.

Or think of the implications, as exemplified at Machan, in the attention to community and to connection with the experience of families and children in the following premise:

People should perceive the learning process as related to their own sense of reality. . . . Schools cannot expect the trust and understanding of their students if agriculture is discussed in terms of the stereotype family farm, when these same students perceive around them huge agriculture combines and underpaid migrant labor. (p. 9)

At Machan that reality wasn't, of course, the family farm or agriculture capitulated to big business. The reality at Machan was a community located in an impoverished neighborhood in which many languages were spoken, with Spanish as often as not a child's primary language. Equally, it was a reality in which day labor and service jobs, with pay to match, were the rule.

In the context of the exploitative and rigid testing system that in the world of now holds each child to the same standard, consider what was being strived for in that other world of 40 years ago—and was also being strived for at Machan. In the words of the Vermont Design,

Evaluations, based upon standardized expectancies, force students to adopt standardized learning in order to compete. Many of today's expectancies are influenced by publishing concerns and hardware vendors.

> We must develop personalized ways of assessing an individual's progress, his [or her] strengths and weaknesses, keeping in mind that the ultimate purpose of evaluation is to strengthen the learning process. (p. 14)

In the future world projected in the Vermont Design, the approach to what in the world of now is called accountability was outspoken in its flat rejection of pandering to so-called research-based methods or the profit-motivated textbook and testing industry. As at Machan, the role of evaluation, in keeping with the word *value* at its root, was first and foremost to support the child's learning process, and specifically to do that by maximizing the child's own strengths as a learner.

Kind of wonderful, isn't it—an official state document that speaks with such caring and respect for the child? What stands out 40 years after it was first issued, and in the wake of decades of official and sustained negativity toward children, families, schools, and the community, is what also stands out from Jenny's story: respect for the learner, trust in the person and in the child's "strong, inherent desire to learn," insistence on the positive value of diversity and stout defense of doubt and reason, outspoken affirmation of the right and obligation to question authority, appreciation for originality and creativity, and the explicit requirement that the school connect with the reality of students' lives and the communities they come from. What also stands out is how readable the document is. Free of jargon, free of angry denunciation of what it opposes, it sets forth directly, positively, and forcefully what it is *for*. In brief, what stands out is clarity of vision and the spaciousness, generosity, and rigor of the ideas.

And there is more. As commendable as the Design's commitment to children and to learning for all and at all ages may be, its respect for local knowledge and local conditions is equally so—and equally refreshing. The Vermont Design was not a top-down directive, enforced with threats and reprisals. There is a passage toward the end of the booklet that after decades of imperial mandates seems especially worthy of note. It has to do with how the Vermont Design was introduced to local districts and implemented:

> It should be emphasized that acceptance of this philosophy and its implementation must be *voluntary*. . . . [And for this reason] No amount of legislation or administrative mandate will provide beneficial and permanent educational changes for students." (p. 25; emphasis added)

Extending and underscoring that passage, a cover letter tucked into the booklet, apparently written when the Vermont Design was reissued in 1971, advises local communities as follows: "The local district design [for educational change] can be that of the Vermont Design but it can also be of its own choosing." And, continuing, the letter assures districts that *whatever the community's decision,* the State Department of Education will make available to the local community not only "its [own] total resources [but also] those of a mutually agreed upon consultant." In these passages, trust in children and learners of all ages is matched with trust in those closest to the scene to have and bring to bear knowledge valuable for reshaping and particularizing the state's mission to better match local conditions.

AN UPSTART ERA

The Vermont Design for Education set a standard. Other states took interest. The Prospect School also set a standard. Other schools and educational centers took interest. In ways direct and indirect, what happened over 20 years later at W. T. Machan and other Phoenix schools was influenced by the movement in which Vermont's—and Prospect's—stories are inextricably entwined. Told in microcosm, a sampling of the elements of that history follows. An era has no exact starting or ending point. Things happen—a war, an election, a march, a demonstration. Boundaries previously observed are breached—and others follow. Energy is released. What wasn't dreamed of yesterday seems suddenly doable, even if unsanctioned, today. There is an element of instability, a frisson of fear mixed with exhilaration. Eras tend to be named after the fact. "The Sixties" is now synonymous with such an era, one that initiated a societal upheaval of dramatic proportions. For any who experienced it, and for many who didn't, it is remembered—favorably by some, deplored by others—as a time virtually unparalleled for its headiness: bursting with energy, ideas, and, yes, confidence, even if, in retrospect, sometimes that confidence was unwarranted. Most important, it was a time when the possibility of a more open, more pluralistic, more heterodox society seemed almost within reach. The winds of change were blowing hard.

There was an awakening to injustices and to dreams of change previously unvoiced, which, when spoken, fell on receptive ears. Opposition to a misbegotten war, the Civil Rights Movement, at the time 10 and more years in action, the Feminist Movement, the War on Poverty, the Gay and Lesbian Liberation Movement, and the rights of people more generally, energized large segments of the population and, most especially, young people. A struggle was commencing for schools that put the well-being of children, and the populace at large, ahead of the ambitions and excesses of what was called at the time the military/industrial complex.

What these movements had in common was a vision of society and of human possibility—a vision of horizons spacious enough for the populace at large, without exception, to pursue their dreams, to contribute to society, to better their own lives. Let it be said that the Civil Rights Movement, by seizing national attention in the 1950s, by the fortitude and courage of an able people, led the way all the way. It was in the wake of that immense undertaking by an entire people, and at times intersecting it, that the push for ending the war, for remaking the schools, for women's rights, for civil rights, for the elimination of poverty was re-energized. I choose *re-energized* as the apt word, for these movements themselves had roots in the history of struggle—struggles that at other times, even if only briefly, yielded the sweet fruit of success. It was an upstart era, rambunctious, given to excesses, at times erupting in violence, even as nonviolence was for many an inviolable ethical principle. Yet, for all these flaws, it was an era inspired and buoyed by the vision of a more open, more humane society.

By the late sixties, making change in the schools was happening in locations across the country—change that among other things aimed at leveling the educational hierarchy. It was during this era that decentralization of power and demand for community schools revolutionized governance of the public schools in New York City. By 1970, with the child's learning at the center, Lillian Weber's Open Corridor program was bringing previously isolated teachers together, with the corridors providing space and opportunity for interactions among teachers and children. From that inspired adventure sprang the Open Education Movement. In North Dakota, Vito Perrone launched the New School, later the Center for Teaching and Learning, with its aim to alter top-down governance by establishing a reciprocal collegial relationship between the university and the schools, one in which, as Perrone phrases it, "universities and schools can develop meaningful relationships in which each influences the other's direction (cited in Carini, 2006, p. 33).

In 1965, Head Start awakened the promise for early education for all children. News of the British Infant School Movement invigorated a vision of more open and equitable schools—a vision enacted in a subset of National Follow Through Programs sponsored by the University of North Dakota, the Education Development Center (EDC) in Boston, and Bank Street College in New York City. Inheritors of the history embodied in early childhood and progressive education, these programs were united by commitment to an education that starts from the child, the learner. Like Head Start, Follow Through included among its goals not only academic gains but the betterment of children's nutrition, health, and well-being. Parallel to the creation

PLATE 1
Portrait of girl
with red sun

PLATE 2
Collage portrait
of girl in yellow

PLATE 3
Note to dad

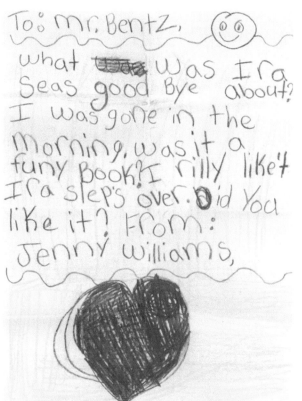

PLATE 4
Letter to
Mr. Bentz

To: Mr. Bentz,
what was Ira
Seas good Bye about?
I was gone in the
Morning. was it a
funy Book? I rilly like't
Ira slep's over. Did You
like it? From:
Jenny williams,

To Cecilia
This is all
The
anf of my love
This I made
Becose You
You very like
much
Love Senny

PLATE 5   Note to Cecilia

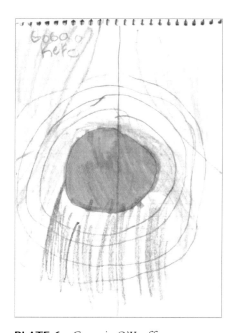

PLATE 6   Georgia O'Keeffe

PLATE 7 Mother's Day acrostic

of National Follow Through, commitment to these same principles put into action New York State's Experimental Pre-Kindergarten Program, sponsored by the Bureau of Child Development and Parent Education, under the able leadership of Ruth Flurry.

Emerging on the scene was the Teacher Center Movement, its seeds already sown in the creation of local teacher centers that brought teachers together, across schools and sometimes districts, all with hunger for a curriculum and classrooms able to nurture the child's agency in his or her own learning—including among many, many others, the Philadelphia Advisory Center (subsequently, the Teachers Learning Cooperative); The Durham Center, also in Philadelphia; the Workshop Center at City College (New York City); and the Mountain Towns Teacher Center in Wilmington, Vermont. Meeting together in these centers sprinkled across the country, teachers historically isolated from each other came to share their experiences, to buoy each other's efforts, to speak out on educational issues—and through their efforts to mark out a path for teacher control over their own professional development.

In my memory, two events in the 1970s stand out for mobilizing common aims among the many and disparate locations in which change was happening. Both are in keeping with the premises and the spirit of the Vermont Design. The first was what turned out to be the charter meeting of the North Dakota Study Group on Evaluation (NDSG), convened by Vito Perrone in 1972. The second was the 1975 Roots of Open Education Conference led by Lillian Weber at the Workshop Center at City College. These events are not unrelated. There was overlap in terms of participation. More importantly, both Vito Perrone and Lillian Weber were dedicated to history as legacy and resource for the current movement. Both conferences were held as the undertow of federal and state demands for accountability were threatening to undo the work just beginning to flower in the schools.

A potent theme of the NDSG meeting was the urgent need for alternatives to standardized testing as the sole measure of school success—for individual children and for the school as a whole. What Prospect contributed to that meeting were the fruits of its descriptive documentation of children's growth and learning, including collections of children's works (visual and written). Rooted in observation, it was documentation that by 1972 spanned seven years. The response to that documentation from others at the session led directly to summer institutes, conferences, and workshops on Prospect's descriptive methodology both at Prospect and in many other locations.

The Roots of Open Education Conference was a profound experience, bringing together those then at the forefront of a movement in company with the pioneers who had paved their way. In plan it was simple. In scope it was comprehensive. Beginning and ending with plenary sessions, there were small groups led by, among others, Myles Horton, Dorothea Cotton, Cornelia Goldsmith, and Sakakohe Cook. A sampling of the proceedings names a wide swathe of educational innovations, including Settlement Houses, Citizenship Schools, Highlander, the first Day Care Program, and under the wing of the WPA, arts programs for poor children.

It was a once in a lifetime experience. For those who drove down from Vermont, the conference confirmed our efforts and strengthened our resolve. We weren't alone. We took away with us exactly what the conference so vividly etched in our minds: the rich legacy of history.

PAST PRESENT

Today, the era, the ideas, the struggle that inspired the Vermont Design are history—though not for that reason irretrievable or without influence. As Vito Perrone tells us in his important book, *Teacher with a Heart* (1998), the visions that inspired change in other eras, and the struggles of those who strove to enact those visions, are touchstones to the future. To keep these visions and struggles ever present is, in Perrone's words, "a reminder that our work as educators is not without a history; that many of the problems we currently struggle with were faced by others before us, sometimes confronted differently, often more intelligently" (p. 1). And continuing, he tells us the value of connecting with this history:

> Maintaining better connections with history, making it part of our ongoing reflection about teaching, learning, and schools, keeps the dignity of teaching and its broader social context within our gaze, providing us with larger sets of possibilities for our practice, leading us to a more discriminating stance about what is put forward as reform. (p. 1)

Movements for social and educational change on the small and the large scale, even when exhilarating, are beset with tensions and misunderstanding, burdened by lack of adequate resources. This was true at W. T. Machan even as the school moved steadfastly from strength to strength. It was true at Prospect School. Prospect's founding aim to become a wing of the public schools was never realized. There were setbacks. Local political conditions altered and earlier support from the public sector faded with the tragic loss of four educators key to that effort in a plane crash. The school was confronted with difficult decisions. Money was in short supply. There were disagreements and tensions within and without. Yet the commitment to enroll children from all walks of life was not abandoned.

At the same time, the state effort to enact the vision set forth in the premises of the Vermont Design met with stiff resistance. For a scattering of schools and districts across the state, the vision embodied in its premises was liberating, generating intense debate leading to real changes in the schools. In other schools and districts, not only the Vermont Design itself but change of any kind was resisted. Was it worth the struggle, that intense effort to make the Vermont Design a reality? Certainly, the struggle didn't succeed on a broad scale. Was it then a partial success? A partial failure? Or, perhaps neither. I would ask the same of Prospect. Perhaps "imperfect" better describes the fate of both. Even in the darkest days of No Child Left Behind, there were still schools in Vermont that clung to elements of the vision. Multi-age classrooms for young children were still in evidence here and there. Learning experiences rooted in reality, in the life of the child, were findable. Equally, there were and are districts and schools in Vermont in which rigid, top-down mandates rule the day and testing dictates the content of study.

Further, there is no denying that nationally testable achievement and accountability were gaining ground even before the ink on the Vermont Design was dry. The idea that there is more to learning than achievement was not widely accepted. Prospect's descriptive methodology, embraced by many teachers and administrators, didn't satisfy the bureaucratic drive for certainty of measurable outcome. This was also the case in locations across the country, even as the struggle for more open, community-based schools was at peak pitch. Since that time, Prospect's methodology has accrued a solid history— a methodology expanded and deepened through the continuous use, examination, and remaking of the Descriptive Processes, not only at Prospect but in locations across the country—as Jenny's story and the story of W. T. Machan School in Phoenix attest.

Yet even so—even with evidence, even with the fruits of careful documentation—it was then, as now, exceedingly hard to make the case for learning that exceeds or subverts measurement. It is not stretching the point to say that now, in 2009, state-mandated school policy has effectively eclipsed the value and, in too many instances, the opportunity for learning intrinsic to the learner's interests, and even its very existence. By making visible the depth and positive value of learning propelled by the child's own passions across a significant span of years, *Jenny's Story* effectively challenges both the negation of the child's agency and the equation of learning and achievement that now dominates educational dialogue (L. Carini, 2009). This is the heart of the matter. As Louis Carini says,

> Educating consists of discovering what the child's experiencings are, and where his or her interests lie, and ... expand[ing] the child's current experiencings into educationally sound knowledge that is meaningful to [the child]. (p. 52)

By making the case for founding education and the schools on the child's interests and inherent desire to learn, *Jenny's Story* focuses attention on the particularities of perspective and the complexities of capacity each and every individual child brings to learning, to the school, and to the world. By making that case, *Jenny's Story* reaffirms, highlights, and particularizes the positive democratic value the Vermont Design accords to difference. Swept to the sidelines by the ever-proliferating business of diagnosing and labeling children for suspected pathology, what has supplanted the democratic value of differences, and the educational value of expanding on them, is a relentless quest for certainty, correctness, and uniformity of product. Yet the principle of the high value of difference is as fresh, as inviting, as the day the Vermont Design was published. It is as fresh and inviting as the story of Jenny—one child, not uniform, not correct, unbowed by the system.

IMAGINATION UNLOOSED

The story of the Vermont Design, like the story of Prospect and the story of W. T. Machan School, is an old story, one told many times over, and well documented in the wider history of struggle for a more open society. In these harsh times, the history of struggle for visions, partially realized at best, and the philosophy set forth in the Vermont Design may well ring hollow. This history teaches the lesson that hard struggle doesn't assure an altogether successful outcome. Isn't this a history better set aside? Isn't the Vermont Design merely a quaint relic of a bygone time? Isn't the Design's philosophy, a philosophy in a bubble? In the clear, hard light of now, doesn't its history teach that it is a fool's errand to struggle against such odds?

I don't think so, for it is the vision of what might be, of what once was, of what still might be, that drives, as it ever has, the struggle for better schools, for an education big enough for the enormity of human capacity, for horizons spacious enough for that capacity to discover its own fruition in works generative of future works not yet dreamed of. It is not a vision in isolation. That same vision joins the struggle for better schools with other struggles for a more spacious vision of human possibility, now and historically—for affordable child care, for quality health care, for fair wages, for employment safeguarded by workers' rights, for equal access to opportunity and justice, to name only a few.

In *Freedom Dreams,* Robin D. G. Kelley (2002) quotes these lines from the poet Keorapetse Kgositsile: "When the clouds clear / We shall know the colour of the sky" (p. 11). And goes on to say, "It has been the poets—no matter the medium—who have succeeded in imagining the color of the sky, in rendering the kinds of dreams and futures social movements are capable of producing" (p. 11). Unpacking those lines, the potency of imagination is its visionary capacity—to see beyond the clouds, to see beyond what passes for reality at any given moment, to a future that exceeds it. To see beyond, to see what might be, moves the seer to action. Imagination unloosed has a spreading effect; there is an excitement of possibility. The history of social movements testifies to the power of vision to awaken—and the challenge of that awakening to the status quo.

To experience that power is life changing. Words embodying dreams only whispered before spring to the lips of many. In the urgency to enact what yesterday was merely a dream, there is the tendency to rush ahead, to take things too quickly, to overreach. There is equally the slow, steady work, the struggle to make something sound, something of beauty, something that though imperfect will itself be generative of works, ideas, calls to action as yet undreamed of. There is the tragedy of lost ground, of the unmaking of what was painstakingly made. There is the history of the ground gained and the story of the struggle to claim and remake it. There is the memory of the visions and dreams that inspired the struggle—a wellspring for dreamers and visionaries for generations to come. Visions enacted, dreams pursued, hover on the horizon of the limitless sky.

CHAPTER SIX

Memory

Making and Remaking Ourselves as Teachers

Cecilia Espinosa

As a child in Ecuador, I knew I wanted to be a teacher on my first day of kindergarten. As I entered into the 50-year-old gray school building with endless walls made of stone and cement, I was struck by the sight of several kids desperately crying as their parents left them in the charge of a nun who was paying no real attention to the emotions that filled the room, but instead wanted us to be quiet and in order right away. I think it was the mixture of a lack of attention to the emotional tone in the classroom and the absence of bright colors in the building that made me realize that one day I was going to create a classroom where kids wouldn't cry, but instead couldn't wait to come to school—a classroom filled with colors. I never abandoned that desire, although the vision of the kind of space I wanted to create as a teacher has taken a long time to evolve.

LEARNING IN SCHOOL

I still have a few images of my life as an elementary school student. I remember that we started first grade with a notebook where we had to fill in pages with circles and lines, straight or inclined, before we even tried to make any letters. The correct and way to hold the pencil was stressed by the teacher, as was the cleanliness of the page. I remember that the next step in our path toward learning to read was using the silabario *El Coquito*. We had to divide words into syllables and read sentences that were put together in order to match a certain consonant/vowel sound: for example, *"Mi ma-má me mi-ma."* Reading was connected to writing by having us copy these syllables and make them into sentences. Both reading and writing were devoid of meaning.

As we learned to write with more proficiency, we were assigned a weekly composition—which we were never asked to revise. Aside from this weekly composition, most writing assignments consisted of memorizing rules and taking dictation from the teacher. I remember having to endlessly conjugate verbs for each tense in Spanish, from present to subjunctive to past participle, and for all six pronouns, even "*vosotros*," which is used only in Spain. We had to study the rules of spelling, the rules of the accent mark, the parts of a sentence, mostly in isolation. Language was studied as something that was "out there." The rules we learned were those given to us by the Real Academia Española; thus they were very much male-oriented, and they privileged only a certain kind of dialect. We learned, for example, that if there were ten females and one male, we still needed to use the masculine ending of an adjective or noun.

At school, it was ignored that in daily life the Spanish we used had words from the indigenous language Quechua, such as the names of the volcano Cotopaxi, the city of Latacunga, and a river named Cutuchi, or the expression "*achachai*" which we used when it was very cold or "*arrarai*" when something was too hot. The language of the curriculum emphasized only Castilian Spanish. English, our foreign language, was taught the same way, devoid of meaning and expression, and instead to be learned through drills and memorization.

Except for my second-grade teacher, Srta. Esperanza, I don't remember that the teachers read to us very much or that they told us very many oral stories. Srta. Esperanza used to tell us Ecuadorian legends. From her I learned stories like "*Marcelino Pan y Vino.*" This was the only time when we could sit away from our assigned seats and were allowed to sit on the floor around her. Quietly we heard her stories with the lights in the classroom turned off and the curtains closed. She would tell us these stories with such great voice, intonation, and gesture that it was impossible not to be immersed completely in the story. We heard a lot of stories from Srta. Esperanza, but we never learned about her life, and I don't think she knew much about our lives either.

With the exception of first grade, when we used the reader *El Coquito,* we always used a textbook called *El Escolar Ecuatoriano.* It was a very thick textbook that contained all of the subject areas we studied. Each grade level had its own *Escolar Ecuatoriano* containing the material the Minister of Education said needed to be covered that year. In high school, literature was covered by reading summaries of books and the analysis of experts. The only whole book I was asked to read was *Marianela* by Benito Pérez Galdós (1878/2008). Even though we all read the book, the interpretation we were given and expected to know was the one provided by an expert in a textbook. There were only a few public libraries, and we weren't allowed to check books out. Yet, I remember going to those buildings, which were mostly located downtown, just to look and touch the old books that were covered with dust.

On weekends, our house was always filled with friends and a constant stream of first cousins, so I was able to practice being a teacher almost on a weekly basis with kids of all ages, some of them older than myself. Often my "students" became rebellious, for in this play we reproduced what we were experiencing in school—completing laborious writing assignments like copying syllables, doing dictation, and writing on topics for compositions. I filled their papers with red ink and led them in endless memorization.

LEARNING IN THE WORLD

We spent our summers and holidays at the family farm, a place close to the active volcano Cotopaxi. We grew up both admiring and fearing the volcano. Stories of the last eruption were repeated over and over by the elderly. From these stories we learned the path that the mud and the lava might take in the case of a new eruption. We were always going over our plans for evacuation—as we visited the sites where the lava from the last eruption was still evident. Through these stories we learned the names of the other volcanoes, the hills, the rivers, the valleys, the towns. Learning geography and history had its own purpose at the farm.

Our days at the farm were spent mainly learning about the farm animals (horses, dogs, cows, chickens, sheep, goats, as well as the different kinds of birds and fish native to the area), the weather, the effects of the moon on the weather, the shapes and colors of clouds, the quality of the soil after a volcanic eruption, and the life cycles of plants and animals. We had secret places where we had our "tadpole farms." We would organize the tadpoles by stages of development once we figured out that their bodies went through such an amazing transformation. The people who worked at the farm or lived close by were very generous in sharing their knowledge with us. They taught us to read the sky and to tell how weak or strong a storm was going to be just by feeling the wind and watching the clouds. With them we saw how baby calves and baby colts are born. We learned how to harvest potatoes, wheat, corn, broccoli, apples, pears, and capulies (a kind of cherry that grows in Ecuador) at the perfect time of maturity. We learned how to get the earth ready for the new season. They took us to hidden places where ancient people had built their homes and their places of prayer. We heard them talking with their friends and families in Quechua, and we marveled at the speed with which many of them could switch from that language to Spanish.

During my years as a student in Ecuador, learning at home and learning at school were strictly separated. Classrooms where the curriculum was permeable to the world were nonexistent. Knowledge was viewed as something static, acquired mostly through drills and memorization. Knowledge was not something made locally, but instead was something created by someone else far away. Other ways of knowing and languages native to Ecuador were ignored. School was not a place where we could explore our own questions. We were there to answer someone else's questions. From this perspective, teachers didn't need to acknowledge that students had different ways of approaching the world or that each family had particular "funds of knowledge" (Moll, Amanti, Neff, & González, 1992). Observing children, connecting with children, and developing curriculum around children's interests seemed unnecessary. In other words, school was a place where the banking system of education thrived (Freire, 1970/2000). In contrast, my years as a teacher in a bilingual classroom offered me an abundance of possibilities to build on who the children were and what they brought with them. These years also brought ample opportunities to ask my own questions in the company of others.

THE POETRY OF TEACHING

Once I had graduated from college in the United States, I was hired first as a bilingual kindergarten teacher and a couple of years later as a multi-age, bilingual teacher at W. T. Machan School in Phoenix, Arizona. In this new role, it didn't take long for me to realize that in the United States most people who spoke Spanish did not have high status in society. The children brought an abundance of related stories to the classroom on a regular basis. It wasn't rare to hear children tell us that they didn't come to school on a particular day because *la migra* had visited their neighborhood and it was safer not to leave their apartments for a day or two, or that they had heard someone in the street tell one of their family members that "they should not speak Spanish, because this is America!"

Yet, the Spanish-speaking children weren't the only ones exposed to these attitudes. Once, for example, during the time when Jenny's Dad was running for a seat on the local school board, Jenny came back to school very disconcerted by what had occurred the night before. She shared with us during morning meeting that while they had gone to gather signatures for her Dad's candidacy, she had heard several people ask "if he believed in educating illegals" and "if he believed in bilingual education." As I heard Jenny share this unsettling experience with us and continued to hear about the experiences the children and their families had as immigrants and as speakers of a language other than English, I began to see with new eyes the complexities of what it means to create a space in my bilingual classroom for a more humane education, one that links with the world. I sought a caring democratic space, as Dewey would envision, where "students could exercise 'intelligent sympathy'" (DeStigter, 1998, p. 272); space developed around strong relationships and built around trust, honesty, and a willingness to engage in difficult conversations, essential conversations; space surrounded by deep dialogue, caring dialogue (Peterson, 1992).

Creating Curriculum

The children were certainly asking questions that dealt with larger issues about society. Our curriculum needed to do the same. Our study of The Sonoran Desert, for example, went beyond a study of its flora and fauna. It also included the work of Cesar Chavez and his advocacy for the rights of migrant workers (Espinosa, Moore, & Serna, 1998). These studies achieved deeper layers of meaning when we accompanied them with Pablo Neruda's passion to make poetry accessible to everyone, even the common person, and Tish Hinojosa's songs for social justice. Aside from studying the beauty of the language and craft of the poet or of the songwriter, we realized that both Pablo Neruda's and Tish Hinojosa's work can help us ask deep questions about what it means to be human. Hinojosa's song, "There Is Something in the Rain," for example, deals with the effects of pesticides in the migrant worker communities surrounding the fields of grapes in California. "*Bandera del Sol*/Flag of the Sun" is a bilingual song that reminds us that, in spite of all the artificial borders, we all share one flag, the sun. Over time, this song became known by all classes at Machan, as we often sang it not only in our individual classrooms but also at school-wide celebrations. Neruda's poetry, alongside the poetry of Rafael Alberti, Federico Garcia Lorca, Gabriela Mistral, Langston Hughes, and Nikki Giovanni taught us that poetry has the potential not only to help us reflect on our realities but also to serve as sites for transformative dialogue (Espinosa & Moore, 1999).

At Machan our principal, Lynn Davey, resisted for years all efforts to treat teachers as technicians and children as empty vessels to be filled. In this setting, literature, poetry, making and exploring things, and intellectual discussions became integral components of our ways of doing school. Our decisions as to what books to read with the children were based not only on what the children needed because they were in a particular grade or reading at a certain level, but also on the kinds of "thinking" possibilities the materials offered (Espinosa & Fournier, 1999). These decisions were based on our observations of what was happening in our classrooms and the kinds of connections the children were making. Through our carefully selected books for read alouds, and our deep conversations about the story world, we witnessed the ways in which characters often inhabited the space of our daily conversations (Espinosa & Fournier, 1995). It wasn't rare to hear the children ask, when faced with complicated issues in their social world of the classroom, "What would Vitita or Rosa do?" Both were the main characters of the story by Pico (1991) called *La Peineta Colorada* (translated as *The Red Comb*: Pico, 1994). Over time, these characters had become living examples of the need to take action against injustice, rather than just bear witness to it. "You gotta do something about it, don't just stand there" was a comment the children often repeated to each other when faced with an ethical decision. Quality literature allowed us opportunities to explore our own worlds as we examined other worlds. From our work with Arizona State University (ASU) professors Ralph Peterson and Mariann Eeds (1990), we knew these were generative spaces for "grand conversations" to occur.

Engaging in Inquiry

As young bilingual teachers, our wonderings were always taken seriously, no matter how absurd they might have seemed to the more experienced eye. In my first year of teaching, for example, two other newly hired kindergarten teachers and I formed a study group around issues of emergent literacy. In our study sessions, under the guidance of administrative associate Kelly Draper, we argued for weeks about the best ways to support children's emergent literacy development, particularly about the issue of kindergartners and drawing. Kelly observed in our classrooms and studied children's work with us, and we read from the relevant professional literature. She gently led us to see the importance of drawing and the dangers of narrowing the curriculum to letters (or print). This inquiry study also had huge implications for our curriculum because it helped us to recognize that children *do* engage in purposeful literacy early on in their lives, and thus we needed to offer them real reasons to engage in reading, writing, and drawing in our classrooms (Edelsky, Alwerger, & Flores, 1990; Y. Goodman, 1984).

Professors Sarah Hudelson and Irene Serna helped us to solidify our understanding of the role of the native language in the development of a child's second language, as they engaged in a five-year research study at our school and made presentations of their findings to the faculty and administrators at the school, the parents, and the school board community. Through their child studies, they helped us understand the uniqueness of each child's process in becoming bilingual/biliterate (Hudelson, 1994; Hudelson & Serna, 1994; Serna & Hudelson, 1993, 1997). In addition, these studies also influenced our decision-making with regard to our early-exit bilingual program. This work was instrumental in helping us to envision a late-exit bilingual program at Machan. This shift gave the children the necessary time to learn a second language, as evidenced by the work of Hudelson, Serna, and other researchers.

The strong relationships we had with faculty at ASU offered us further possibilities to explore other, larger pedagogical questions. Teachers and students at Machan had questions, but so did professors at the university. There were ample opportunities for each of us to ask and explore our own questions, "to live in the question" (Traugh, 2000). As the years went by, some of us at Machan became interested in finding out ways to open up our mathematics and science curriculum to offer the children additional possibilities for exploration. This interest was first supported by mathematics professor Alfinio Flores, who engaged with us in a year-long inquiry about geometry, with a focus on symmetry and its use in different cultures, as well as science professor Herb Cohen, who, once we came to the realization that our curriculum was too focused on life science, helped us strengthen our understanding of physical science through a study of simple machines. Both professors spent hours supporting us in deepening our knowledge of the content and helping us think about appropriate materials for the classroom.

And so we learned "to love the questions" themselves (Traugh, 2000). Throughout the years, many thinkers came to our school, to ASU, and to the Center for Establishing Dialogue (CED) to share their thinking with us, support us in our inquiries, help us shape our curriculum, read with us relevant professional literature, and challenge us to ask deeper questions about our pedagogy (Edelsky, 1991; K. Goodman, 1986; Hudelson, 1987; Perrone, 1998). We asked, for example: What is the role of poetry in a teacher's life and in the life of the classroom? How can a child's world be connected with the world of school? What does it mean to develop an organic curriculum that asks larger questions about issues of social justice, given the realities of the lives of the children in our classrooms? In what ways do concern time and meeting time support the development of a more democratic space? (Bachman & Fournier, 1999.) What is happening with regard to the publishing of Spanish language children's literature in Mexico and in the United States? (Hudelson, Fournier, Espinosa, & Bachman, 1994.) What is the difference between standards set by an outsider versus the standards the children hold for themselves? What does it mean to build on a child's strengths? What does it mean to develop a rich curriculum for second language learners that has multiple points of entry?

The first time I attended a Prospect Descriptive Review organized by CED in Tempe, Arizona, and led by Pat Carini, I was completely captivated by the teacher's description of the child, as well as by the questions and recommendations after the teacher's presentation. As I listened to the detailed stories told through each section of the Descriptive Review, I was impressed by how much she knew about the child and how respectful the other group members were of both the teacher and the child. Other children came to my mind as I heard the teacher's descriptions—children who had a love for language, or who loved to play with words, or who memorized jokes, nursery rhymes, riddles, chants, or music, but who also appeared to be shy and hard to get to know. I was reminded that each learning opportunity I offered the children mattered—how I created the learning environment, how I selected the materials for the class, how I organized the schedule, how I positioned myself as the teacher, how the children had choices about what mattered to them. My responsibility as a teacher was to find out what mattered to each child, what awakened him or her, and to build from there.

The years I spent in the classroom working with the children were years in which I was completely absorbed in my teaching. The classroom was a place where children rarely misbehaved, not because there was tight control, but because there was so much that mattered to inquire about. In addition, our multi-age classes offered us large blocks of time, opportunities to revisit curricular studies, along with a curriculum that offered multiple entry points, as well as the opportunity to develop strong relationships with families and among colleagues. In contrast to my childhood years at school in Ecuador, where memorization and drills were the daily work, my years as a classroom teacher were filled with learning deep and engaging content along with the children. Ours was a school responsive to the diverse range of needs, interests, and potential of children and adults.

WORKING WITH BEGINNING TEACHERS
AND THEIR BURNING QUESTIONS

Currently, I work as a teacher educator at a college in which the student body is largely minority and immigrant, many of them first-generation college students. Although they come to class every semester filled with questions about teaching and learning and a strong desire to engage with and change the world through their teaching, sadly these questions are deeply constricted by the harsh conditions they often experience in the schools. The spaces for resistance are elusive and often need to be carved and recarved on a daily basis. This resistance might take the form of building a relationship with a child around work by giving the child a few minutes a week to work with materials of her or his choice. A teacher might give the child a book she or he loves instead of a leveled book. The art of teaching currently might lie in recognizing and carving out those small and momentary spaces of resistance.

In my work with the bilingual graduate students in a course I teach on biliteracy, I begin the semester by asking them to engage in an inquiry project about a biliteracy question of their own interest, which they will explore throughout the semester. (Some of the students in my class already have their own classroom; others do not.) During one particular semester, 14 bilingual students attended the course. Participation in the study was voluntary. My decision to document and study my bilingual students' work came from an opportunity offered by The Institute for Literacy Studies at Lehman College/City University of New York through the program "Writing Across the Curriculum." Each faculty member who participated in this semester-long program was asked to develop an inquiry around his or her own practice and document it. Marta (a pseudonym), the student whose work I describe later on, was one of the students in this course who agreed to participate in my study.

In the biliteracy course we begin the project together by challenging ourselves to find that tension or current wondering in our teaching. It often takes most of the students' time to reconnect with their own questions. Some of them, at times, find the process even uncomfortable, and ask me, "Why don't you just give me a question? It would be so much easier." After all, they say, "there is very little space in my teaching for my own questions. I am being told what do every minute of the day." Over time, as the students reflect and interact with one another, they begin to connect with their tensions and turn them into possible questions for their evolving inquiry. They soon start to see possibilities, even if these are only fleeting possibilities. As a teacher educator/researcher, I find that by studying the bilingual teachers' individual inquiry questions, not only am I able to gain insights about their current practice, but the process also allows me to support them at a point of need in their individual inquiry journeys.

After a couple of weeks of searching for her wonderings about biliteracy, Marta, a bilingual student who didn't have her own classroom yet and who had had very few experiences working with children, chose to work in a fifth-grade bilingual class. After consulting with the classroom teacher and me, she worked on a weekly basis with a small group of bilingual students. She began her inquiry project with the following initial "evolving question":

What happens when bilingual children have opportunities to talk and write with their friends (not just the teacher) about their reading? I want to know if they read more.

She chose this question, she explained, because although she loves to read, she had heard that often Latino children struggle with reading. So she wanted to think about ways to make reading more enjoyable for her future bilingual students—once she had her own classroom.

Throughout the semester, Marta kept weekly notes on her interactions with the small group of fifth-grade bilingual students. Each time she met with the students, she documented both her observations and her interpretations. In one of her observation/interpretation papers (dated February 25, 2008), she wrote:

In the last couple of weeks, I have realized that I need to pay attention to how they read, not just how much they read or whether they read more or less. Today, I noticed that I was surprised that Angel had a lot to say about the story. He was even going back into the book to show the pictures. In my eyes, he seemed restless and was moving a lot. I thought he was not into the story at all.

At this point in her observations, Marta is beginning to see that it matters that teachers take the time to look further and question those initial assumptions. She is discovering that it is critical that one takes the time look closely, to re-look and reexamine and reevaluate.

On her March 10, 2008, observation, Marta wrote:

Lately I have felt a bit frustrated in some of my sessions with the children. Both children have seemed rather disengaged or uninterested in the last few sessions. I have been thinking that I also need to pay close attention to my actions as a teacher and the kinds of engagements I might prepare. I heard in class the other day that I am not just observing the children, I am also observing myself. I can't just say to the children, "read." I am beginning to think that I also need to read with them.

Marta is now wondering about the integral connection between observation and reflection. She has recognized that as an observer, the meaning she brings to the observation really matters. She is opening up her teaching to possibilities of room for growth. On one of her next observations (April 10, 2008), Marta wrote:

> Today I asked the children to do something different. I don't want our sessions to be monotonous. I asked them to make a sketch about an image they had in their mind as we read the text. We stopped at different parts of our reading; we spent a few minutes sketching, and talked about them. It seemed to me the children found this activity very interesting. It seemed to me they understood more of the story also.

As a bilingual teacher, Marta is recognizing the possibilities of offering the children more open-ended engagements. These engagements certainly provide more appealing opportunities for interesting talk. She is becoming in tune with the ways in which her students think and learn. She is beginning to "grapple with the complexities of understanding children's worldviews and, more particularly with making classroom activities permeable, open to children's language and experiences" (Dyson, 1997, p. 72).

At the end of the semester, Marta wrote an extensive paper in which she told the story of her inquiry project and made connections to readings from class:

> I end my inquiry thinking that I as a teacher can do a lot to inspire the children so that they will love to read. As a teacher, I need to know not only lots of strategies, but I can, for example, provide choices as to what books they can read and in what language they can read, just like Karen Smith (1995) wrote in her article. I can take notes of the choices they make and about what they say of the books they read.
>
> As a teacher, I have learned that I need to read with them. The children need lots of opportunities to talk about what they read. I can also integrate the arts more, as I read in the article "Art and Literacy with Bilingual Children" (Carger, 2004), and bring more interesting materials. I end this semester with new understandings about the importance of valuing bilingualism/biliteracy, after all what matters is that children don't lose their love for reading and that they experience the beauty of their first language.

Marta is beginning to find and define for herself the poetry and art of her teaching through the questions she asks. She knows that as a bilingual teacher and, in this case, a teacher of reading, it matters that she takes an inquiry stance toward her actions and initial assumptions, as she observes her students and herself "in motion," as Patricia Carini says. It is, after all, through her questions, reflections, and dialogue that she will recognize and carve out those small spaces for resistance—generative spaces for big and deep thinking; spaces where she can resist looking at children solely through scores of numbers and levels; spaces of possibility where in spite of institutional constraints, she might one day come together with other teachers and talk about kids from a perspective of strength.

As a bilingual teacher educator, studying Marta's work challenges me to remember that all beginning and experienced bilingual teachers have burning questions about issues of bilingualism/biliteracy. I need to take their evolving questions seriously, and I need to do my best to support each one of them by helping them take an inquiry stance, just as Kelly Draper once did with us when we were beginning to teach. As a teacher educator, I need to ask myself: Do I care enough to give serious attention to their questions and wonderings? To what is on their minds?

CHAPTER SEVEN

Conviction
The Teacher I Want to Be

Julia Fournier

꧁꧂

As I looked over the reviews Cecilia and I did of Jenny over a decade ago, I was hit with an overwhelming sense of nostalgia and loss, because of the kind of teacher I was at that time, the kind of school I worked in at that time, and the climate of education in general at that time. I was also hit with a powerful sense of anger, as I was not certain I could now be the kind of teacher Jenny had needed me to be then.

COMING OF AGE

I came of age as an educator during my fourth year of teaching, in 1985. This is when I started attending workshops and reading professional publications that were outside the circle I had been exposed to as an undergraduate. I met other teachers who had similar views about teaching and learning. The Center for Establishing Dialogue (CED), the organization that planned and sponsored these workshops, was teacher led. The energy and focus of the work of this organization was inspired for the most part by the work of Ken and Yetta Goodman, whose theory of reading development suggested that rather than learning language and reading through exercises, we learn through meaningful exposure to language and text (K. Goodman, Shannon, Y. Goodman, & Rapoport, 2004; Y. Goodman, Watson, & Burke, 2005). This way of thinking about learning was known as Language Experience. The idea that learning takes place through meaningful experience and not rote exercises was not confined only to learning language. Teachers eventually used this philosophy to shape the entire curriculum in the school day.

At the time, I was teaching in a Native American community located just outside the Phoenix area. My assignment was a self-contained classroom of children from the ages of five through nine who were labeled Learning Disabled, Educable Mentally Retarded, or Emotionally/Behaviorally Disabled. Some of the students spoke three languages. The materials and textbooks that were available to me were not appropriate for the group of children in my classroom. The ideas and activities I learned about from other teachers who were interested in Language Experience made sense to me. As I tried them out in my classroom, the response from the students was immediate.

It was during this time I realized I needed to stop relying on most of what I had learned in college and start paying attention to my own experiences and instincts. Once a teacher discovers the power of a classroom filled with children who are learning based on curriculum designed for them by their teacher, it is impossible to imagine ever reverting back to manuals and skill sheets.

WHAT HAS BEEN LOST

Now the process of how yearly, weekly, and daily plans are made is even more removed from the children than those basals and textbooks were back then. The children are given tests. The state creates standards based (by and large) on what the children are tested on. The textbook companies create a collection of materials designed to teach to these standards (in other words, to the test). No matter how narrow the focus of each item and each standard, learning has been reduced to these bits and pieces. Unfortunately, for poor and struggling children especially, this means the way they are taught now will most certainly guarantee their failure on these tests, despite what No Child Left Behind (NCLB) has in store for them.

The kinds of classrooms in public schools that promote independent thought and learning in young children have been all but phased out of existence. We have disconnected learning from life and life from learning. We are told to plug in each mathematics, language arts, and reading skill and teach it as if it were not connected to anything else, many times even within the discipline itself, and certainly not across disciplines.

We have gone back to skill and drill; the curriculum has been pushed down to ever more developmentally inappropriate lessons for young children. We teach children for the most part to rely on algorithm, and so when they come to the test item, they don't recognize it as something they are familiar with unless the item has been presented to them in exactly the same way. And because the now accepted (mandated) methods of delivery of instruction do not promote problem solving, students have difficulty taking what they have learned and broadening it to include what they see on the test. In other words, since children are not encouraged to make natural connections in mathematics, but to rely on algorithm to solve problems, they also rely on the structures the textbooks put in place for them. So, for example, if they have learned how to add three-digit numbers with carrying in the context of a traditional "stacked" addition problem, they might do well on the test if given the problem presented in the same manner, but if confronted with the same task in the context of a word problem, or in the context of a missing addend question, the child may have difficulty arriving at the correct response.

I now work in the school library and with middle-school children, mostly in the area of language arts, as a collaboration teacher. I have been fortunate in a way: I don't think I have had to deal with the loss of control over curriculum choices that regular classroom teachers have had to deal with. However, from the vantage point the library affords, I have a wide-angle view of the effect NCLB has had.

Despite the extreme focus on reading, writing, and math, children are reading less, not more; writing less, not more; and less able to understand complex mathematical problems than before. The prescripted formula for teaching subjects has removed the individual from the process and the joy from learning. There are still good students, students who try hard and do well, but the thrill is gone. Kids are in and out as soon as possible, and it's the same for most teachers. Teacher-led and -directed study groups are few and far between. Virtually every minute of every day is devoted to bringing up test scores, *or else*.

The "or else" means being "taken over" by an outside entity who apparently will come in and "change everything." What's left to change?

And, of course, the schools caught "underperforming" on tests are schools who teach poor children, English-learning children, and children who live on Native American reservations.

TELLING STORIES AS ACTS OF RESISTANCE

Last year a study group in Phoenix read together the book, *The Truth about Stories* by Thomas King (2005). King, a Native American writer and storyteller, asserts that we not only are defined by the stories we tell, but we in actuality *are* the stories we tell. I have come to believe this is true. With this in mind, I do not want to tell the story of loss and the outrage I feel for politicians who have eviscerated the profession of teaching and stolen away from children the kind of learning that fosters independent thought and decision making.

This is not who I want to be.

This is not who I want teachers to be.

The story I want to tell right now is the story of my classroom at the time Jenny was a student in our school. Other experienced teachers, like me, will be familiar with many aspects of that classroom. My memory of teaching at that time was the extreme pleasure and joy I felt walking into the classroom each day, turning on the light and wondering what great learning and fun we would have that day.

Jenny was a third-grader in my multi-age, Grades 2–3 classroom in 1996. At that point, I had been teaching for 14 years. I had been working without textbooks for 10. Our school year began, as always, with play. The room was large for a Phoenix public school classroom (about 25 × 35 feet). About a third of the room was sectioned off so that large block construction projects could be left standing as construction continued. Most schools in Phoenix are one-story, stand-alone buildings that back up to or are within neighborhoods. Doors open to the outside. Rather than corridors or hallways, we walk down sidewalks outdoors to go from place to place.

Inside the classroom, there were organic materials available for junk construction—materials such as cardboard boxes, tape, tubes, and egg cartons. There were building materials and tools such as nails, screws, boards, hammers, screwdrivers. There were markers, stamps and ink pads, paint, all sizes of paper, and large tubes and connectors that could be used to make playhouse-sized structures. We had a steamer trunk full of costume and dress-up materials. Two wires hung across the room. One supported lightweight curtains used for performances; the other wire was used to display artwork. There were puppets, stuffed animals, and an overhead projector the children used to make shadow puppets and hand shadows. Discarded household items and appliances were brought in for deconstruction: a typewriter, telephone, or toaster might be examples. We had pets—usually a bird or two, sometimes a family of finches, as well as turtles, fish, or snakes in a very large aquarium or terrarium. And we had plants.

The students worked at tables that were comfortable for four to six students in chairs. It was also possible for students to work on the floor, as we had ample floor space and enough clipboards for each child. There were huge cubbies, big and deep enough to hold backpacks and ongoing projects. The large open area for circle time could be made larger easily by moving tables back. The seating and workspace was flexible and was in flux throughout the day.

The official school day began at 8:30, but the classroom was open at 8:00. Students were allowed on the playground or in the classroom, working on projects or socializing.

I had an aide for most of the day, and very often a student teacher or intern. I team-taught with the teacher next door.

For the first week or two of the school year, students entered the room as they arrived at school and went to work on whatever project they had under way or activity that interested them. I can't emphasize enough how important this was to the way children approached learning for the year. Children were given time to play and to get to know each other through this kind of work, through choice, and through strength. They bonded as thinkers and doers.

After play, each day began with a morning meeting. Two students were in charge of running the meeting, which started by taking an account of who was present and making sure assigned jobs had been completed and homework was collected. Then the question of the day was asked. The material for the question came from *The Kids' Book of Questions* by Gregory Stock (1988). We came upon this part of the morning meeting by accident. We pulled questions from the book as time fillers, but then recognized the power of the content of the questions and their potential for strengthening discussion and participation in the classroom.

The questions were provocative (Who has it easier? Girls or boys?), and even the most reluctant of whole-group talkers would give an opinion. Many of the questions led to larger, more philosophical discussions. During the course of the year, students would begin to create their own questions. In a multi-age classroom there can be an uneven feel at the beginning of the year due to the fact that there are continuing learners and older learners. But this daily ritual set up the expectation that each person would participate and be listened to at the beginning of each day.

Reading consisted of a read-aloud and discussion. We were very careful in the books we chose, especially read-aloud chapter books, recognizing the importance of selecting a book that could be read and discussed for a length of time. It had to be a great book, for any number of reasons. A book could have a theme we were interested in exploring, beautiful language, or a really well-drawn character. The book could be funny or tied to a cultural study. Often the characters or situations in books we read would come up in meeting time or concern circle. I remember one time a student's brother had been shot and killed in a drive-by. We were sad, and also feeling a great sense of loss for our classmate, Monica. When she had still not returned to class after two weeks and the children were wanting her back and asking when would she be back, one student suggested that maybe Monica was like Jiya in Pearl S. Buck's *The Big Wave* (1986), not ready to live again yet. Since all students understood what Jiya had gone through in *The Big Wave*, they accepted this as a possibility.

Students also were involved in literature study, which could be based on a theme or author we were getting to know. Students emergent in literacy read books with repetitive, predictable text in small groups. They created their own books based on the pattern of the book they had mastered. Language arts was studied through journal writing and writer's workshop, which consisted of mini-lessons focusing on conventions that needed introduction or reinforcement.

Our mathematics program was based on research by the National Council of Teachers of Mathematics and the National Science Foundation. In this program, TERC, an education research and development organization, introduced students to concepts through activities and games that built on prior knowledge, experience, and logical progression. There were no student workbooks. Teachers were given guidebooks and manipulative materials from which to select appropriate lessons. I remember so many "Ah-Ha!" moments in using this program.

Homework was nightly and consistent. Tuesday night was news. The students were asked to watch the news and write about an event that was specified—international, national, state, or local. During morning meeting we would discuss anything of interest. Wednesday night was poetry. A poem that related to something in the current curriculum theme or season would be selected. The child would have the option of responding to the poem with prose, poem, or an illustration. They were also given the choice to memorize the poem and recite it to the class. Thursday night was math. The students were given a word problem to work out at home.

We had three science investigations to get through each year. The investigations could be very thin or go very deep. We usually worked within the guidelines of the investigations either until they collapsed naturally with time or until the students took up a new interest. I remember, for example, that the rocks and minerals investigation took a turn when a child asked, "What is dirt?" This took us into a new investigation led by the children's, rather than the district's, agenda. This investigation was one of the most interesting in my memory, and I remember realizing I would never have thought to study dirt and how great it was that the children had decided to do it.

Social studies projects were frequently connected to our science investigations and very often focused on one particular scientist related to the area we were studying. At other times we did a cultural study, working hard to make it authentic by drawing on one person's experience as a native of particular culture, rather than engaging in a generalized holiday or food type of study.

Field trips at our school tended to be the culminating experience or reward activity. One year, at an end-of-the-year pool party, we talked about the fact that we learned so much about a child's "other world" strengths outside the classroom when we had them in a different environment. We decided field trips like going to the pool should be done at the beginning of the year as well, to help us get to know the child. In addition, rather than having the field trip be the end of the study experience, it should be at the beginning or middle to inform whatever content was being studied. Since we were allowed only one field trip per class per year, we needed to look for outside ways to fund these trips.

We approached the Art Museum at Arizona State University about setting up a series of field trips. They were thrilled with the idea. We communicated monthly with museum staff to keep ahead of the schedule for the visits. At the beginning of each season, we went over the planned exhibits and discussed the appropriateness of the works, deciding which artist or exhibit to focus on each month. Over the course of time, the museum began including activities at the end of each tour where the students would create art based on the exhibit they had seen and the art or artist they had learned about. In addition, other classrooms began to become interested, until there were eight classrooms visiting the University Art Museum on a monthly basis.

We realized during a trip to a nursing home one year how much more meaningful "community service" would be if we could make visits to a nursing home on a weekly or biweekly basis. With the support of our district we were able to make this happen, and our relationships with the residents of the nursing home became an important extension of our school community.

Perhaps the singularly most important part of the day was compliment/concern circle. These daily meetings took place just after lunch. The students had an opportunity to discuss problems or to give compliments at this time. Although these meetings were led by the teacher at the beginning of the year, the students took over by the second semester. All concerns and consequences were recorded. Consequences were natural and were meant as an opportunity to learn or repair a relationship rather than punish. Because we took time each day to discuss concerns, we cleared the air every day, keeping small problems from becoming big, and at the same time modeling for children ways to solve problems and take ownership for good and bad decision making. During the course of the year, we could see a shift taking place as students began solving their own problems during recess. When it came to circle time, instead of describing the problem, the children involved would describe how they had worked to solve their problem together. All classrooms had a concern circle, so children could go to any classroom where there was a student they had a concern with.

Writing this, reading it, and rereading it, has driven home to me how truly child-centered this education was. Virtually *every* decision was based on the children we were teaching at the time. Our lessons were based on a theme or exploration, and we expanded the theme to include each student and all subject areas. We even had the Art Museum working to include our themes in the tour the docent took with the classes each month.

This description of my classroom could apply to most of the classrooms at W. T. Machan School at the time. Each teacher's individual personality and strengths in addition to students' interests gave every classroom a distinct character; however, what was common was the importance placed on consideration of the individual.

One element that influenced this focus on the individual was our work with Prospect's Descriptive Processes. We met in small groups as a staff at least once a month to do Descriptive Reviews of Children. These reviews were used to inform the entire staff on issues related to classroom structure or curriculum building. It became apparent during one review, for example, that it was important that a particular child have food on hand in order for him to feel more comfortable in the learning environment. All of the teachers began thinking about this idea for children in their own classrooms, and the next thing you knew, classrooms had begun a snack program. And so it went.

CONFRONTING CONVICTION

The writing of this book about Jenny has been in process for more than nine years. Every time I edit and revise this chapter, I am forced, however willingly, to revisit the past and a time and place that no longer exist, and I am struck by the night-and-day difference between then and now. Things have gotten much, much worse.

I will not return to Machan in the fall.

On June 2, 2009, I read my letter of resignation at the Creighton School District board meeting, to silence from the board and a standing ovation from the parents and teachers at the meeting:

> For the past 22 years I have been a dedicated, hardworking, and, in my opinion, really good educator at Machan School in Creighton School District.
>
> Creighton School District and particularly Machan School have been a large part of my life. Creighton in years past has been well known for its innovation and willingness to try new and different ideas in the interest of helping all of its learners reach their full potential. Over the years we have had visitors from across the nation, as well as international guests, eager to observe our wonderful teachers and students.
>
> I have published work and presented at conferences across the United States and have been proud to point to Machan and Creighton as my home, my inspiration.
>
> This has all changed over the past year.

I know that certain changes occurred due to the federal mandates of No Child Left Behind and the state mandates of English Language Development.

I am appalled at what has been allowed to happen and what is being done to our teachers, our parents, and especially our children. "First do no harm" is a term used in the medical profession, but it's a good fit in education as well.

Arizona State University, for example, has had a classroom at Machan for many years, and our teachers have been flooded with requests for interns and student teachers. The other day, however, I overheard a group of students talking about where they would doing student teaching this fall. I heard them specifically say only one from their group would be doing their student teaching at our school.

My first instinct was to jump to the defense of our school, but on second thought I wondered: Who in their right mind would chose to be a part of the stilted and repetitive delivery system that has been imposed in the past year on our good teachers?

The rhetoric defending these national and state mandates asserts that our 21st-century classrooms need to prepare our students for jobs that we cannot even imagine will exist in the future.

Do we really think these jobs can be filled by people who were trained in elementary school to give answers primarily to yes or no questions or by putting thumbs up or thumbs down as responses for the majority of the day?

We are not helping these children prepare for the future; we are harming them.

In my opinion, practices that have been implemented by our district are harming our teachers, who are scared and angry instead of excited and inspired about their work.

In my opinion, practices that have been implemented by our district are harmful to children and families as they have taken away the joy of discovery, collaboration, and dialogue, keystones for an education worthy of all children.

I was offered a job yesterday at a nearby charter school. I accepted a position where I will be working 50 days longer for $4000 less per year. I believe the direction of this new school is founded on principles we have lost here.

It gives me no great pleasure to offer my letter of resignation to you this evening, but I find myself in the position of wanting to do no more harm.

CHAPTER EIGHT

Courage and Trust
Acting on Behalf of All Children

Carol Christine

My most recent work as a teacher educator at Arizona State University (ASU) connects me with prospective teachers for both elementary and high schools and sometimes their parents. Uppermost in my mind during these meetings are the experiences, ideas, passions, and knowledge of self that for each person will ground the desire to teach.

Last August I met with Jonathan, a potential applicant, and his family—mom, dad, and brother. He had made the decision to teach history, and was looking for a program that provides teacher certification as part of a master's degree. ASU has such a program, and what Jonathan was eager to find out were the program structure, the requirements, and the opportunities for teaching positions in the Phoenix area.

What I was eager to find out was what Jonathan knew about himself that made teaching, and in particular teaching history, seem to be the right choice. In response, Jonathan described a classroom where he had been assigned to observe, and then was encouraged by the teacher to work with students and to teach. Jonathan's excitement and obvious joy in this experience was confirmed by his parents. As his mother put it, "He was hooked and we could see it." In the conversation that followed, I learned that Jonathan's interest in history was long-standing. On family vacations, he was the one who had insisted on stopping to read historical markers. His recreational reading while growing up had centered on historical and social events and biographies. What the experience in the history classroom had done was to create the opportunity for Jonathan to tap into his passion for history and to convey it to others.

As I listened to Jonathan and his family tell their stories—and was reminded of my own—my question of what Jonathan would bring to teaching was answered. This was the kind of passion, self-knowledge, and excitement that, in my experience, provides the resource and capacity for the courage that teachers need each and every day in their classroom lives in order to teach for the benefit of each child and all children.

TEACHERS MATTER

I am a teacher now because particular teachers recognized needs and talents I had as a child and as an adolescent. I had attended six elementary schools by the time I started fourth grade, and what I remember about that year is sitting under the keyboard of the piano for talking too much. I'm certain I was trying to figure out how the classroom space worked and where I fit in. I remember the teacher's name, the piano, my discomfort as I sat hunched over my knees, and my frustration with not understanding why I kept being put there. I was to sit at the end, head down, so I couldn't see the other children, and my knees were bent because the pedals didn't allow me to stretch my legs.

On the playground of the school, I swung on the bars, played hopscotch in the dirt, where deep wells had formed from repeated jumps, and invented games and contests that led to forming clubs with the other girls. Our playground was divided into two parts—boys on one side of the wide concrete sidewalk and girls on the other. My first club was the "wiggle worm club." To be in the club, a girl had to wiggle on her tummy, pulling her body along by her elbows from one corner of the playground all the way around to the sidewalk that separated us from the boys. We actually did this. We must have been very, very dusty when we went back to class (maybe that was partly why I was under the piano!). I remember nothing academically from that year.

In fifth grade, my teacher let me sit in the back of the room and paint. Our desks were in rows, bolted to the floor, and the paper I was given to paint on was as big as the desk surface. We sang a lot in our classroom, and one of my paintings was sent to the state fair. I remember no academics from that year either, but I was one happy child. I made friends, and I was in the same school. I also started an embroidery club, as this was something my mother was teaching me, and we met on Saturdays. I still have a toaster cover from that year.

By sixth grade, I had begun to enjoy school and gain confidence that I could learn along with the other children. I idolized my teacher and was saddened she was not coming back the next year, even though I was moving on to junior high school. The world had become my place.

Certainly I had grown into a social self, and my memories before high school are filled with time I spent in the library with my friend from childhood—the friend I still see almost every year—and the independence I had to go from place to place on my bicycle. It surprises me that I can see the streets and trees, the cars, the neighborhoods, and even some of the people, so clearly in my mind.

In high school, the personal confidence I had was not reflected in my report cards from school. I was an average student, and what kept me going to school were my friends and the activities. I played in the marching band, participated in intramural sports, and finally made it into the synchronized swim club—the Mermaids—after three tryouts. The physical education teacher, the coach for the Mermaids, said she had let me in because of my persistence, not my ability, and she wrote in my yearbook that she had never met anyone who could talk so much. This is puzzling to me, because I don't remember myself as talking a lot. I do know I joined every club there was, and I was doing something every day after school and on the weekends. My journalism teacher assigned my best friend the post of editor of the yearbook, and I was disappointed to have been appointed advertising manager. Yet this position helped me to grow into my self in many ways. I had to make connections with adults in the community, and I learned to ask for what was needed for the yearbook. I had to be convincing because the size of the ad determined the money gained for our publication.

I can imagine now that the journalism teacher, my English teacher (who was also my former sixth-grade teacher), and my physical education teacher talked with each other about me as well as about other students in their classes. I hadn't thought about my teachers in high school making decisions about opportunities they gave me. I had assumed all along that I made my own way and made the best of what was there. My own agency was certainly important, but others may have seen possibilities for me. In high school I had been writing weekly themes in my English classes, and my teacher had come to know me well. She knew the dreamy me, my teenage longings, my hopes for my future, and many aspects of my family life. My physical education teacher knew me as a team member and competitor. It is entirely possible that the decisions and choices that served me so well as a teenager were helped along by teachers who knew me in different contexts, who watched what I did well, and who purposely gave me responsibilities that would challenge me to learn to use my strengths.

In college I set out to be a journalist. In high school I had read a book called *The Hidden Persuaders* (1957/1980) by Vance Packard, and I was absolutely certain I wanted to go into journalism—advertising in particular. I was very taken with the idea that a shape, or a color, or packaging influenced consumers. As a teenager I wasn't thinking in terms of pro or con. Journalism didn't work out for me, although it is most honest to say I had no idea what college would be like and I wasn't prepared to study for my classes. I continued to join numerous clubs and participate in many activities (but I didn't succeed when I tried out for the synchronized swim team in college), and I began working with youth groups through my church. By the middle of my sophomore year I still didn't know what I wanted to do. But I knew I was broke, so I quit school.

I returned to my hometown and worked in a factory office for two years before moving to Phoenix, where I found a job in the personnel department of a bank. I remember one day standing at a filing cabinet and knowing that I was not cut out for office work. I continued working at the bank, but I also returned to college as a part-time student. I planned to teach English. Yet, by 1967 when I graduated, I had changed majors from teaching English to special education and finally to early childhood education. I was beginning to find my way.

VISION AND VALUES

From my life and from my school experiences, there were things I already knew when I first entered the classroom as a teacher. I knew teaching is more than training. Training is rote and practiced, repeated until mastered. Training is what I did as I practiced and practiced in order to get into Mermaids. My own teachers, by their thoughtfulness, surely influenced me to reject the negative view of teaching as rote application of rule-driven models and formulas.

I believed then, as I do now, that it is my first desire and my biggest responsibility to act on behalf of children. For me then, as now, to imagine or consider what is possible for a child or for anyone is what inspires teaching that supports the learner. Though everyone has vulnerabilities, I believe a child, an adolescent, or a preservice teacher learns more when the teacher focuses on his or her strong points. I knew from an early age that I couldn't learn for anyone else, and I continue to believe that learning is the right and responsibility of the learner. What I can do is trust the learner and support the learning. These beliefs—in possibility, strengths, trust—are with me now as a university teacher just as they were when I first began teaching young children.

Believing what I believe, I was fortunate to start teaching in a Head Start classroom in 1967 with an administrator who respected me as the teacher. It was a different school, but not unlike W. T. Machan when Cecilia and Julia began teaching there. The administrators I worked with listened. They supported my work and my interests. They recognized my strengths, and they left the responsibility for how to teach with me. They trusted that I had the ability and the capacity to learn. It may be that these attitudes were reflective of the relationship of administrators to teachers in the 1960s.

ACTS OF RESISTANCE

Does this mean all that happened even in this first school where I taught was for the benefit of the children? No, it doesn't. I remember very well the times when these beliefs placed me in opposition to common practices and administrative requirements. For example, children were not allowed to speak Spanish, and I saw other teachers tap children on the head or hands with a ruler for doing so, as I was walking with my own class to the playground. This made no sense to me, and I continued to allow children to speak Spanish in my classroom. This observation, along with others in my first year of teaching, created despair and disillusionment in me with regard to my chosen career. Had I not had the opportunity to listen to Jeanette Veatch, author of numerous books and articles about individualized reading and about teaching reading with children's literature (Veatch, 1959, 1978, 1984, for example), speak passionately about the rights and responsibilities of teachers as advocates for children during that school year, I might have changed professions. I left Dr. Veatch's talk in November of 1967 understanding that my convictions had power only when I chose to act upon them.

I taught in public school classrooms in five schools over the next 19 years. Each brought its own issues and collisions with my beliefs. A few years after the Head Start experience, a child in my kindergarten was tested because someone thought her development indicated "language delay," and she was recommended for special "language instruction." I couldn't see how daily 30-minute one-to-one interactions and calling out names of pictures on cards would develop her language, and I refused to let her be taken from my classroom. Another year, when I was teaching first grade, the speech and language therapist wanted to take a six-year-old Spanish speaker out of the classroom daily to teach him English words with a machine that "spoke" and displayed one word at a time. This time I adamantly refused first the therapist and then my principal.

When I moved on to teaching fourth grade, my principal required a year-long lesson plan at the beginning of school one September. I refused to comply, although a colleague offered hers for me to copy. I did leave the principal a detailed overview of our year's curriculum when school ended—a curriculum informed by children's interests and experiences as well as the district requirements.

These are examples of school practice I resisted and of choices I made because I thought they were best for children in relation to how they learned and what I knew about teaching. I remember feeling frustrated and angered by these demands, but as I continued to teach, I became increasingly confident that resistance and choice were my responsibilities as a teacher. I see, in retro-spect, how my actions and behavior were at times argumentative and noncom-pliant. But I can also see that I took a stand for what I believed right for the child in each instance. Speaking and finding acceptable ways to express myself helped me to develop confidence. Cecilia responded in very much the same way on behalf of Jenny Williams when the reading specialist in her school diagnosed Jenny as needing remediation for reading.

I also remember how difficult it was to say and describe my resistance beyond "it doesn't make sense to me." Later, the work I did with Prospect and with Patricia Carini helped me develop a vocabulary to describe what I was thinking and learning. At earlier points in my career I could sense, but not describe, that a child's learning was driven by curiosity and interest and that learning was continuous, cumulative, and increasingly complex over a period of time. What I had been doing as a classroom teacher and now am doing as a teacher educator has become increasingly clear to me as I have used Pros-pect's Descriptive Processes. I can now articulate the significance and inter-relationships of my personal beliefs, values, and knowledge of children's learn-ing and can convey how these factors impact my teaching and my work in teacher preparation.

THE POWER OF COLLABORATION: "SHEER ENERGY"

Teaching itself, as well as teacher education, has always been affected by the national media and by local and international political events. In the 1960s, there began an increased flow of federal monies into education—in Arizona growing to 39 million dollars by 1970–1971 and to 142 million dollars by the 1980s. There was increasing public awareness of disparities related to eco-nomic, racial, and social class boundaries. The War on Poverty, declared by President Lyndon Johnson, funded Head Start, a national program for children and parents (my first classroom was in a Head Start program for five-year-old children). Arizona legislated financial support for kindergarten as part of pub-lic education in 1967, allowing school districts five years to prepare for this requirement.

With the increase in federal and state funding, however, the tenor of schools began to shift dramatically. By the mid-1970s there was an increased call for accountability and control, as the public recognized that "public schools could not fulfill the many expectations that had been expressed for them in the 1950s and 1960s" (Berliner and Biddle, 1995, p. 130). A downturn in the econ-omy and inflation adversely affected funding for schools, and school districts had to compete for dollars. By 1972, the same year all five-year-old children in

Arizona began attending kindergarten, legislators were advocating yearly measurement of outcomes to justify the spending, and state legislation required that all school districts develop and implement a Continuous Uniform Evaluation System (CUES). I remember arguing with colleagues at the time about the appropriateness of using "outcome" as the word to describe what teachers taught and children learned.

There was more to come. The first iteration of CUES for first-graders in my district required children to identify nouns and adjectives. For example:

> The red flower is in a vase. Color the circle that tells
> which word is an adjective:
> ○   a) flower
> ○   b) vase
> ○   c) red

I believed, along with other teachers in my school, that there was little value in teaching our first-grade children to identify nouns, verbs, and adjectives for a test, as they would be able to easily name and use these conceptual terms by the time they were seventh- and eighth-graders. We worked together to keep this from becoming a first-grade test item; our goal was to prevent the testing of an unnecessary and inappropriate skill in first grade. At the same time, district administration was striving to comply with legislation enforced by the state Department of Education. Looking back, I think it was then that teaching began to shift to production, as children bubbled in their answers on test forms, as the tests were scored, and as learning was reduced to or reflected by what could be counted.

By the late 1970s, a group of teachers from several school districts gathered at the home of Ralph Peterson, a professor at ASU, to talk about the increasing tension in our schools as a result of CUES. What can be done? How can we secure our role as teachers who are listened to by administration and parents? *Why are we so timid?*

We shared our classroom experiences as we described our children's excitement with learning. Alongside were our "horror" stories of posting CUES requirements by grade level in our classrooms, dealing with the increasing demand for lesson plans that stated the CUES objectives, and submitting weekly and yearly plans to the building principal, presumably to approve what was to be taught for the week or the year.

By the end of that first Saturday morning we had named ourselves Support and Maintenance for Implementing Language Expression (s.m.i.l.e.), and we had decided to host a workshop to increase our numbers. This auspicious beginning in March 1979 brought 50 teachers together with a demand for more workshops.

Our presentations that day included bookbinding, puppetry, language experience resources for teachers, learning center ideas, and ways to use children's literature. Each of these was a part of a bigger focus on children. Children across Arizona were writing and publishing their own books, and authors of children's books came to conferences for children and teachers. Teachers sought multiple venues for using and enriching children's language—writing stories and making books, charts, journals, songs—and children's language was used to teach reading and writing. Many teachers were teaching reading with an individualized reading approach and language experience activities. Published programs, or basal series, were prevalent, but they did not dominate classrooms. There were no widespread mandates to teach reading in a particular way, but many of us were being pressured by administrators to use programs with detailed lesson plans for teachers that included questions to ask and responses to accept from the children. These, of course, could be easily aligned to the objectives in CUES.

Word spread quickly from this first workshop, and our group began to meet monthly to share our teaching stories. Shortly after s.m.i.l.e. began meeting, we learned of the Teachers Applying Whole Language (TAWL) groups in Tucson and Columbia, Missouri. Networks formed as educators began talking about this grassroots movement in their communities at conferences and workshops. Individual teachers and groups from Minnesota, Kentucky, New Mexico, California, and Canada began to contact each other about ways to protect and to develop their work.

There was no formal membership in s.m.i.l.e., there were no dues, and there were new faces at each meeting. We represented a range of school districts across the Phoenix area, and we taught all ages of children. We began developing a network of resources and of people who helped us spread the word about our workshops, and we began to identify school administrators who supported our work. Schools and districts hosted our workshops at no cost. Teachers were invited from one school to another to provide in-district workshops for teachers. The state Department of Education paid the substitutes for these consulting teachers.

Prominent educators and authors spoke at our workshops for nominal fees. In 1984, Donald Graves spoke to a crowd of 700 teachers at one of our workshops about writing and teaching as a process (Graves, 1983). He compared our challenge of creating change to disassembling "brick by brick" what had been built, and in a letter written after his talk (February 5, 1984) he described his experience with us in this way: "You are in the forefront of what is needed in the United States, a rebirth for teachers, a rebirth for the dignity of the profession itself. You are showing the way. I marveled . . . [at] the sheer energy you give each other." Our audiences continued to grow.

In 1985 I took a leave of absence from my school district to work on filing for nonprofit status for our organization, which changed its name to the Center for Establishing Dialogue in Teaching and Learning (CED). The Center was a direct result of the professional activity of classroom teachers and university faculty working together to understand, support, and develop classroom teachers' views of curriculum and their own learning. Our primary purposes for the Center were:

• Support and develop educational practices that use children's experiences and their modes of expression as the means of learning
• Encourage and support research and writing by teachers
• Provide opportunities for teachers to link research and classroom practices in cooperation with public and private educational institutions
• Provide opportunities for individuals and groups to form coalitions to carry out common goals and purposes

CED experienced steady growth after incorporation in 1986, and by 1989 we had introduced a school membership. By 1992, we had 14 school and district members and over 400 individual members. Our first director, Alice Christie (now President's Professor in the College of Teacher Education and Leadership at ASU), coordinated a statewide committee of parents and teachers, called the Community for Effective Student Evaluation (CESE), that set out to learn about and to challenge state legislation that required testing of children in first and second grades. We were successful, and local school districts were permitted to make this decision for themselves.

Through our workshop programs, Patricia Carini and Prospect's Descriptive Processes were introduced to teachers from the Phoenix area. By 1993, Principal Lynn Davey at Machan School described the number of Machan teachers involved in study groups, workshops, and seminars as a "critical mass"—all of which directly contributed to the overall well-being of the staff, families, and children in the community.

The excitement of this collaborative, grassroots labor of love generated and regenerated the "sheer energy" that Donald Graves had observed in his 1984 visit. Nevertheless, that energy proved not to be sufficient to prevent the eventual disintegration and erosion of all that CED provided. A Nation at Risk (1983), with its message of a failed public school system, took a toll. And money was certainly a factor. The local opportunities CED provided for teachers were increasingly in competition with conferences and workshops provided by professional organizations, publishers, and for-profit businesses. Requirements for "district training" increased as schools adopted programs to "train" teachers to use the district's approach to discipline and the district's methods for teaching particular content and the district's prescription for how to plan the time required for various subjects throughout the day. Teachers' contracts mandated participation in these training sessions, and the time they once had to pursue individual interests was no longer available. The nationwide push toward standardization established a presence in the media, with almost daily reports on outcomes. The educational climate in the nation by the end of the 20th century had shifted to one of uniformity and conformity.

THE COURAGE TO CONTINUE

Losing CED was a hard blow, but the work was labor intensive and had always been more than paid staff at the Center could handle. Harder yet was the realization that CED was not an isolated casualty of changing attitudes and educational policy. Those changes were, and continue to be, felt at every level. Julia's description (see Chapter 7) of the losses at Machan is emblematic of the hard times in schools, especially for schools that serve the poor, the English language learners, and all those who are most in need of a rich school experience. Here at ASU, where I now teach, the disconnects are wrenching.

It isn't that there aren't eager applicants like Jonathan. It isn't that there aren't committed faculty or individual teachers like Julia eager to match his passion with their own. Too often what our students in the ASU teacher education program see and hear in the schools they are assigned to, for their field experiences and their student teaching, is fractured and fracturing. The demands made for accountability and compliance from national and state agencies, and for teaching with scripted methods and approved materials, dominate the schools' curricula. Failure to reach and maintain test scores at particular levels in classrooms and schools has resulted in public labeling of the achievement of children by individual classrooms and schools.

The graduate students in my children's literature course (each one a classroom teacher) are a reminder of a not-so-long-ago conversation with a school principal. All teachers in "her" school were required to follow the reading program and teach the same script, in the same way, for 90 minutes each day. In the fall of 2008, the teachers in my class, from six different schools, were teaching with this same restriction. Teaching was reduced to delivering or administering a product to a captive group of children. At the same time, I learned that students admitted to our college of education were changing their majors, dropping out of teaching before they even got to the classroom. They were disillusioned by the conformity required in how teachers teach and by the pressures they see on teachers in schools.

I do love teaching, and it is in part because of the challenges individual "teachers to be," like Jonathan, face in this most rewarding of professions. Ben Okri, the Nigerian storyteller, says that "In a fractured age . . . we are living the stories planted in us early or along the way, or we are also living the stories we planted—knowingly or unknowingly—in ourselves" (1997, p. 46). As a teacher myself, I owe to others the story of how I came to teaching, what I struggled with, and how I recognized that my voice as a child and an adolescent was the same voice I had as teacher. To tell their own stories, each teacher needs to imagine and explore what it is that fires his or her desires and possibilities as a teacher. When they hear about experiences and choices in the stories of others, teachers can imagine their own actions and formulate their own thinking about why they might act in particular ways when they face similar scenarios. Teacher education must be sufficiently rich in frames of reference to allow new teachers to articulate what they are doing and why it matters to the learner and to education writ large. I owe them opportunities for learning that are rooted in inquiry so the habit of self-questioning and questioning of authority becomes engrained: Is this task appropriate? Is it necessary? Is it right for this child at this time? Are the child's best interests served by the school—and by me?

It is impossible to find a "perfect" school, but teachers can and do work together to make changes that matter for the children they teach. All beginning teachers need to know that teaching and learning come as one. My experiences with the value and necessity of establishing collegial relationships can be sought in their own teaching. They owe it to themselves and to the children they teach to participate in workshops, conferences, and book study groups to support each other and to continue their own learning. Those preparing to teach, and teachers just starting out in the classroom, need to understand that they must have authority/authorship of their teaching if they are to see themselves as advocates for children—even if that means questioning and speaking out against prevailing models and policies.

Teachers need to know, too, that programs designed by publishers to teach science or math or reading will come and go as they have come and gone for generations. They need to know that administrations change, that the composition of teachers in a school changes, that communities change—that change itself is the constant. They need to know that the courage of our convictions is what allows us to face change, uncertainty, and difficulty and to continue doing and trusting what we know is best for children.

For myself, I have learned that what I *can* trust to be constant is children and the families who love them, as well as the teachers and educators who care for them. The continuous thread among these three—children, families, teachers—is our humanness. The work we do in response to what is possible continues to be what is most important in teaching and what makes teaching really matter.

I have a passage in my writer's notebook from Barbara Kingsolver's book *Animal Dreams* (1991) that describes where I think we are now: "The daily work—that goes on, it adds up. . . . Good things don't get lost" (p. 299). The daily work of education is that accomplished by classroom teachers, and in the best of circumstances the qualities and direction of that education are a responsibility shared with each child's family. No one of us is like another. No child is like another. It is my firm conviction that our responsibility as teachers is to see the uniqueness of each child and to support that particular child's process of learning and growing. I trust the next generations of teachers to tell their stories of what it means to live up to and act upon their own convictions in circumstances that continue to be less than favorable for children and adolescents in our classrooms.

PART III

Moving Forward

Refusing Conformity/
Creating Possibility

HE TWO CHAPTERS that conclude the book carry forward and apply the main lessons we have learned from Jenny to envision a future for our schools. The first lesson Jenny teaches is resistance to the conventional and routinized roles assigned by the schools and by society at large. The second lesson is to ask hard questions persistently, with the aim of digging deep and breaking free from predetermined boundaries. The third lesson is to reach out to others with trust and with the conviction that from the active inclusion of diverse points of view novel possibilities and new paths forward are created. The fourth and perhaps most important lesson is not to lose heart and courage if the path is long and hard and the struggle demanding. For surely this is Jenny's greatest lesson: that the lives of all those preceding us who acted from the belief that it is possible to make a better school, a better world, are our own greatest and most reliable resource.

CHAPTER NINE

Poiesis

Life on the Uptake

Margaret Himley

I really like Jenny as she emerged through the spanning studies—her embrace of the world, her insistence on social justice, her love for others, her generosity and courage, and her learning through memory and value. But mostly I smile when I think about Jenny's letter to Mr. Bentz, or her probing questions to Julia Fournier about her family, or her decision to invite a troublemaker and his target to join her for lunch with the teacher, or her request that people at the Prospect Summer Institute not read her prayers, or her desire to talk openly about menstruation in her fifth-grade class. I smile, because Jenny *takes up* these potentially highly conventionalized interactions in surprising ways. In this chapter I explore how Jenny's *uptake* becomes a form of agency, a process of ethical self-making, or *poiesis*, and how her uptake demands a response and a responsibility from us.

Originally borrowed from speech act theory, the concept of *uptake* comes from scholarly work being done in rhetorical genre theory. The idea is that "as people orient themselves toward particular social spaces, they enact the genres valued in that system" (Kill, 2006, p. 217) by doing certain kinds of things, by thinking certain kinds of thoughts, by saying certain kinds of words, and by performing certain kinds of identity or senses of self. It's part of our sociality—to fit in, to share ground rules, to perform expected roles, to engage meaningfully and coherently with others. Most of this happens automatically, but we've all had the experience of not knowing the genre rules and roles at different times and places in our lives, and then at least temporarily losing our sense of who are or how we fit in.

When Austin first introduced the idea of uptake in *How to Do Things with Words* (1975), he was referring to comprehension—a speech act is completed only if the receiver takes up, understands, and acts on what the speaker has said. The teacher asks the class to open their books to page 5, and they do. The child asks a question, and the teacher answers it. But what's missing from this is how uptake has history and memory (Kill, 2006, p. 220). For example, children are taking up the teacher in the classroom not just in the most immediate way of that one particular teacher, but within the context of a long line of teachers, experienced directly as well as mediated through cultural representations such as movies, novels, family stories, and music videos. The teacher enacts a kind of institutional and cultural role, and the children recognize that. Mostly this process proceeds smoothly, even seamlessly—until something disrupts it and reveals greater complexity and new possibility. Here's an example of the interactions of uptake, identity, and communication:

> One day, a boy named William came to [a friend working at a day care center], crying and infuriated, to report that one of his peers had said that William was not four years old. The fact that William *was* four years old was of little consolation to him; he wanted an adult not only to confirm his age but also to make the child who had challenged him acknowledge it. At one level, this demand can be dismissed as childish, but, at a relatively profound level, William understood that if he couldn't get other people to respond to him as a four-year-old, then, in practice, the actual fact of his age was of little or no significance (Kill, 2006, pp. 221–222).

We secure our sense of ourselves by securing uptake from others, by being legible within already established genres, meanings, signs, rituals, discourses, communities, and institutions.

Jenny, like many creative and courageous people, challenges the predictability of this process, thereby opening up space for desire and design, reflection and response, intention and change. More specifically, as we learned in the spanning studies, Jenny refuses a narrow or conventional identity of student—and in so doing gives us all a chance to rethink our own often too conventional thinking about students and schooling. I think that's one reason the participants in the spanning studies like Jenny so much. Me too.

FINDING A BASS LINE

Let's go back to the letter to Mr. Bentz (Plate 4). Although I don't know the context for this note, I wonder if Jenny missed the class discussion or reading of *Ira Seas [Says?] Good Bye,* and now wants to make up for that absence in some way and perhaps to get herself out of any trouble she might be in. In her earlier review, Julia Fournier noted that Jenny often missed out this way, but made up for it by reading the book herself (see Chapter 2). In any case, this is not a typical student note. First, she deploys the formality of a memo—"To: Mr. Bentz" and "From: Jenny Williams"—with its focus on communication, not apology or even explanation. She takes charge of the communication, by first asking him a question, as if it's *his* job to tell *her* about the book. She asserts without excuse her absence in the morning. She then generates a larger conversation about whether the book was funny and about how much she liked an earlier book apparently in the same series—*Ira Sle[e]ps Over*. And then she takes on almost a teacherly role herself, by asking Mr. Bentz if he liked that book. It's an interesting speech act—one that requests the teacher to take her up as a partner in a discussion about books, one that asserts agency in the communicative context, and one that mimics the kind of book talk found on television shows. And, finally, the smiling face and the big red heart move this memo into the realm of art—into the expressiveness, sociality, joyfulness, presence, and aesthetics that are so representative of Jenny's body of work.

This assertion of agency, this play with convention, this refusal to be (just) "the student" pushes teachers into a little self-reflection. I don't know how Mr. Bentz took up this memo from Jenny, but we do have some accounts in the spanning studies of teachers being startled by Jenny into rethinking their own teacherly identity and performance.

When Jenny came up to her fifth-grade teacher, Kitty Kaczmarek, with a book in hand and a frown on her face, and wanted to know right then and there about gynecological exams and Pap smears, Kitty's first thought was to suggest Jenny take this question home and talk with her mother, and her second thought was, "I felt like I was not being up front with this information" (see Chapter 3). Kitty still talked with Tisa Williams later, but in that moment she took Jenny up more directly and more honestly than she might have with another student. Perhaps this was because Jenny had already demonstrated her ease with sensitive topics when she explained informatively and without embarrassment how menstruation works to a boy named Douglas in her class. Perhaps this was because Jenny brings her whole self to her questions, as part of her embodied engagement with the world—as her mother notes in describing Jenny as positioning her whole body around the cash register at the grocery store and standing there until the clerk answers her questions about how things work (see Chapter 1).

Julia Fournier, Jenny's third-grade teacher, observes that Jenny's three years with Cecilia Espinosa and her mother working in the school "lessened any teacher/student dependence. It was never like Jenny belonged to me. Our relationship was more like swapping stories or kidding around with each other" (see Chapter 2). Again, Jenny pushed up against the conventional student role, buoyed by her sense of belonging in the whole school and not just in Julia's classroom. She left jokes in her journals, and she wanted to know about Julia as a person (if she's Catholic, if she goes to confession, if the men in her wedding pictures are her friends). In the final interview at the end of the book, Jenny talks about how she remembers Julia by her first name and how much that surprised a friend of hers, who only knew teachers from a more conventional distance—last name only. Jenny moved easily, if sometimes annoyingly to those on a different schedule, from classroom to classroom. And as she prepared to leave Machan, she asked folks in the school to write in her autograph book, so she could take "a little bit [of Machan] with her" to her new school (see Chapter 2). Jenny had made a place for herself at Machan, had taken up a place, and had engaged the school as a community with identity, relations, and history. And Machan was open to Jenny as a person with her own particular style and values, which gave her the opportunity to express and further her way of being in the world. The school was not what it is for too many children and even teachers—a *non-place,* a place you are moving through only to get to the next place, a place that you don't engage and change or that engages and changes you (Augé, 1995, p. 52).

Jenny took up assignments in the same way that she took up the school, as Julia Fournier observes, when she says, "Jenny makes meaning of the world by knowing who she is. She becomes what she learns, and then that becomes more of how she makes sense of the world" (see Chapter 2). That's quite a profound approach to schooling, one that insists on the process being social and significant—and one that often results in her doing her work so fully that she doesn't always have time to finish it on time. I am reminded of a story that Cecilia Espinosa told me about asking Jenny, then a second-grader, what she was going to study, to which she replied, "Foxes." Cecilia was a bit perplexed by the fact that Jenny was choosing the same animal she had studied in kindergarten and must have looked at her with a strange eye, because Jenny responded by saying, "I still have a lot to learn about foxes, Cecilia. I am not done yet."

Of course, Jenny's insistence on her own time frame could perturb teachers who were faced with a classroom of students, curricular goals, and administrative demands. Jenny's teachers, though, recognized that her being late, or transitioning in her own way, or returning to a subject such as foxes, was about her desire to engage deeply and meaningfully and thoroughly, and they typically worked to accommodate her. As one of the participants in the review said, "What's different is that Jenny takes responsibility for her own learning." Participants in the spanning studies were also moved by Jenny's claiming her own time. They were encouraged to rethink their own relationship to time in their personal lives as well as their teaching practice, as they connected it to the rapid acceleration of history and the condensation of time and space that result from our living in a globalized world, startlingly transformed by information technologies and instant mass communication.

Jenny asked lots and lots of questions—passionate questions, serious questions, unembarrassed questions, questions that often involved how things got to be the way they are. She wanted to know about history and historical figures, especially ones involved in social justice. She wanted to express and address feelings. She wanted to really get to know topics and people and events and places and adult life . . . and so on and so on. In a time of a superabundance of information, events, and what Augé (1995) calls "the growing tangle of interdependences" (p. 28), it has been a pleasure to be reminded by Jenny to slow down, dig deep, immerse—to know something and not just (barely) recognize it. And it has been important to be reminded of the power of passionate engagement in learning and teaching, and of the contexts in which that can happen again and again.

In all these ways, Jenny refused the conventional role of student in a classroom and the values (re)produced by enacting that role, and she demonstrated what it means to take up schooling as well as the world as an agent, a real learner, someone confident in herself and insistent on meaningfulness in her own education. The teachers at Machan understood, valued, and supported how Jenny functioned in the world, how she learned, and how, to use a familiar Prospect phrase, she took up schooling "from another angle"—and that made all the difference for her and for them.

MAKING A DIFFERENCE

In this passionate dialectic of self and world, Jenny has a bass line, a rhythm, a line of continuity, a sense of self that remains constant, that carries her forward, and that opens up spaces for social critique. We hear this in her final interview at the end of the book, as she contests the injustice of segregating students in eighth grade into cores, circulates petitions, takes on a leadership role in high school, criticizes teachers who disrespect and demean students, and argues against testing. From within the everyday, as an ethical response to the world around her, Jenny makes and remakes herself—and holds on to that self in the face of voices and attitudes that threaten to diminish her, to ignore her, to misread her, to make her docile. This is a task we all face—making and remaking of ourselves in the face of powerful threats to self-hood and agency, as well as addressing and critiquing those threats.

In assessing what it is like to teach under the regime of No Child Left Behind, Julia Fournier says, "This is not who I want to be," this is not the story I want to tell, one of "loss and . . . outrage" at the eviscerating of the profession of teaching (see Chapter 7). She refuses the uptake of the discourses of high-stakes testing, conformity, and standardization, and turns instead to the story of her early teaching experiences, with classrooms full of materials and potential and with colleagues full of energy and excitement, to remember when "Virtually *every* decision was based on the children we were teaching at the time." In Chapter 8 Carol Christine recounts the moments when she began to really think about children, their learning, and her teaching—when she encountered Prospect, when she took pleasure in reading good books to the children in her classrooms, when she taught in a school that trusted teachers and that acted on behalf of all children, and when she worked with others to prevent testing from taking over the schools. And Cecilia Espinosa in Chapter 6 draws on her memories and passions from her childhood in Ecuador as well as her joyful teaching experiences at Machan School, with its brave principal and unyielding commitment to multi-age and bilingual classrooms, in order to confront the challenges of her current job as a teacher educator in the New York City area, where teachers are mandated to be on the same page, at the same time, saying the exact words developed by someone else who is outside of classrooms and far away from schools. These turns to memory are not about nostalgia, but about resource.

Always at Prospect we have worked to create contexts in which we can draw on story, memory, value, and idea in order to make and remake ourselves as better teachers for all children, in even the most constricted circumstances— and to refuse those circumstances as much as possible. At Prospect, we use the phrase, "inches matter," an expression which first came about in the description of how a teacher named Ann Caren (now President of the Prospect Board) rearranged a room to facilitate easier movement. In fact, this whole book serves as an argument for how the Descriptive Processes developed at Prospect, along with its philosophy and its commitment to taking a philosophical stance, can be used to create such a context, to make even a little space, to give teachers and parents a place to stand as they work together as advocates for children and as they say "no" to practices and prescriptions that deny an education based on children's strengths and capacities. This book is about how to help teachers learn to hear and act from their own bass line, to join in philosophic questioning and discussion with others, in order to make a difference in the schools and the world.

POIESIS

It is this intimate connection between ethical self-making and agency—between finding a bass line and making a difference—that I will explore a little further through a discussion of poiesis.

I begin that discussion with a line of argument from *Giving an Account of Oneself* (2005), where philosopher and theorist Judith Butler takes up questions of moral philosophy within the contemporary social and historical scheme of things, by asking how we can negotiate this world in "a living and reflective way" (p. 10). She draws our attention to the later books of Michel Foucault, a well-known French philosopher and historian of ideas, where he no longer sees the self as only the effect of discourse, but presents a more nuanced, a more hopeful argument about the reflexive formation of subjects. As Butler concludes:

> The subject forms itself in relation to a set of codes, prescriptions, or norms and does so in ways that not only (a) reveal self-constitution to be a kind of *poiesis* but (b) establish self-making as part of the broader operation of critique. (p. 17)

I take this to mean that we are, of course, not totally free agents, untouched by history and unaffected by material realities. We come into being—and continue to come into being—at particular historical moments and in particular geographical places, always within a complex matrix of conflicting forces and pressures, norms and prescriptions, desires and demands. We all know this, because we live it every day in our struggles with and against institutions, images, and ideologies. But I take Butler to mean that while we do not stand apart from "the unchosen conditions of one's life" (p. 19), we are also not merely an effect or an instrument of those conditions, and that what matters is *how* we take them up, *how* we delimit a place to stand and act in relation to those conditions, and *how* we ourselves are on the uptake. The *how* has everything to do with the project of self-making as an aesthetic and ethical-political practice.

Butler goes on to say that for Foucault this self-making is "not a radical creation of the self *ex nihilo*" (2005, p. 17), but "a process in which the individual delimits that part of himself [or herself] that will form the object of his [or her] moral practice" (Foucault, 1990, p. 28). This mode of self-creating takes place in the context of those interpersonal or proximate exchanges that put us in contact with the larger social scene of what Butler calls "normativity" (p. 24), that is, the oppressive and dominant forces of conformity and docility.

I think this often happens when there is a breakdown—something small perhaps, like the Title I teacher's judgment about Jenny's *slowness,* or something bigger, like a school's failing test scores—something that disrupts the everyday, that challenges the givenness of what we consider "normal" or "the norm," and that offers a critical opening for reassessing the assumptions and practices that govern that norm.

In that moment of breakdown, for Butler, there are two reciprocal questions: Who am I? and How should I treat you? We are immediately faced with our relationship to the norm, to the socially and historically given, and we have to make a decision about that relationship by crafting who we want to be and how we want to treat others who are also produced by/within that norm. At Machan, for example, teachers put a lot of pressure on themselves to think hard about both questions, to analyze what happens when they and the children were not recognizable within the narrow prevailing discourses and practices, and to confront rather than concede the struggle. Once addressed, these questions took the Machan teachers to a point of no return, because they had been compelled outside of themselves and had in effect become social theorists and political activists. This happened to Jenny's parents too. I don't mean that they all took to the streets or wrote angry letters of protest to the state legislature (though they might have done that too—and Tisa Williams certainly became a very active and effective school board member!), but rather that they recognized that there was more to this breakdown than the immediate and local interaction. When the Title I person swung through the classroom and saw Jenny as *slow* and as needing remedial help or special tracking, her teacher's and her parents' and the school's response was to look critically at the assumptions and ideologies at work in that swift judgment. Returning to Butler:

> We are not mere dyads on our own, since the exchange is conditioned and mediated by language, by conventions, by a sedimentation of norms that are social in character and that exceed the perspective of those involved in the exchange. (2005, p. 28)

Through these "proximate and living exchanges" (p. 30), we come in contact with the workings of those very norms that establish who we are and how we are to behave. Ann Laura Stoler's edited collection *Haunted by Empire: Geographies of Intimacy in North American History* (2006) is not about contemporary classrooms in the United States, but it prompts further thinking about what happens in these exchanges. Her book analyzes the many ways colonial power worked through both the requisitioning of bodies as well as the molding of structures of feelings. As Stoler says, "Colonial authority rested on educating the proper distribution of sentiments and desires" (p. 2) and on reordering the intimate spaces in which both the colonizer and the colonized lived—who slept with whom, who lived with whom, who was acknowledged as one's child, who nursed and reared and cared for whom, who was educated and who was not, who was taken in and who was abandoned.

Among other things, this provocative idea of the politics of intimacy draws our attention to the blurred boundaries between care and coercion. I have no doubt that the Title I teacher believed, and more importantly was trained to believe, that what she was doing in passing this judgment, in making this classification, in reproducing this hierarchy was ultimately in Jenny's best interest. *That* is what scares me—the ease with which we become agents of norms. The insidious and everyday ways that norms capture us, fasten us all too securely within them, squelch our aesthetic and ethical desire to be a certain kind of person, and cause us to disavow our capacity for finding our bass line and making a difference.

I will come at this from one more angle. As noted earlier, in his later work Foucault (1990) turned to the question of how to render the present more livable and proposed the idea of the "arts of living" as the right and the ability of the person to choose a way of being in the world and a way of relating to others. This mode of self-making was a way to pursue one's life as art and to tear oneself free of discourses that colonize one's experience of the self (Paras, 2006, p. 126). In *The Uses of Pleasure* (1990), for example, Foucault starts his inquiry into desire and the desiring subject by looking at what he calls "the arts of existence" in ancient Greek and Greco-Roman culture—those techniques of the self that [then] men deployed not only to set for themselves rules of conduct, but also to transform themselves and to make their lives into a body of work or aesthetics of existence.

Foucault presents an interesting and rich account, but for my purposes I would like to draw from just one of his analyses. He notes that within the code of marital fidelity there are many ways to "be faithful"—as strict observance of the code, as self-mastery, as the quality of the relationship binding the two spouses, as part of the larger project of being an ethical person. What I find compelling about this discussion is the continuum of choices we may have in following what seems like a fairly rigid code—especially the choices at the end of the continuum that involve the larger project of becoming a certain kind of person. Yes, we can follow codes and rules, and we can feel good about that. Yes, we can find pleasure in self-mastery in being a code- and rule-follower. But more importantly, the choice leads to a larger project and connects with ethics, as it becomes a commitment to a way of living and a way of *"liv[ing] with each other*" (Paras, 2006, p. 131; emphasis in original). Hints at what a modern art of living might look like can be garnered from Foucault's comments in an October 1981 interview in *Christopher Street,* where Foucault deflects a question about legal changes in the status of same sex couples and argues instead for efforts to "imagine and create a new right of relations" (cited in Paras, 2006, p. 131)—that is, a creative rather than defensive effort that goes beyond tolerance and rights and moves into new cultural forms and new kinds of relationships. "The distance between an existential ethics and an aesthetics of existence had, for Foucault, shrunk to nothing. To constitute ourselves as moral agents through the living of life as an art-object: these were two sides of the same coin" (p. 132). This is not a narcissistic self-making, but an ethical one that responds to and has the capacity to transform the world.

Here are two quick examples of such a self-making. In the feminist classic "Identity: Skin Blood Heart," poet and activist Minnie Bruce Pratt (1991) describes and analyzes in powerful detail the contours of her growing up in the South, and her struggles to become a different kind of person than the one she would have become had she not engaged in this philosophic exploration of the self. It was not an easy thing, this poiesis: "Yes, that fear is there, but I will try to be at the edge between my fear and the outside, on the edge at my skin, listening, asking what new things will I hear, will I see, will I let myself feel, beyond the fear" (p. 35). This reminds me of the crisis four students faced at Syracuse University after their Facebook group's demeaning of a writing teacher drew the attention of the student judicial affairs officer. As then Director of Undergraduate Studies in the Writing Program, I met with each of the four students one-on-one, and I was struck by how quickly the discussion turned from one about breaking the rules of a social networking site and violating the university's hate speech code, to one of who I am and how I want to be seen and how I want to treat others. This is not who I am, they kept insisting; this does not reflect my real values. This is not how I want to be taken up by others. The episode was a big breakdown for these students, and I admired their honesty and their struggle.

It is in the struggle with/in the uptake where we carve out ethical ways to craft a relation to our unchosen world. Sometimes we are in situations that enable that struggle, and even reward it, as when Carol Christine talks about schools that trusted teachers, or when Cecilia Espinosa describes what happened when a brave principal gave teachers their own budgets, or when Julia Fournier recalls her decision to turn away from textbooks. Sometimes we aren't, and the struggle seems impossible, the outcome depressingly determined. But the challenge remains, and the uptake matters.

RESPONSE AND RESPONSIBILITY

As we near the close of this book, I am left wondering about Carol Christine's haunting question: "Why are we so timid?" (see Chapter 8). With this question, she draws us into a scene of address, where we are required to give an account of ourselves. She is not looking for excuses or defenses or confessions. She is not naive about the context and realities of public schooling. Rather she is calling us forward into a social and ethical practice of self-making on behalf of ourselves and the children we teach. I too call on us to take up her question—with others—as we craft a self as part of the broader operation of critique—for the benefit of children, all children, and for the education they all deserve. This is poiesis—a way of being, a mode of acting, a kind of ethical self-making. It's what Jenny asks of herself in a poem she wrote when she was in first grade:

i Love the wrol	I love the world
i will kep it saf	I will keep it safe
For avvrey one	for every one.

Jenny sets the bar high for all of us, and I trust we will continue the struggle to meet it.

CHAPTER TEN

Making and Doing Philosophy in a School

Patricia F. Carini

The founders of the Prospect School (Joan B. Blake, Louis Carini, Patricia Carini, and Marion Stroud) were steeped in the philosophy of John Dewey. Marion Stroud brought as well her considerable experience in the British Infant Schools, a movement substantially influenced by Dewey. Jessica Howard, who had been involved in the planning stages for Prospect while still a student at Bennington College, returned with a Master's Degree from Bank Street College and teaching experience in New York City to be the school's second teacher. This is now history. The story that follows from that beginning is long and complex—too complex for any one of the many, many people who have made Prospect what it is to tell.

The piece I have chosen to recount here is the story of Prospect's philosophy as it was enacted and as it evolved—and as it continues to evolve in locations across the country. I tell this story for the resource it may provide for schools that are at this moment in the making. I tell it with particular gratitude as a resource for administrators, teachers, families, and communities struggling to remake schools that have suffered immeasurable loss under the severe reprisals of No Child Left Behind and that are now struggling to return to what President Barack Obama calls our "better histories" for the vision of a school regenerated from its own roots.

LOCATING PHILOSOPHY IN A SCHOOL

Locating philosophy and the making of it in a school for children lifts philosophy down from the library shelf and out of the ivory tower. It is a consequential relocation. It claims that the work of making and doing philosophy can and does happen in daily life, and further that it can happen in the midst of a school, part and parcel of busy classrooms brimming with energy and activity. Locating philosophy in a school, in the midst of life, I am saying that philosophy is bigger than a specialist activity or an academic pursuit. I am asserting that the making of philosophy isn't dry or tame stuff or a domain barred against those other than scholars. With that assertion, I am affirming a philosophy active and in action. I am saying the source from which philosophies spring is a *burning human desire*. This desire, the human longing to make sense of the world and our own place within it, fuels a driving force in the world—a force with very real consequences for good or for ill. I am saying that it is a passion no less strong than other human passions. I am saying that we humans are philosophizers by nature. Children are no exception.

Jenny is herself a powerful example of a child pondering, wondering, questioning, pushing hard on the boundaries of what passes for justice and what it means to have a voice to speak out for what you believe. Her teacher, Julia Fournier, says of Jenny that she has "questions, questions, questions," and rightly relates this habit of questioning to her strong desire to learn, to know. The questions that compel a child's attention are ways of probing the world. They tap persisting themes and interests. They invite imaginative exploration. These are not the order of questions that can be answered once and for all and then set aside. These are questions of sufficient magnitude to power further thought, further exploration.

The bigness, indeed the profundity, of the questions young children pose and hazard to make sense of can startle. A very little girl—not yet in school—asserts, pointing her finger skyward, "Before I was born I was a star." A boy, age 5, standing up, gesturing the length of his body asks, "Is *this* me? Is *this* who I'll always be?" My own son, Peter, at age 6, observed to me one day that he knew where we were. I didn't quite get what he meant. In response to my questioning look, he told me, "We are all on a green grassy head and we just can't see the body and the feet." When he was about 10, his thinking about where we are took a different turn: "Remember that head I told you about? I don't think I like it so well anymore. I've been thinking that maybe we're inside and someone is dreaming us. What if he wakes up?" Another boy, age 10, a student at Prospect School, when asked about a vial of water he had taken to carrying around, responded that he was trying to start life in a bottle. Further conversation revealed that the basis of his quest was knowledge of the origins of life gleaned from a documentary. The same boy's persistent and absorbed interest in dissecting road kill found and brought to school took on a somewhat different meaning when viewed from the angle of a search for life—as did his fascination with Mary Shelley's *Frankenstein* (Himley, 1991, pp. 22–25).

All those acquainted with children—their own or others their paths have crossed—could add their own examples of children doing the same: *pondering, thinking twice (or more) about something, wondering about it, trying it out in play or gesture, letting a question percolate, reevaluating it.* That is, exercising what I am going to call a philosophic attitude. It is that attitude on which this essay pivots. I take it to be a distinguishing characteristic of humans everywhere since time immemorial—or there would be no myths of origin and struggle, no philosophies of knowledge, no metaphysical philosophies in search of ultimate answers, and so on. And, equally, returning again to daily life, there would no philosophies particular to our personal lives—the values and creeds by which we live, tested and retested in experience—without which, or should they fail us, we suffer the pain of being without anchor, adrift, bereft, a plaything of fate.

Dewey writes in *Democracy and Education* (1916/1997) that "Philosophy might almost be described as thinking which has become conscious of itself—which has generalized its place, function, and value in experience" (p. 326). Especially in that first part about "thinking . . . becom[ing] conscious of itself," I take Dewey to be referring to the attitude at philosophy's root, without which none of the philosophies I referred to, or his own, would exist.

When I make the claim that philosophy can happen in the midst of a school—can be a part of daily classroom life—I am talking about exercising that philosophic attitude. I am talking about practicing "thinking becoming conscious of itself." I will describe how that happened at Prospect School, though with the broader intention of spelling out how that can happen in other schools—as indeed it did among a group of teachers and administrators at W. T. Machan School at the time Jenny was a student there. The same exercising of "thinking becoming conscious of itself" happens now in Prospect-related inquiry groups in many other locations. A teacher can do this practicing on his or her own through reading, through journal keeping, or through reflection on questions arising from the classroom—though admittedly to do this kind of sustained practice alone is harder.

In the following quotation, I speak of what I call Prospect's "great advantage"—an advantage that locates the practice of a philosophic attitude in the descriptive methodology that is a main theme of this book and that is integral to Jenny's story as it is told here:

This was perhaps our great advantage at Prospect: Starting from the commitment to examine our own practice, we were oriented from the first toward noticing, with a responsibility to record, reflect on, and describe these noticings. (Carini, 2000, p. 16)

Prospect—by fostering noticing, by fostering questions, by releasing the passion to make sense of what was happening for children and in the school—created a context in which a philosophic attitude could flourish.

And there was more. Because Prospect was a school, not a laboratory or a model school for a select population, it brought together in one place a rich sampling of human complexity and variety. There were the children only just beginning in life and families from all walks of life. There was the staff dedicated to a new venture in education. Within four years of its founding, there were interns from Prospect's Teacher Education Program eager to join in that venture. There were members of the wider community attracted by the school's philosophy who joined in staff and intern seminars. It was an ever-expanding circle. By 1971, it would expand yet again to include conferences and summer institutes connecting Prospect with schools, mostly urban, across the country.

PAYING ATTENTION TO WHAT *IS*

Strong opinions and intense feeling abounded at Prospect and so did the whole array of human dilemmas and conflicts that came up on a regular basis, all contriving to provide ample opportunity to practice "thinking . . . becom[ing] conscious of itself" (to cite Dewey again). When I think of Prospect as it launched itself, I am flooded with the ferment and excitement I experienced then, a bubbling over of observations, questions, and intensity of feeling.

There is disagreement among staff about what constitutes bad language on the playground and what the response should be. Observations of children building disclose, among other things, that children with strong preferences for blocks often aren't the same children who go for cardboard construction or Legos. Reading looms large on the school agenda, and there is recurring parental anxiety about reading and the teaching of reading. We have a new entry to the school—a nine-year-old boy who can't read. There are children in seemingly larger numbers than before who can't bear to lose at a game and who are inclined to be contemptuous of adult intervention. There is a young child who unpredictably but regularly flies into a rage, making lightning strikes around the room that disrupt the whole class. What children make during choice time displays a high degree of internal consistency child by child. Looking at a bundle of houses, suns, and trees made by children, it is striking that there is no duplication within the totality of work or in an individual child's renderings. An accrual of observations of children playing outdoors calls to attention the depth and intensity of this play, some of which is collective and resumed from one outdoor time to the next. For the most part, painting, drawing, block construction, sewing and other fabric-related activities, cooking, and working with clay and other moldable materials have no observable upper age limit. Children have strong preferences among these activities, and materials most preferred continue to absorb the children over a span of years, their skill expanding with experience and age.

Each of these observations, assorted as they are, invokes a trio of pivotal questions: *What is the meaning of what we are seeing? What of value about children, about learning and teaching, about the school can these observations tell us? What do they make us think about?*

So: What is swearing anyway? What about it brings such strong adult response? How can working on these questions help us to respond to the children in ways meaningful to them and to us?

What is it about the outdoors, about nature that calls out to so many children? How can we as a school respond to that strong interest?

What is happening to set off that little boy's lightning strikes? Is it rage, as it appears to be? What is rage anyway? How do we as a school get beyond merely stopping him?

What is at stake in losing a game—and in loss more generally? What do these games mean to the children so intent on winning? Are there some children involved who aren't so do-or-die about the whole thing? When we adults experience a child's responses as contemptuous, what are we talking about?

What is reading and how does it happen for different children? How will it happen for a nine-year-old who has failed many times? What does it mean about reading that there isn't a technique or method that guarantees success?

What does it mean that children have strong preferences for certain materials and activities? What does it tell us about the child and about the material itself? What is it about blocks that make them not interchangeable with Legos or scrap material? What does it mean and what does it tell us about children and about ourselves that blocks and drawing and sand and clay and cooking and sewing hold compelling interest for 13-year-olds as well as 5-year-olds—and for adults, too?

What does it mean that for all the houses and suns and trees drawn by children, no two are the same? What does it mean that a child's work is identifiably hers or his even though it also changes with age? What does that tell us about the relation of change to continuity in human lives—and about learning? How might continuousness and change be described not separately but together and inter-animating?

These are all philosophical questions. That is, they are questions that don't have answers and don't respond to ready-made solutions. Instead, by breaking the cake of custom and convention, they demand a second and considered look at what might otherwise be dismissed either as obvious or as unimportant or as both. They are also questions redolent with the textures and descriptive of the parameters of the particular school in which they arose.

For example, there are all the questions about materials and children's choices. For them to arise there had to be the opportunity to see children in a relatively uncontrived learning surround engaged with blocks, sand, painting, and so on, and to witness the choices children made. Similarly, to notice the continuities in a child's works across time, there had to be the opportunity to observe and keep a record of a child's production and choices of mediums over that span. For reading to be a live issue, it follows that there wasn't allegiance to a standard, prescriptive reading program designed to take each child from A to Z and beyond. As I have written elsewhere, the big idea driving this activity and fueling intellectual fire sufficient to sustain it was that "a school and a staff could create a comprehensive plan for doing this kind of observational inquiry . . . that a school could itself generate knowledge of children, of curriculum, of learning and teaching" (Carini, 2000, p. 9).

By virtue of diligent observation and ways to reflect on what we saw; by trial and error; by making mistakes; by not giving up; by re-looking at our own efforts; by multiplying descriptions of children across time; by learning to take a child's "works" as seriously as we took the child, and so as worthy of close, caring attention; and especially by increasing confidence in the power of process and of looking itself—from this fertile ground evolved what are known as Prospect's Descriptive Processes.

It was exciting and taxing work spanning many years, many crises, many changes. Drawing on my own experience, what most helped us to sustain the effort was trust in the children as persons and learners. It was that trust which oriented us to seek and to particularize the capacities and strengths of each child, confident that those capacities and strengths were there to be found. It was an inquiry guided by this trust, and continued over many years, that yielded a picture not only of the individual child but through descriptions multiplied many times over, of humanness itself—a picture startling in its complexity, in its contradictions, in its variety, in its generative potential.

PHILOSOPHY IN ACTION: THE STORY OF A CHILD

I have been speaking of how a philosophy in the making folded the doing of it into practice. I have told how prompted by puzzlement, or conflicting opinion, or confusion, we learned to frame questions that required us as a staff to re-look and to reconsider, to forgo solutions in favor of a search for the meaning of whatever had caught our attention. To illustrate how this happened and what it taught us, I will expand on one of the examples I offered earlier: the little boy who unpredictably but regularly flew about the room in an apparent rage, leaving a trail of destruction in his wake. Merely stopping Sean, which was itself no easy matter, didn't seem sustainable over the long run. The teacher in particular, and others of us in support of her efforts, were in search of a way to understand what was setting off these rampages, with the short-term goal of anticipating them and the longer-term aim of channeling all that energy before it flared out of control. Some of us weren't sure just what we meant by naming what we observed "rage," and wondered if by assuming rage we were prejudging the situation and effectively blocking our own capacity to see outside that frame.

That wondering led to a decision to widen the lens by focusing attention on this little boy *not* when he was expressing what we were calling rage—but when he *wasn't*. It proved a fortunate move. When we gathered a week or so later, using a fledgling version of the descriptive review process to assemble our observations, the picture yielded was remarkably consistent. What we observed was an exceptionally productive child, engaged with a wide variety of mediums, experimental in his approach, who mostly worked alone and with a remarkable intensity of focus over protracted periods of time. Sean's facility with an array of mediums was particularly noted by those who observed him making things during choice time, as was his habit of embellishing what he made and his pleasure in telling about the process. For anyone who happened to look in at story time, it was his stillness and total absorption that stood out. Sean's teacher added to this picture his sensitive appreciation for the meaning of what was read and his equal appreciation of humor, often seeing the point of a joke missed by others. Reflecting on Sean's concentration, his ingenuity, his high productivity, and his love of story, one of us observed that, explosions aside, this was a child who was daily using what the school had to offer to the optimum.

In the context of this picture, it was, as is usually the case, an observation of the teacher's, the one among us who knew him best, that provided the insight we were seeking. It was seemingly a coincidence of timing that offered the fortuitous glimpse, though I suspect from my own experience that most of these so-called chance observations are more a function of heightened awareness than otherwise. On this particular day, shortly after we had shared our assembled observations, the teacher noticed how intently Sean was working on one of the larger puzzles in the room, one she would have thought too difficult for a not-yet-five-year-old. He was putting in the last piece as she approached to comment on his prowess with puzzles when in a flash Sean leapt to his feet, deliberately overturning the table, sending puzzle pieces flying in all directions.

In the time it took to observe what happened, and with the assembled observations fresh in her mind, what she was seeing snapped into place. Wasn't it likely that what sent the child flying around the room was the intensity and persistence with which he poured himself into his work—an intensity that then erupted as pent-up feeling and random energy? This was, it seemed to her in that moment, not so much rage as need for an emotional release—an outlet for overwrought feeling.

That insight opened the way for highly productive conversation. Now that we had an inkling of what was going on, we could together generate some ways of easing the intensity. Among these, humor was high on the list, along with conversation, improvised breaks for stretching exercises, and plentiful invitations to talk about his work—all the while staying on the alert for other opportunities to balance concentration with relaxation.

Did all this looking and reflecting *solve* the problem? Were there no more lightning strikes? No, that didn't happen, though they did diminish, and when they did occur were easier to interrupt. What did noticeably change as a function of our changed perceptions was how the teacher and the rest of us appreciated Sean. We appreciated him for his determination and his passion to learn, to do, to create and for his insatiable hunger for stories. We appreciated him, too, for the complex intermingling of passions channeled in abundant creative activity and sometimes so intensely felt they overwhelmed him.

That is, we appreciated Sean for being human, possessed of human desires and longings woven fine, some of them contradictory and not always reconcilable, and equally for the volatility that is passion's nether side. We appreciated him for what he taught us about humanness, about ourselves, about the struggles and longings of other children he called to mind. It makes a world of difference to know a child humanly, to appreciate the complexity and intensity of what it is to be fired by desires and longings, and to recognize the educational potency of these passions. Over the span of nine years at Prospect, it was valuing the child in these ways that proved sustaining.

For us, the adults, refocusing from rage to passion and desire—to what it is a child is longing for—turned our heads around. Now a new question hovered on the horizon: What do these strong desires, these passions, mean educationally and how do they play out in a person's life and education over the longer span? How does a school respond to these strong desires intelligently and supportively?

This is a story of a child. It is also a story of philosophy in action. It is a story that particularizes Prospect's philosophy of the person, as it happened in the making of it, as it grounded and also propelled the whole of Prospect's educational mission for both children and adults. As in the story just told, it is each child, and each of us, who experiences the world, who seizes on it, who discovers in action its meanings, no two of us finding it precisely the same. Each child, and each of us, highly particular, confers value on the world, each capable of choice, altogether human and altogether unique in our interests, our passions, our yearnings. Each lends to the world a novel dimension, a particularized noticing that in the experience of it through the eyes of each of us has an enlarging effect on all.

These were big and lasting lessons: What it is to be a person. What it is to grapple with the complexity of human passions and conflicting purposes. What it is to choose. What it is to value and to be valued. And there were more such lessons. We learned that to see a child or a child's work afresh and from multiple perspectives not only changed how we saw the child but how we acted in response. We learned that to be awakened, to have one's eyes opened, to see what was previously not observable has a transforming effect on the observer. We learned that for the child who is valued for who she is, for her unique contributions and capacities, that appreciation has a potent releasing effect. Space to grow, to learn, and to be is expanded. There is room to take a deep breath. Possibility abounds.

READING TOGETHER

For all this learning, there was still more: lessons learned by reading books that often seemed in their aptness to have been written especially for our benefit. To tell the story of how, early on, some of us met on Sundays to do that reading is to tell how in those gatherings the seeds of what later became more formal seminars were sown. It is hard now to explain the upsurge of excitement we felt over the discovery that Friedrich Froebel's (1826/1899) observations of children's outdoor play from the first quarter of the 19th century matched so closely what we were observing in the 1960s. The two together, our own observations and Froebel's, spurred us on, inspiring intensified attention to the sufficiency of small things—twigs, mud, stones, acorns, puddles—and to what these natural materials meant to the children and for their education.

Seeing the children—noticing their hands and their gestures as they arranged found objects, built with them, discovered in what was at hand what they needed—honed our perceptions of the body, challenging the mentalistic cast of contemporary developmental theory. One thing led to another. Searching for expanded ways to think about this knowing in the body, and about the body's nexus with the world, made the dual discovery, in close compass, of Alfred North Whitehead's *Modes of Thought* (1938/1958) and Maurice Merleau-

Ponty's *The Phenomenology of Perception* (1962) seem almost magical. Ripe with our noticings of the children in nature, Whitehead's conceptualizing of the human body as "that region of the world which is the primary field of human expression" (p. 30) made immediate sense to us. I can remember hardly being able to read the book fast enough. With the children all around us doing and making, and on a daily basis delighting us with the beauty of what they created, and with our appreciation of how the works of each child bore that child's imprint, we could not have been more ready to hear Merleau-Ponty when he writes,

> In the home into which a child is born, all objects change their significance; they begin to await some as yet indeterminate treatment at his hands; another and different person is there, a new personal history, short or long, has just been initiated, another account has been opened (p. 407).

It was an interplay of animating ideas, with us filled to the brim with all that we were seeing, and so *on the ready* for thinkers who could push us further in our search. Then, as is so often the case, one book or author led to another. For example, reading Merleau-Ponty led us to Max Scheler's *The Nature of Sympathy* (1913/1973), the book almost jumping off the shelf of its own accord when I spotted it in, of all places, the bookstore of New York City's Port Authority bus terminal. With these few references, I have touched only the tip of the iceberg (see Note below for a further listing of philosophers who impacted our thinking). It was a period of energizing intellectual intensity equal to the intensity of the questions spinning from what the children were showing us on a daily basis.

WHAT IS PHILOSOPHY FOR?

I have left the question of philosophy's uses and value for last. For Prospect in all its dimensions, across the many locations where Prospect-related work happens, philosophy's value and function is measured by the value of what it protects and nurtures. Without it, the Descriptive Processes are left unguarded. Without it, the child is left unguarded. Without it, practice is left unguarded. What is left unguarded can be burgled, undermined, left to dwindle away, distorted, or violently uprooted. I count among the most serious damages of No Child Left Behind the preempting of standards by agents remote from schools. It is that action against the schools and against local communities that deprives them of a fundamental educational right and obligation—

the right and obligation to develop and enact a basic philosophy particular to a school's history and to its founding ideals and principles.

Schools are never good enough. There has never been a perfect school and there never will be. There is always more to be done. Education is always bigger than what schools can provide. Neither is it predictable as to its outcomes. Big learning, learning that propels a learner to new heights or sustains the stamina to dig deeper, is immeasurable. To reduce learning to measurable achievement according to standards external to that learning degrades the learner and shames the school. When that happens, tiny ideas, generalized conventional wisdom, and wing-clipping adherence to rules trump variety, roominess of thought, and the generative potency of imagination—in short, the particularized perspective each learner brings to the world.

A philosophy neglected withers. Scores of school mission statements, cobbled together by a committee, featuring nice words like "whole child" and "child-centered," gather dust at this moment in countless file drawers. The nice words themselves too often paper over strong and actual differences of value and principle within the school community—differences left unspoken for the sake of the appearance of consensus. Better to let them lie. The fatal flaw, though, is that mostly these mission statements reflect philosophies adopted ready-made. There is no process or method for the making of a philosophy, for enacting its principles, or for evaluating it in action as it actually affects the education and lives of children, as it actually influences the life of the school. *A philosophy that isn't enacted fails at the most basic level: it cannot serve as an educational, social, political, and ethical guide for action, for resistance, and for the revitalizing of the school.*

This is terribly important, and more so now than ever. Schools, teachers, and families are bombarded with conflicting demands and expectations. In recent years, the bombardment has accelerated to a blitz, a firestorm, with children the victims, as children always are when violence reigns. Teachers in schools across the country have been held hostage to mandates, with surveillance and intimidation the means for forcing them to submit. What is miraculous is that even so, *even so,* schools, principals, teachers, and families have continued to struggle for the sake of the child's rights to dignity, well-being, and an education big with ideas and possibilities.

It is terribly hard to sustain these struggles. Compromises are made and trade-offs transacted. Sometimes the compromise or the trade-off can be accommodated without a total sellout. Sometimes not. The burning question posed each time a compromise or a trade-off is forced is, What is it that I as a teacher or parent, or all of us collectively, is losing? It is one thing to give up choice or activity time for children—or recess or play or time for stories or for circle meetings to talk through problems—with full knowledge of what it is the children and you and the school are losing. It is entirely another to give it up, feel regretful, yet shrug and move on to the next thing. To know what I or you or all of us are losing in situations of forced submission to external authority is a political, educational, and ethical obligation.

To be in the habit of questioning, of exercising a philosophical attitude, is invaluable in times of duress. It is by sustaining a philosophical attitude, by reflecting, recollecting, questioning, that it is possible to face threatened loss and to reach decisions on when to resist, on how not to give one more inch than necessary, and on how to make what inches you have count for a lot. I can't have choice time. Perhaps I have said the day I give that up I leave teaching. I am torn. So: What is choice time anyway? What does it mean for the learner to have choice? Where can I continue to create spaces for choosing and to free the child's own capacity for making knowledge? Where can I still catch glimpses of this child's interests, of that child's strengths? How can I, and others, keep choice present even in these tightened circumstances? How can we keep it talkable? Can this be a recurring conversation in the school—or if not in the school, with other teachers who share this commitment?

These are philosophical questions—they are also politically, educationally, and ethically charged questions. These are questions that chart a course, that exert a high-value pressure. *They are questions that, by not begging the question of the child as both starting point and end point for education and school, provide a reliable moral compass for both.* It is a radical idea to put the child—the person—first: ahead of the system, ahead of "achievement," ahead of school business, ahead of economic concerns. As the political philosopher Isaiah Berlin (2006) tells us, the individual and the individual's "free self-expression, the infinite variety of persons and of the relationships between them, and the right of free choice" are ever under threat "in the name of an efficiently working order, untroubled by agonizing moral conflict" (pp. xxix–xxx).

To close, I turn again to Dewey, this time to acknowledge a debt of gratitude for a comprehensive body of thought that makes a philosophy in action possible—a body of thought that was the single most important influence on Prospect at the time it was founded.

NOTE

Several philosophers are mentioned in the text. The following is a sampling of other philosophers, theorists, and educators, as well as poets, novelists, artists, whose works have been explored in Prospect seminars in a variety of forums and locations: Michael Armstrong, Jimmy Santiago Baca, M. M. Bakhtin,

Owen Barfield, John Berger, Albert Camus, Louis Carini, Ernst Cassirer, Paul Cezanne, Edward Chittenden, James Clifford, Edith Cobb, Marjorie DeVault, Mark Doty, W. E. B. Du Bois, Eleanor Duckworth, Philip Frank, Paolo Freire, Friedrich Froebel, Clifford Geertz, Johann Wolfgang von Goethe, Nadine Gordimer, Stephen Jay Gould, Shirley Brice Heath, Martin Heidegger, bell hooks, Myles Horton, Lewis Hyde, James Joyce, Carl Jung, Paul Klee, Milan Kundera, Audre Lord, Barbara McClintock, Toni Morrison, Lisel Mueller, Howard Nemerov, Kenzaburo Oe, Octavio Paz, Vito Perrone, Jean Piaget, Adrienne Rich, Muriel Rukeyser, Oliver Sacks, Edward Said, Jose Saramago, Ernest Schachtel, James C. Scott, W. G. Sebald, Lewis Thomas, Lev Vygotsky, Lillian Weber, Eudora Welty, Heinz Werner, Cornel West, Raymond Williams, and William Carlos Williams.

Interview with Tisa Williams
and Jenny Williams

Fall 2007

Conducted by *Cecilia Espinosa*

Cecilia Espinosa: Of course, what I am most curious about is what the book brings to mind for each of you. What stands out? What are you hearing that surprises you or reminds you of what was happening then—more than 10 years ago for you, Jenny, at the time you were at Machan?

Tisa Williams: I noticed that there were a lot of things that are still the same, like the kind of music Jenny listens to, the way she dresses, the things she's really concerned about, and just the way she sees the world.

Jenny Williams: For me, it was weird that people were saying they could see signs of my being *slow*, because I would never have felt that in high school at all. I did Student Council for four years, and I was President of my freshman and junior classes, and Vice President in my sophomore and senior years. I did notice that my reading was slower than most of the other students, but that didn't hold me back in any of my classes, because I could learn and do everything else just as fast.

Cecilia: Looking back on your years at Machan, what do you remember? What about that time is still with you?

Jenny: I remember feeling like back then it was more like everyone was equal (not to the teachers), but we were more respected—not fighting, not being judged, not being lower.

Somebody at work the other day said something about one of their teachers from grade school, and she asked me my third-grade teacher's name. I said, "Her name was Julia." And she said, "You know her first name? I have been out of school for so long and don't know my teacher's first name." I said, "That's what we called them when we were in school," and I couldn't for the life of me remember her last name but I remember it now—Fournier. I couldn't remember then.

Cecilia: Talk a little about what school was like after you moved from Machan—maybe when you were in fifth grade and later.

Jenny: I remember not having any friends in seventh grade. I was an outcast, and I was in the orchestra. But in eighth grade I had more friends, and I was a peer mediator, which made me more friends with everyone else.

I remember in eighth grade they decided to make a special core for the more advanced students, and that was the core I was put in at first, but then they moved me to another core after a couple of months, one that that was made up of mostly minority kids. I liked going into the other core, because I was already listening to alternative and rock and that kind of stuff, and that core was into rap music and gangster and stuff. But these were the so-called "bad kids."

Tisa: Yes, I remember fighting that, and there were a lot of teachers there that wanted to segregate and put the "bad kids" in one area. The demographics in Glendale had changed, with more Hispanic, Black, lower income coming in, and as that population grew, so did the separation. In eighth grade, Jenny initiated a petition.

Jenny: When they separated us into the cores, they did it based on math scores. That didn't show everything about being smart, because someone who gets good math scores isn't necessarily good in English. The whole thing was not good.

Cecilia: How about high school?

Jenny: In terms of my academic classes, I got close to the teacher in "Thinking Science." He was a really good teacher, sarcastic, a good guy, who made sure we got our work done. I don't remember much more from freshman year. I didn't like the teacher in my math class, but I didn't fail. The thing was the teacher played favorites. Through high school it was a lot like that. I remember in high school people saying teaching was all about politics, not about education, and some of the teachers didn't like some of us. It was different than when I was growing up.

Tisa: Jenny was a leader in every sense. She was on Student Council, and she put on the carnival. She was a real go-getter. Some of the teachers didn't like the Student Council kids, because the Student Council did all this stuff, and some of the teachers didn't want to participate because it was extra stuff.

Cecilia: How did these kinds of issues connect with the ones that were compelling for you from childhood, Jenny?

Jenny: A big issue in high school was the test required for graduation. Not that I couldn't do the test. I passed it the first time I took it; it wasn't hard. But I felt it was stupid that I needed to pass the test to graduate. I didn't agree with it at all. Too broad of a test to see if a child was prepared for life outside of school.

Tisa: I seem to remember that you used to get upset at some of the contests where people deserved certain things and they didn't get them. They would run for homecoming or a scholarship or something. You know, the people that didn't get enough attention.

Jenny: Yeah, I felt that all the time. I was always different than everybody else, but I was popular different—everyone knew me, oh, Jenny Williams, because I was loud and outgoing. I was different, but I was personable. But there were always kids in the class that were different, but they didn't know anybody, they didn't talk to anybody. I remember one of those kids—we met freshman year—we were both trying out for the drum line. He didn't talk to anybody. I still see him sometimes. He stayed in the drum line, but he didn't even seem too much into that group either. He was never completely accepted.

Cecilia: Now and looking ahead, what do you see as the big issues confronting your generation and what do you see as possible for young people to do about them?

Jenny: Global warming is major. That's bad. People should choose to stop wasting and start helping out. There is also the robot of the everyday, people just getting up and going to sleep, getting up and going to sleep. It is what is making people lose their compassion for other people, for helping the earth, and for things like that.

I think that the war is hitting my generation a lot, because a lot of the guys who are going are people my age, or a few years older, in their middle twenties. I think people don't realize that. It's not close to home for me, because I don't have people in my family who are there or who have died, but people are dying. I think people don't see it and realize it is a war like World War II and the Korean War, wars that were big. They don't realize like this could be like one of those wars too. It is like one of those wars. It's not here, not in the textbooks, but people don't realize it now, especially my generation. I don't think they know it's so serious.

And I think about segregation, not just between the races but between pretty people and skinny people and between fat people and people who exercise—just segregation between everybody. Just because there are no signs, "skinny people eat here, fat people here there," it's still out there. The media, magazines, models, even with like plus-size modeling.

Cecilia: How about you? Where do you see yourself in the next five years?

Jenny: I'm just working right now, trying to make some money. I'd like to go back to school for photography, and I'd like to do some traveling. I've been living by myself with two roommates for nine months now. It's been good. I like paying for things by myself. I would like to build my own business doing something with photography. I really like being in charge, I really like planning things, and getting things done, and once it's done, I love it.

The Vermont Design for Education

Under the aegis of the Vermont State Board of Education, the State Department of Education developed The Vermont Design for Education, which was first published in 1968. In 2005, the Prospect Archives and Center for Education and Research electronically republished a version (without original illustrations) based on the 1971 fifth reprinting of the document. The version reproduced here is derived from the 2005 Prospect Archives edition.

VERMONT DESIGN FOR EDUCATION

THE CONCEPTS set forth in this Design represent the position of the State Department of Education, and were developed in cooperation with lay and professional groups throughout Vermont. This Design directs itself to the process of education, but supports the Seven Cardinal Principles of Education stated in 1918[1]—Health; Command of Fundamental Processes; Worthy Home Membership; Vocation; Civic Education; Worthy Use of Leisure; and Ethical Character.

This Design is not to be taken as final, but should be reviewed periodically and be subject to change. Recommendations for improvement will be appreciated and should be directed to the Commissioner of Education, Montpelier, Vermont.

[1]Commission on the Reorganization of Secondary Education, Appointed by the National Education Association, A Report of the Commission, *Cardinal Principles of Secondary Education,* Bureau of Education Bulletin, 1918, No. 35 (Washington, D.C.: Government Printing Office, 1962).

VERMONT THE PROCESS FOR IMPROVED LEARNING OPPORTUNITIES

EDUCATION IN VERMONT, if it is to move forward, must have a goal toward which to move, a basic philosophy which combines the best which is known about learning, children, development, and human relations with the unique and general needs and desires of Vermont communities. It is entirely possible to discuss goals and ideals in terms of more and better classrooms, expanded library facilities, health services, audio-visual equipment, and such. The Vermont Design for Education takes the position that, although these are certainly justifiable concerns, an educational philosophy should center around and focus upon the individual, his learning process, and his relationship and interaction with the teacher. Toward these ends, the following premises are offered which, taken in summation, constitute a goal, an ideal, a student-centered philosophy for the process of education in Vermont.

1. **THE EMPHASIS MUST BE UPON LEARNING, RATHER THAN TEACHING.**
   Education is a process conceived to benefit the learner. Central to any focus is the individual and how his learning process may be maximized. This idea is basic and provides the foundation of all other elements of quality education.

2. **A STUDENT MUST BE ACCEPTED AS A PERSON.**
   His feelings and ideas deserve consideration and his inquiries an honest response. He should have the right to doubt—he should even be encouraged to doubt with responsibility, to question, to discuss with teachers, textbooks authors and other authorities. He must, however, do more than doubt; he must strive to seek solutions to those issues which he questions. Each individual must be free to determine whether a position being advocated by an authority or another student is justifiable and rational.

3. **EDUCATION SHOULD BE BASED UPON THE INDIVIDUAL'S STRONG, INHERENT DESIRE TO LEARN AND TO MAKE SENSE OF HIS ENVIRONMENT.**
   Desire to learn is accentuated when the experiences are stimulating and non-threatening. Learning about things is a natural part of a child's life, and in the process of growing up, the better part of learning is done independently.
   The inherent motivation basic to this natural learning experience is internal, based upon a child's desire to answer a question, solve a problem, fill a gap in his knowledge, make things fit together, glimpse a pattern, or discover an order. When a child thus extends his knowledge, it is sufficiently rewarding in itself to make him happy to have learned and eager to learn more. This internal motivation must also become the basis for learning in the school situation. If school work is to absorb his interest, he must know something of its purpose. Involvement in planning and true decision making will help

retain the initial enthusiasm with which a child enters school. The structure of the school must complement the natural way in which children learn.

4. **ALL PEOPLE NEED SUCCESS TO PROSPER.**

Youth is no exception. A continual series of failures, if experienced in the school, can lead to a negative self-image, loss of face, loss of desire to continue to participate, and an urge to seek this needed success outside of the school situation. A school situation should be flexible and divergent enough to allow each person regularly to find some measure of success.

5. **EDUCATION SHOULD STRIVE TO MAINTAIN THE INDIVIDUALITY AND ORIGINALITY OF THE LEARNER.**

The school's function is to expand the differences between individuals and create a respect for those differences.

6. **EMPHASIS SHOULD BE UPON A CHILD'S OWN WAY OF LEARNING— THROUGH DISCOVERY AND EXPLORATION—THROUGH REAL RATHER THAN ABSTRACT EXPERIENCES.**

At no time in a person's life does one learn more or better than during early childhood. It is most revealing to watch a young child in this learning process—exploring, testing through trial and error, manipulating his environment, questioning, repeating.

The opportunity for this type of natural learning should be provided in schools. How much more meaningful for a pupil to be able to see the relationships in a numerical system expressed in concrete objects which he can manipulate to discover their interactions, rather than being faced with a set of numbers in an arithmetic textbook.

Compare the learning which can take place if a student can study trees in a wood lot, discover the interdependency of life in a pond, collect and analyze rocks, minerals, and soil from the surrounding area, rather than struggle through a series of charts and exercises in a workbook. Compare the meaning a student derives from involvement in the actions of a legislative committee with a textbook account of the same process.

7. **THE DEVELOPMENT OF AN INDIVIDUAL'S THOUGHT PROCESS SHOULD BE PRIMARY.**

Rote learning of facts should be de-emphasized—facts should become the building blocks for generalities and processes.

The ability to solve problems—whether social, mathematical, or economic— must be given preference.

A person equipped to function adequately is able to relate his knowledge to new situations in order to solve new problems. He can use judgment and forethought—he is able to reason and imagine. Such a person can perceive problems as well as solve them.

8. PEOPLE SHOULD PERCEIVE THE LEARNING PROCESS AS RELATED TO THEIR OWN SENSE OF REALITY.

There must be a conscientious effort to make the readings, discussions and issues faced in school relate to the world which people experience—to what they see when they look about and read the newspaper.

Schools cannot expect the trust and understanding of their students if agriculture is discussed in terms of the stereotype family farm, when these same students perceive around them huge agriculture combines and under-paid migrant labor.

9. AN INDIVIDUAL MUST BE ALLOWED TO WORK ACCORDING TO HIS OWN ABILITIES.

Students are as diverse intellectually as they are physically, having different backgrounds and experiences, feelings, ways of thinking, personalities, and ways of working and learning.

In order to be effective, schools must allow and encourage students to work at their own rate, to develop their own unique style of learning, conceptualizing and piecing together the parts to form coherent patterns.

Learning experiences must be geared to individual needs rather than group norms.

10. THE TEACHER'S ROLE MUST BE THAT OF A PARTNER AND GUIDE IN THE LEARNING PROCESS.

The role of the teacher must not be one of an imparter of knowledge, someone who knows all the answers and is never wrong, but rather one who possesses those skills necessary to establish an appropriate learning climate, both in atmosphere as well as equipment and materials. The teacher must constantly be aware of each person's abilities and accomplishments, lead that person from one level of conceptualizing to the next, from his immediate interests to a logical learning process, involve him in the planning and decision making process and allow him the freedom and responsibility of becoming deeply involved. The teacher must extend the student's horizons beyond the limitations of the interests and abilities of the student, or even beyond those of the teacher. The teacher must help the individual realize what he has learned, and channel random discoveries into systematized learning.

The role of the teacher might be illustrated by the following example. Consider a child who expresses interests in whales through a freely created clay model. The teacher must be aware of the great number of learning experiences in which the child might become involved deriving directly from his self-expressed interest in whales.

These experiences might include numerical work through measuring, weighing, and developing of the ratios of various parts of the model to each other or in comparison to the real animal. Science, prediction and logical thinking can be involved through forecasting the model's daily loss in weight, questioning why this loss, what is lost, where it goes and in what form. Language development can be furthered through writing stories about one's own whale, or reading stories involving other whales, and research through exploration of different types of whales, their culture, classifications, habits and environment. The teacher must help the child determine which of these experiences would be most appropriate to move toward an individualized set of expectancies.

Consideration should be given to allowing students to set up their own course of study in a subject matter field if it is not relevant to a particular learning situation. For example, in the pursuit of knowledge in the field of chemistry, a student's needs might be better met through the development of a program acceptable to him and the teacher-counselor rather than the existing textbook-laboratory course.

The teacher does not abdicate his leadership role in the student-centered approach, but indeed assumes a far more important role of leadership, one responding to the individualized needs of each person with whom he works.

11. THE DEVELOPMENT OF A PERSONAL PHILOSOPHY, A BASIC SET OF VALUES, IS PERHAPS ONE OF THE MOST IMPORTANT OF HUMAN ACHIEVEMENTS.

The school must assume an active role in helping each individual to evolve a set of personal values which will be most meaningful in helping him meet the challenges of life as a student and later as an adult. The teacher must not dictate a particular set of values or try to impose his own, but rather must help each person sort out his own experiences and seek a set of truths which can provide a tentative philosophy, one which can be re-evaluated in terms of further experiences and knowledge.

12. WE MUST SEEK TO INDIVIDUALIZE OUR EXPECTATIONS OF A PERSON'S PROGRESS AS WE STRIVE TO INDIVIDUALIZE THE LEARNING EXPERIENCES FOR EACH PERSON.

Evaluations, based upon standardized expectancies, force students to adopt standardized learning in order to compete. Many of today's expectancies are influenced by publishing concerns and hardware vendors. We must develop personalized ways of assessing an individual's progress, his strengths and weaknesses, keeping in mind that the ultimate purpose of evaluation is to strengthen the learning process.

13. THE ENVIRONMENT WITHIN WHICH STUDENTS ARE ENCOURAGED TO LEARN MUST BE GREATLY EXPANDED.

The classroom, or even the school, is an extremely limited learning environment.

The total culture surrounding each individual should become his learning environment. The surrounding parks, forests, lakes, homes, businesses, museums, factories should be as widely used as the resources of classrooms and libraries.

The wealth of personal talent in the community should be utilized. The talents, crafts, hobbies, travel experiences of persons of all walks of life should become resources for the learning process. Students should be encouraged to taste life, to become actively involved in the activities and the decision making processes of the community.

14. THE SCHOOL SHOULD PROVIDE A STRUCTURE IN WHICH STUDENTS CAN LEARN FROM EACH OTHER.

Much learning takes place naturally through association with peers or older siblings, and much of the motivation to learn and explore comes from this association. Students who have developed certain abilities can provide models for those less developed. Those engaged in some activity often provide the needed stimulus to interest others in becoming involved in that learning activity.

Schools should encourage students to work together cooperatively, to realize that individual efforts can often be improved through the combined effect of what each has to contribute to the common project.

15. TO PROVIDE A MAXIMUM LEARNING EXPERIENCE FOR ALL STUDENTS REQUIRES THE INVOLVEMENT AND SUPPORT OF THE ENTIRE COMMUNITY.

In order to make maximum use of available learning opportunities, students need the support and understanding of teachers, who in turn need the support of the school administration to allow students to operate effectively. The administration is responsible to the community and the State.

If any of the links in this chain operate independently and resist efforts to maximize learning for students through lack of understanding, the students themselves suffer. All parties must work cooperatively toward a common set of concepts and goals if students are to reap maximum benefit from the learning opportunities which should be theirs.

16. SCHOOLS SHOULD BE COMPATIBLE WITH REALITY. LEARNING WHICH IS COMPARTMENTALIZED INTO ARTIFICIAL SUBJECT FIELDS BY TEACHERS AND ADMINISTRATORS IS CONTRARY TO WHAT IS KNOWN ABOUT THE LEARNING PROCESS.

The interdependencies of real life, which involve the combined use of a number of skills, should suggest a direction for school activities such as math, reading, science, social studies. it is unrealistic that math, or any subject, be limited to a certain period during the day, to be turned on and off by a bell.

How much more meaningful if math can be explored as one of a series of factors necessary to solving real problems as they arise during the course of the day. If we again look to the natural learning of preschool children as a model, it is apparent that they do not compartmentalize learning into neat little packages.

17. INDIVIDUALS SHOULD BE ENCOURAGED TO DEVELOP A SENSE OF RESPONSIBILITY.

A student's school should be HIS school, one to be proud of. He should be actively involved in its direction, its maintenance, and its care. The attitude of belonging and being an important contributor can do much toward establishing a spirit of cooperation and respect. This sense of responsibility should be further developed to include peers and adults. It is vital that students realize other people are individuals with feelings, ideas which may conflict with their own, strengths, weaknesses, and problems. A sense of responsibility and respect for the individuality of each person is necessary for better understanding and cooperation.

VERMONT—SOME WAYS FOR IMPLEMENTING THE PROCESS FOR IMPROVED LEARNING OPPORTUNITIES

THE FOREGOING PHILOSOPHY should serve as a guideline for all activities directed toward the improved learning opportunities, as well as establishing priorities among the school's needs. Keeping the philosophy in the fore, the following are offered as possible activities which will help a school move toward its implementation.

A. THE SINGLE MOST IMPORTANT FACTOR IN IMPLEMENTING THESE IDEAS IS THE TEACHER, AND THE QUALITY OF THE INTERACTION BETWEEN THE TEACHER AND LEARNER. Without a sympathetic and skill-ful teacher, most efforts of improving are doomed to failure. Teachers should be supported and involved in a number of ways—inservice training, workshops, individual consultant help, and the opportunity to visit and discuss other programs. These activities should strive to assist the teacher in understanding and accepting the basic concepts of the philosophy and implementing them to provide the best possible learning situation for his students. It is possible, even desirable, that teachers interpret and implement these basic concepts in various ways to best suit their own traits, and the unique individuals, school and community which they serve.

B. **TEACHERS WHO SEEM TO HAVE DEVELOPED TO A CONSIDERABLE DEGREE IN TERMS OF IMPLEMENTING THIS PHILOSOPHY SHOULD BE GIVEN INTENSIVE ASSISTANCE TO WORK IN MODEL OR DEMONSTRATION CLASSROOMS.** It is vital to the development of teachers that they be able to visit and evaluate good examples demonstrating a particular concept, as well as observe teachers who have been able to work successfully with these ideas in situations similar to their own.

C. **IT IS IMPERATIVE THAT PRE-SERVICE COLLEGE STUDENTS BECOME CONCERNED WITH AND EVALUATE THESE IDEAS.** If the students find these ideas appropriate, they should be given the opportunity to develop the necessary skills and attitudes to allow them to utilize effectively these methods upon beginning to teach. The process of working only with inservice teachers will be tremendously complicated if it must include those coming into teaching from our colleges each year.

Although it has been stated that the teacher and his interaction with students is primary, a teacher is powerless to work in accord with this philosophy if not supported by the school administration. This support must be provided.

D. **CURRICULUM GUIDES AND REQUIREMENTS SHOULD CONTAIN SUFFICIENT LATITUDE TO PROVIDE THE TEACHER THE OPPORTUNITY TO MEET INDIVIDUAL NEEDS.** To expect all individuals to complete or utilize certain prescribed texts and workbooks in the course of the year violates that which is known about the learning process.

E. **THE DAILY SCHOOL SCHEDULE SHOULD BE RELATED TO THE MAXIMIZING OF LEARNING OPPORTUNITIES.** Whenever possible, teachers should be allowed to develop an educational program according to the needs of their students without interference from bells or other scheduled interruptions. Every attempt should be made to provide flexibility, including the hours of attendance. Teachers must be free to allow individuals time to explore, create, work, and interact without being cut short by bells.

F. **STUDENTS MUST BE PROVIDED WITH A STIMULATING ENVIRONMENT, CONSISTING OF A WIDE AND APPROPRIATE SELECTION OF CHALLENGING EQUIPMENT, MATERIALS, AND READING MATTER SUITED TO THEIR PARTICULAR INTERESTS AND ABILITY LEVELS.** Equipment need not be particularly expensive or elaborate—often those items made by the teacher or students are best suited. The equipment should not be classified according to subject matter, such as math or science, but students should be allowed to develop and use equipment for a variety of purposes. Schools must be prepared to support teachers by providing at least a minimum of basic equipment and materials appropriate to encourage the kind of learning compatible with this philosophy.

G. **CONSIDERATION SHOULD BE GIVEN TO PROVIDING A FLEXIBLE SCHOOL ENTRANCE SCHEDULE.** Children should begin their school experience at varying times throughout the school year, rather than on the same magical day in September. This schedule might be arranged to allow children to enter school on a certain day of each month, on their birthday, or at the beginning of a quarter or term. Not only would this arrangement provide the opportunity to get children into school at the most appropriate time relative to learning, but would also compel teachers to individualize instruction rather than moving a class of children as a group. This step, however, is not realistic if a school is still operating within a graded framework.

H. **ALMOST ANY SCHOOL FACILITY WHICH HAS ADEQUATE SPACE AND IS SAFE FOR CHILDREN IS COMPATIBLE WITH A STUDENT-CENTERED APPROACH TO LEARNING, ALTHOUGH SOME ARE MORE CONDUCIVE TO LEARNING THAN OTHERS.** This factor becomes of particular concern when a new building or major addition is being contemplated. Flexibility should be the single most important consideration, with a maximum of space so designed to be utilized for a variety of activities.

I. **COOPERATION AND COMMUNICATION AMONG THE SCHOOL STAFF SHOULD BE ENCOURAGED.** Communication can lead to a sharing and strengthening of ideas and a comparison of techniques, according to their strengths and weaknesses. Cooperation is vital in allowing teachers maximum flexibility through sharing duties and responsibilities.

J. **FOR A SCHOOL TO BE TRULY A CENTER FOR LEARNING, IT MUST BE REALIZED THAT INDIVIDUALS DO NOT CONFINE THEIR LEARNING TO THE WEEKDAY HOURS BETWEEN 8 A.M. AND 3:30 P.M. FROM SEPTEMBER TO JUNE.** The school must work toward providing a learning center which is available to all persons, children through adults, into the evening hours, weekends and vacations. A student-centered approach may alleviate some of the biggest drawbacks to extended operation, in that students accept the responsibility to work independently, making a minimum of adult supervision necessary.

K. **CREATIVE USE OF PARA-PROFESSIONALS CAN HELP FREE TEACHERS TO SPEND A GREATER PROPORTION OF THEIR TIME CONCERNED WITH LEARNING AND KNOWING THEIR STUDENTS.** Providing the most beneficial learning situation is a full time activity for teachers. Those duties not essential to maintaining this learning situation, such as collecting milk money, mimeographing, or taking attendance, can only detract from a teacher's effectiveness.

L. **THE CONTINUAL ASSESSMENT OF EACH STUDENT'S PROGRESS IS VITAL. THIS ASSESSMENT SHOULD BE APPROPRIATE TO HIS CAPABILITIES, DESIRES AND GOALS.** Rather than categorize a student into one of a given series of groups, evaluation must describe his activities, strengths and weaknesses. Meaningful assessment should provide the basis of a teacher's work with each student.

M. **THE ADMINISTRATIVE ORGANIZATION, TO UTILIZE MOST EFFECTIVELY AVAILABLE SPACE, TIME AND TALENT, THE VERMONT DESIGN FOR EDUCATION MUST BE REORGANIZED.** The K–12 organization is essential for the most efficient utilization of administrative time and talent, for the greatest assurance of articulation in the learning process from a child's entrance into school through graduation, and for the most economical appropriation of funds for the total educational program.

THE VERMONT DESIGN FOR EDUCATION will not emerge without a greater understanding of the need for a change in the role of the teacher—indeed, all people concerned with the education process. Programs have been developed in isolation and with insufficient funds. In many instances, there has been insufficient effort for the coordination of appropriate activities related to improved learning opportunities. It is essential that all parties and agencies connected with education in Vermont develop a team approach toward its common goal—that of improving the learning opportunities for persons of all ages.

At first glance the educational philosophy described herein would appear a departure from that which is familiar to most people and certainly different from that practiced generally. However, a study of educational philosophy in general from Plato and Aristotle to Dewey and Piaget, and of the interpretation and implementation of an educational program based upon the concepts expressed in their writings, will give the reader a basis for understanding the strong foundation upon which this Vermont Design for Education is being developed.

It should be emphasized that acceptance of this philosophy and its implementation must be voluntary if there are to be improved learning opportunities in schools. No amount of legislation or administrative mandate will provide beneficial and permanent educational changes for students. However, for those systems and teachers interested in implementing appropriate program changes, there should be available financial and professional assistance. Such assistance can be provided by the various educational agencies cooperatively coordinating resources to this end.

STATE OF VERMONT

Governor—Deane C. Davis

State Board of Education—1971

Marion C. Taylor, Chairman	Bennington
Robert Corley	Wolcott
E. Dean Finney	St. Johnsbury
Arline P. Hunt	West Charleston
Robert S. Jones	Springfield
Barbara W. Snelling	Shelburne
John F. Willson	St. Albans

Joseph H. Oakey—Commissioner of Education

Daniel G. O'Connor—Deputy Commissioner

[*Note:* *In the original booklet produced by Queen City Printers in Burlington, Vermont
(1968, 1971), the Vermont Design for Education included artwork by Mitch Hager
as well as cover drawings from Woodstock Elementary School
under the supervision Francis J. Gyro, Jr.*]

[ENCLOSED LETTER]

STATE OF VERMONT
DEPARTMENT OF EDUCATION
MONTPELIER
05602

May 1, 1971

THE VERMONT DESIGN: From Philosophy to Practice

The Vermont State Department of Education has stated its philosophy in the
Vermont Design for Education. However, the State Department's planned use of
the Design toward the involvement of the public for educational improvement is
of far greater significance than its mere statement of a functioning philosophy.

The State Department of Education has placed itself on the line to support a
massive program for improving public education in Vermont. Through this
Design and its plan for implementation the Department will center its approach
to upgrading the Vermont schools. Those standards were implemented in 1967
and dealt primarily with specific criteria which emphasize pupil-teacher ratio,

certification, space, and such items as course offerings, minimum length of the school day, and number of school days in the year. In facing the need for improved educational opportunities, the Vermont Department of Education decided to do its utmost to get improvements to bubble up from involved citizens and professionals rather than by edict from the top.

Our current problem is one of implementing the Design into the programs of education in the local districts. We are attempting to bring this about through a three-step procedure.

First, every district has been advised that it must carry on a local assessment of its elementary education program to determine to what degree the concepts in the Vermont Design for Education exist there. The local assessment will involve pupils, teachers, parents, and administrators. The Department of Education will furnish the local district a few sample instruments which it can use for the probe if there is nothing better to use. It is hoped that the local self-assessment will bring about a "happy dissatisfaction" with the existing educational program.

Secondly, the local district after making an assessment of current practices is being placed in the position of creating its own design for education. The local district design can be that of the Vermont Design but it can also be of its own choosing, subject to the approval of the State Department of Education. The Department is making its total resources plus those of a mutually agreed upon consultant available to the local community. The local design committee will include representatives from all segments of the local society.

Thirdly, the local community must submit to the State Department of Education a calendar of commitment outlining the schedule for implementation of each of the items listed in the local design.

In addition, each pupil must have a minimum of 30 square feet of space for learning and the local community must spend $10 per pupil per year for learning resource materials.

Through these efforts, the Vermont State Department has brought the Vermont Design to the attention of each community in the State and has helped encourage its implementation as a working philosophy in the public schools of Vermont.

JOSEPH H. OAKEY
Commissioner
Vermont State Department of Education

References

Augé, M. (1995). *non-places: Introduction to an anthropology for supermodernity* (J. Howe, Trans.). London & New York: Verso.

Austin, J. L. (1975). *How to do things with words* (2nd ed.). William James Lectures, Harvard University, 1955 (J. O. Urmson & M. Sbisà, Eds.). Cambridge, MA: Harvard University Press.

Baca, J. S. (1992). *Working in the dark: Reflections of a poet of the barrio.* Santa Fe, NM: Red Crane Books.

Bachman, R., & Fournier, J. (1999). Building common ground. In J. W. Lindfors & J. S. Townsend (Eds.), *Teaching language arts through dialogue* (pp. 233–250). Urbana, IL: National Council of Teachers of English.

Bakhtin, M. M. (1986). *Speech genres and other late essays* (2nd ed.) (V. W. McGee, Trans.; C. Emerson & M. Holquist, Eds.). Austin: University of Texas.

Berlin, I. (2006). *Political ideas in the romantic age, their rise and influence on modern thought* (H. Hardy, Ed.). Princeton, NJ: Princeton University Press.

Berliner, D. C., & Biddle, B. J. (1995). *The manufactured crisis: Myths, fraud, and the attack on America's public schools.* Reading, MA: Addison-Wesley.

Buck, P. S. (1986). *The big wave.* New York: HarperCollins.

Butler, J. (2005). *Giving an account of oneself.* New York: Fordham University Press.

Carger, L. C. (2004). Art and literacy with bilingual children. *Language Arts, 81*(4), 283–292.

Carini, L. (2009). *Learning.* Unpublished manuscript. Available at http://www.prospectcenter.org

Carini, P. F. (2000). Prospect's Descriptive Processes. In M. Himley with P. F. Carini (Eds.), *From another angle: Children's strengths and school standards* (pp. 8–20). New York: Teachers College Press.

Carini, P. F. (2001). *Starting strong: A different look at children, schools, and standards.* New York: Teachers College Press.

Carini, P. F. (2006). Vito Perrone and the struggle for democratic schools. *Teaching and Learning: The Journal of Natural Inquiry and Reflective Practice* (K. Gershman & G. Olsen, Guest Eds.), *20,* 32–45.

Chittenden, E. (1990). Young children's discussions of science. In G. Hein (Ed.), *The assessment of hands-on elementary science programs* (North Dakota Study Group Monograph Series). Grand Forks, ND: University of North Dakota Press.

Chittenden, E., Salinger, T. S., & Bussis, A. M. (2001). *Inquiry into meaning: An investigation of learning to read.* New York: Teachers College Press.

Commission on Excellence in Education. (1983). *A nation at risk: The imperative for education reform.* Washington, DC: Author.

Dahl, R. (1982). *The BFG.* New York: Farrar, Straus and Giroux.

DeStigter, T. (1998). *Reflections of a citizen teacher: Literacy, democracy, and the forgotten students of Addison High.* Urbana, IL: National Council of Teachers of English.

Dewey, J. (1916/1997). *Democracy and education: An introduction to the philosophy of education.* New York: Free Press.

Dewey, J. (1938/1963). *Experience and education.* New York: Collier Books.

Dyson, A. H. (with the San Francisco East Bay Teacher Study Group). (1997). *What difference does difference make? Teacher reflections on diversity, literacy, and the urban primary school.* Urbana, IL: National Council of Teachers of English.

Edelman, M. W. (1992). *The measure of our success: A letter to my children and yours.* New York: HarperPerennial.

Edelsky, C. (1991). *With literacy and justice for all.* Philadelphia: Falmer Press.

Edelsky, C., Alwerger, B., & Flores, B. (1990). *Whole language: What's the difference?* Portsmouth, NH: Heinemann.

Espinosa, C., & Fournier, J. (1995). Making meaning of our lives through literature, present, past, and future. *Primary Voices, 3*(2), 15–21.

Espinosa, C., & Fournier, J. (1999). Stepping stones: Literature in the classroom. In J. W. Lindfors & J. S. Townsend (Eds.), *Teaching language arts through dialogue* (pp. 84–100). Urbana, IL: National Council of Teachers of English.

Espinosa, C., & Moore, K. (1999). Understanding and transforming the meaning of our lives through poetry, biographies, and songs. In C. Edelsky (Ed.), *Making justice our project: Teachers working toward critical whole language practice* (pp. 37–54). Urbana, IL: National Council of Teachers of English.

Espinosa, C., Moore, K., & Serna, I. (1998). Learning environments supportive of young Latinos. In M. L. Gonzales, J. Villamil Tinajero, & A. H. Macías (Eds.), *Educating Latino students: A guide to successful practice* (pp. 107–138). Lancaster, PA: Technomac.

Foucault, M. (1990). *The use of pleasure: The history of sexuality* (Vol. 2) (R. Hurley, Trans.). New York: Vintage Books.

Freire, P. (1970/2000). *Pedagogy of the oppressed.* New York: Continuum International.

Froebel, F. (1826/1899). *The education of man* (M. Hailmann, Trans.). New York: D. Appleton.

Galdós, B. P. (1878/2008). *Marianela.* Otero Ediciones.

Gatto, J. T. (1992). *Dumbing us down: The hidden curriculum of compulsory schooling.* Gabriola Island, BC, Canada: New Society.

Goodman, K. (1986). *What's whole in whole language?* Portsmouth, NH: Heinemann.

Goodman, K., Shannon, P., Goodman, Y., & Rapoport, R. (2004). *Saving our schools: The case for public education saying no to "No Child Left Behind."* Berkeley, CA: RDR Books.

Goodman, Y. (1984). The development of initial literacy. In H. Goelman, A. Oberg, & F. Smith (Eds.), *Awakening to literacy* (pp. 102–109). Portsmouth, NH: Heinemann.

Goodman, Y. M., Watson, D. J., & Burke, C. L. (2005). *Reading miscue inventory: From evaluation to instruction* (2nd ed.). Katonah, NY: Richard C. Owen.

Graves, D. (1983). *Writing: Teachers and children at work.* Portsmouth, NH: Heinemann.

Himley, M. (1991). *Shared territory: Understanding children's writing as works.* New York: Oxford University Press.

Himley, M. (with Carini, P. F.) (Eds.). (2000). *From another angle: Children's strengths and school standards.* New York: Teachers College Press.

Himley, M. (Ed.). (2002). *Prospect's Descriptive Processes: The child, the art of teaching, and the classroom and school.* North Bennington, VT: Prospect Center.

Hudelson, S. (1987). The role of native language literacy in the education of language minority children. *Language Arts, 64*(8), 827–841.

Hudelson, S. (1994). Literacy development of second language children. In F. Genesee (Ed.), *Educating second language children: The whole child, the whole curriculum, the whole community.* New York: Cambridge University Press.

Hudelson, S., Fournier, J., Espinosa, C., & Bachman, R. (1994). Chasing windmills, overcoming obstacles in Spanish literature for children. *Language Arts, 3*(71), 164–171.

Hudelson, S., & Serna, I. A. (1994). Beginning literacy in English in a whole language bilingual program. In A. Flurkey and R. J. Meyer (Eds.), *Under the whole language umbrella: Many cultures, many voices.* Urbana, IL: National Council of Teachers of English.

Hughes, L. (1995). *The collected poems of Langston Hughes.* New York: Vintage Books.

Johannsen, D. (n.d.). Growing pains. *Centerspace, 9*(2), 1.

Kelley, R. D. G. (2002). *Freedom dreams.* Boston: Beacon Press.

Kill, M. (2006). Acknowledging the rough edges of resistance: Negotiation of identities for first-year composition. *College Composition and Communication, 58*(2), 213–235.

King, T. (2005). *The truth about stories.* Minneapolis: University of Minnesota Press.

Kingsolver, B. (1991). *Animal dreams.* New York: HarperPerennial.

Kundera, M. (1988). *The art of the novel* (L. Asher, Trans.). New York: Grove Press.

Merleau-Ponty, M. (1962). *The phenomenology of perception.* London: Routledge & Kegan Paul.

Moll, L., Amanti, C., Neff, D., & González, N. (1992). Funds of knowledge for teaching: Using a qualitative approach to connect homes and classrooms. *Theory into Practice, 31,* 132–141.

Morrison, T. (1994). *Lecture and speech of acceptance, upon the award of the Nobel Prize for Literature.* (1993 Nobel Lecture in Literature.) New York: Alfred A. Knopf.

Ocampo, C. (1987). *Si ves pasar un cóndor/If you pass a condor.* Ciudad de México: Celta Amaquemecan, A.C.

Okri, B. (1997). *A way of being free.* London: Phoenix House.

Packard, V. (1957/1980). *The hidden persuaders.* New York: Pocket Books.

Paras, E. (2006). *Foucault 2.0: Beyond power and knowledge.* New York: Other Press.

Perrone, V. (1983). *Teacher education at the University of North Dakota: Highlights of a century-long history.* (Unpublished manuscript written for the University of North Dakota centennial.)

Perrone, V. (1998). *Teacher with a heart: Reflections on Leonard Covello and community.* New York: Teachers College Press.

Peterson, R. (1992). *Life in a crowded place: Making a learning community.* Portsmouth, NH: Heinemann

Peterson, R., & Eeds, M. (1990). *Grand conversations.* New York: Scholastic.

Pico, F. (1991). *La peineta colorada.* Caracas, Venezuela: Ediciones Ekaré.

Pico, F. (1994). *The red comb* (A. Palacios, Trans). Mahwah, NJ: BridgeWater Books.

Pratt, M. B. (1991). *Rebellion: Essays 1980–1991.* Ann Arbor, MI: Firebrand.

Said, E. (2000). *Reflections on exile and other essays*. Cambridge, MA: Harvard University Press.

Scheler, Max. (1913/1973). *The nature of sympathy* (P. Heath, Trans.). Hamden, CT: Shoestring Press.

Sebald, W. G. (2003). On the natural history of destruction. New York: Random House.

Serna, I., & Hudelson, S. (1993). Emergent Spanish literacy in a whole language bilingual program. In R. Donmoyer & R. Kos (Eds.). *At-risk students: Portraits, policies, programs, and practices* (pp. 291–321). Albany, NY: SUNY Press.

Serna, I., & Hudelson, S. (1997). Special Feature 3.2: Alicia's emergent literacy development in Spanish. Special Feature 7.4: Alicia's biliteracy development in first and second grade. In J. Christie, B. Enz, & C. Vukolich (Eds.), *Teaching language and literacy: Preschool through the elementary grades* (pp. 79–83, 255–263). New York: Longman.

Smith, K. (1995). Bringing children and literature together in the elementary classroom. *Primary Voices, 3*(2), 22–32.

Stock, G. (1988). *The kids' book of questions*. New York: Workman.

Stoler, A. L. (Ed.). (2006). *Haunted by empire: Geographies of intimacy in North American history*. Durham, NC, and London: Duke University Press.

Traugh, C. (2000). *Learning to love the question*. Unpublished manuscript. Available from the author: Cecelia.Traugh@liu.edu

Turnquist, B. (2008). *Round tables and grids*. Unpublished manuscript.

Veatch, J. (1959). *Individualizing your reading program: Self-selection in action*. New York: G. P. Putnam's Sons.

Veatch, J. (1978). *Reading in the elementary school* (2nd ed.). New York: Richard C. Owen.

Veatch, J. (1984). *How to teach reading with children's books* (2nd ed.). New York: Richard C. Owen.

Vermont State Department of Education. (1968/1971). *The Vermont design for education*. Burlington, VT: Queen City Printers.

Waber, B. (1972). *Ira sleeps over*. New York: Houghton Mifflin.

Waber, B. (1991). *Ira says good-bye*. New York: Houghton Mifflin.

Weber, L. (1994). *Reflections*. New York: The City College Workshop Center.

Weber, L. (1997). *Looking back and thinking forward* (B. Alberty, Ed.). New York: Teachers College Press.

White Deer of Autumn. (1991). *Ceremony—In the circle of life*. Hillsboro, OR: Beyond Words.

Whitehead, A. N. (1938/1958). *Modes of thought*. New York: Capricorn Books.

Yeats, W. B. (1996). *The collected poems of W. B. Yeats* (2nd ed.) (R. J. Finneran, Ed.). New York: Scribner Paperback Poetry.

Index

About the Authors

PATRICIA F. CARINI

- Doctor of Humane Letters from Bank Street College, 1998
- Independent Educator
- Charter Member of the North Dakota Study Group on Evaluation

Patricia F. Carini is a co-founder of Prospect School (1965–1991) and the Prospect Archives and Center for Education and Research (1979–present). At Prospect, she began the Collections of Children's Works and directed the Archives Scholars and Fellows program, which culminated in publication of the *Reference Edition of the Prospect Archives* (1984). Observational, descriptive methods developed at Prospect by Carini and colleagues for the study of children and their works, and for documentation of curriculum and school practice, have been widely shared with public schools across the country. Carini presided over the transfer of Prospect's Archives, including the Collections of Children's Works, to Special Collections at the Bailey/Howe Library at the University of Vermont. A Presidential Lecture, "The Bigness of Education" (March 2007), celebrated the occasion of the gift and Prospect's contributions to education. Publications include three early, seminal works: *Observation and Description: An Alternative Methodology for the Investigation of Human Phenomena* (1975); *The Art of Seeing and the Visibility of the Person* (1979); and *The School Lives of Seven Children* (1982). She joined Margaret Himley in editing *From Another Angle: Children's Strengths and School Standards* (Teachers College Press, 2000). Carini's collection of essays, *Starting Strong: A Different Look at Children, Schools, and Standards* (Teachers College Press, 2001), positions the valuing of humanness as the starting place and center for education—and for society more generally.

CAROL CHRISTINE

• Ph.D. in Language, Reading, and Culture from the University of Arizona, 1997

Carol Christine recently retired from her position as Clinical Associate Professor and Associate Division Director in the Division of Curriculum and Instruction in the Mary Lou Fulton College of Education at Arizona State University. She worked in teacher education, primarily with faculty in preservice teacher education, and taught graduate and undergraduate courses in children's literature and language arts at ASU from 1991 through 2008. She was a founding member and Program Director of The Center for Establishing Dialogue in Teaching and Learning (CED), a not-for-profit organization of teachers and schools, which was established in the Phoenix area in 1986. She has served as a member of the Prospect Center Board of Trustees of since 1998.

CECILIA ESPINOSA

• Ph.D. in Language and Literacy from Arizona State University, Tempe Campus, 2004
• Assistant Professor in the Department of Early Childhood/Childhood Education at Lehman College, City University of New York

Cecilia Espinosa has worked in the field of bilingual education since 1989. She worked for many years as an early childhood teacher in multi-age, bilingual, kindergarten through second-grade classrooms in Phoenix, Arizona. During these years she presented at national and international conferences and published articles and chapters about teaching and learning in a bilingual classroom. She was an active member of the Center for Establishing Dialogue in Teaching and Learning (CED). In 1997 she left the classroom to coordinate a Title VII grant. Espinosa and her colleagues developed a dual language program that strove to put teachers and children at the center. Now as a teacher educator, she continues to work alongside bilingual teachers and children. Her area of focus is on collaborative research, in particular issues of literacies and biliteracies. She teaches courses on observation and assessment, teacher research, and literacy/biliteracy. She has published recently in the National Council of Teachers of English journal *Language Arts* and in international journals such as *Lectura y Vida* and *Revista Mexicana de Investigacion Educativa*. Espinosa served as a member of the Prospect Center Board of Trustees for several years and also as co-editor of the Prospect publication *The Review*.

JULIA FOURNIER

- M.A. in Elementary Education with special focus on Literacy/
  Biliteracy from Arizona State University, 1995

Julia Fournier has worked continuously in public schools since 1981. She has published and co-written work narrating her experiences with children and collaboration with teachers. She began working at W. T. Machan School in Phoenix in 1987. In 2000, after 19 years in the classroom, Fournier became a library/media and reading specialist at Machan. Her introduction to Prospect and descriptive work was as a participant in 1989 Descriptive Review work through the Center for Establishing Dialogue in Teaching and Learning (CED). She was member of the Prospect Center Board of Trustees from 1999 through 2008. In 2009, Fournier resigned her position at Machan to begin work at a new charter school in Phoenix through the University Public Schools Initiative.

MARGARET HIMLEY

- Ph.D. in Composition and Rhetoric from the University of Illinois at
  Chicago, 1983
- Professor of Writing and Rhetoric in the Writing Program at Syracuse
  University

Margaret Himley has been a member of the Prospect community since the early 1980s. She served on the Prospect Center Board of Trustees as Vice President and as chair of Publications and Media, and edited a book with Patricia F. Carini on Prospect's Descriptive Review of the Child, titled *From Another Angle: Children's Strengths and School Standards* (Teachers College Press, 2000). Other publications include *Shared Territory: Understanding Children's Writing as Works* (1991), which puts Prospect's philosophy into conversation with Bakhtinian theories of language use and subjectivity, and *Political Moments in the Classroom* (1997), which explores the affective and political economy of writing classrooms. Her current project is tentatively titled *Mobilizing Desire in the Classroom*. Himley teaches writing and LGBT studies courses as well as graduate seminars in research methodology, composition pedagogy and curriculum, and the history of writing studies. She co-directs the LGBT Studies Program and Minor at Syracuse University.